Reviews

"The economists and the financial experts tell us it can't happen again. Prechter tells us why a depression is not only possible but lays out a convincing case as to why it is a certainty. Very few people see what Prechter sees right now. Of course very few experts saw a bull market back in 1978 when Prechter went out on a limb to predict the greatest bull market of the 20th century. I urge all investors to read this book to understand what is ahead of us. Then read it to prepare yourself financially to weather the storms that are surely coming."

—Jim Puplava, President, Puplava Financial Services, Inc. and Puplava Securities, Inc.

"After reading *Conquer the Crash* carefully, I am saying that this is 'must reading' for anyone who has even the slightest interest in the stock market and his or her own investing. Prechter's fascinating chapters on the Federal Reserve, the debt situation, and what he calls the coming deflation, is worth ten times the price of the book alone. This is an amazing work, and one that is calculated to make you think deeply. I might even say that this book will astound you with its theses and its conclusions."

—Richard Russell, *Dow Theory Letters*

"All investors imbued with the idea that stocks should be bought and held forever should read this book."

—Charlie Minter and Marty Weiner, Comstock Partners, Inc.

"Prechter's understanding of technical, contrary, and economic analysis is exceptional. Once you view events from this perspective, you can successfully anticipate conditions and properly adjust your investment techniques for maximum wealth appreciation and preservation. While most will be crushed by the weight of their own mortgage and credit card debt, readers of this book can take advantage of a once in a lifetime opportunity. Prechter's advice will surely be used in my own investing."

—Lawrence G. McMillan, *The Option Strategist*

"In straightforward language, free of typical Wall Street econo-babble, Prechter builds a bullet-proof case that a deflationary depression of historic proportion is underway. It will devastate the wealth of those who do not read this book and heed its advice. Prechter calmly and rationally lays out the many options a prudent investor should follow at this juncture. *Conquer the Crash* could save your financial future."

—Grizzly, Bearmarketcentral.com

"*Conquer the Crash* is an awesome piece of research based upon intellectual integrity, profound realism and logic. The book lays one of the essential cornerstones of capital preservation. If you argue with its premises or dismiss its conclusions, the price could well be your permanent loss of wealth."

—Jean-Pierre Louvet, founder & CEO, The SafeWealth Group

"This is the most crucial financial period in your life. This book explains why. It also tells you what you should do about it. If you want to preserve your wealth, I urge you to follow Prechter's advice. You will be grateful that you did."

—Ian Gordon, *The Long Wave Analyst*

"*Conquer the Crash* provides disciplined investors with a map, compass and survival guide. Don't leave home without it."

—Henry Van der Eb, President, Gabelli Mathers Fund

"In the field of economics/finance, a clear, intuitive grasp of the larger top-down patterns is vanishingly rare. *Conquer the Crash* is a masterpiece by an ultimate master."

—P.Q. Wall, *The P.Q. Wall Forecast*

"A compelling exposition of how both the mechanics and the psychology of the business cycle can be encapsulated in market analysis."

—Sean Corrigan, Capital-Insight.com

"Prechter knows the facts like few others. Read his forceful argument carefully. It can save you from financial loss."

—James R. Cook, President, Investment Rarities

"*Conquer the Crash* ensures that at least some investors will stay on the 'rational' side of a very emotional future. Patterns are structured and rational, while human emotions are impulsive and sudden. Prechter's genius is to show the exquisite relationship between the two truths, and what those truths mean to our social, economic and financial future."

—Ted Workman, CEO, Asset Allocation Consultants, Ltd.

"*Conquer the Crash* is required reading for anyone who wants to enhance his or her prospects for economic survival in the years ahead. That's not to say that this is a technical book written only for seasoned analysts or would-be experts. In fact, the opposite is true. Bob Prechter is writing for the average folks who probably haven't given much thought to what might happen to the economy in the years ahead. And while some of the insights in *Conquer the Crash* are scary enough, this really isn't a doom-and-gloom piece. It's chock full of practical tips for specific actions you can and should take now."

—Timothy Bost, Editor, *Financial Cycles*

"*Conquer the Crash* is a humdinger. After almost 50 years in the stock market, I can tell you, without equivocation, that Bob Prechter's new book is a must read for every thinking investor. It is chock full of valuable historical data and principled insights not found elsewhere."

—Charles Allmon, President, *Growth Stock Outlook*

"This book requires the usual investor to rethink how he evaluates stocks, market psychology, and the Fed. But most important, Bob tells us *how* to protect ourselves when/if the totally unexpected hits — a deflationary depression."

—R.E. McMaster, Editor, *The Reaper*

"Prechter doesn't leave readers staring at their brokerage statements in a cold sweat. He also presents a strategy for financial survival. Prechter's no-nonsense recommendations would likely benefit investors even if events don't unfold as dramatically as he expects."

—Ron Peebles, PrudentBear.com

"If you have property, a job, money in the bank, debt, a family, a career, an insurance policy, superannuation and place any value in protecting yourself and your loved ones, you need to read this message before bearing the impact of the months and years ahead. It is a message specifically for you because the economic future will happen and you will have to live in it, prepared or not."

—Cameron Marshall, Elliottwave.com.au.

"... the best investment you can make is your own betterment, via education. This book is a very small investment that may pay huge dividends in your understanding of the macro economic picture. I highly recommend this book."

—David Morgan, Silver-Investor.com

"Prechter's latest book is a must read for every serious investor. The research is top notch and his track record impeccable. After you read the book, pass it along to someone you care about. They will thank you."

—John Riley, Cornerstone Investment

"*Conquer the Crash* is one of the must-read books this year, simply because it will jolt us to think, not to follow the crowd blindly, to be more alert to external situations and be prepared."

—Paul Leo, *Chartpoint Magazine* (Singapore)

"Bob combines a remarkable knowledge of history and a deep understanding of the ebb and flow of markets to produce a truly thoughtful, provocative work. Simply put: If you want to gain a new understanding of how the markets...and the world around you...work, read *Conquer the Crash*."

—Brien Lundin, Editor, *Gold Newsletter*

"This timely volume, with an urgent message presented from a uniquely psychological perspective, also provides abundant and appropriate resources that target your concerns of financial survival."

—Susan J. Baretta, webmaster, Beartopia.net

"I'm personally putting Prechter's new book on my gift list for friends and loved ones."

—Martin D. Weiss, Ph.D., author of the national best seller, *The Ultimate Safe Money Guide*

"This book outlines brilliantly and simply the rationale for how and why the bubble developed. Prechter will go down in history as a legend for having predicted the secular bull market and now having provided a lucid description of the economic cataclysm that unfortunately lies ahead. I urge you to read this book and give it to your loved ones. It provides great tactical advice on how to prepare yourself financially. Reading this book could make the difference between agony and comfort over the next 20 years."

—David Tice, President, Prudent Bear Funds

CONQUER THE CRASH
YOU CAN SURVIVE AND PROSPER IN A DEFLATIONARY DEPRESSION

Robert R. Prechter, Jr.

John Wiley & Sons, Ltd

This publication is designed to provide accurate and authoritative information in
regard to the subject matter covered. It is sold on the understanding that the
Publisher is not engaged in rendering professional services. If professional advice or
other expert assistance is required, the services of a competent professional should
be sought.

Other Wiley Editorial Offices

John Wiley & Sons Inc., 111 River Street, Hoboken, NJ 07030, USA

Jossey-Bass, 989 Market Street, San Francisco, CA 94103-1741, USA

Wiley-VCH Verlag GmbH, Boschstr. 12, D-69469 Weinheim, Germany

John Wiley & Sons Australia Ltd, 33 Park Road, Milton, Queensland 4064,
Australia

John Wiley & Sons (Asia) Pte Ltd, 2 Clementi Loop #02-01, Jin Xing Distripark,
Singapore 129809

John Wiley & Sons Canada Ltd, 22 Worcester Road, Etobicoke, Ontario, Canada
M9W 1L1

Wiley also publishes its books in a variety of electronic formats. Some content that
appears in print may not be available in electronic books.

British Library Cataloguing in Publication Data

A catalogue record for this book is available from the British Library

ISBN 0-470-87090-7

Typeset by the author

Printed and bound in the United States of America

Dedication

This book is dedicated to all my friends and colleagues at Elliott Wave International, who put up with three months of my single-mindedness in producing this book.

Acknowledgments

In putting together this volume, I had invaluable help from Robert Prechter Sr., Lou Crandall, Pete Kendall and Jean-Pierre Louvet, who provided expert information that enhanced certain chapters in this book. Rachel Webb and Angela Hall created the charts, Sally Webb formatted the book, and Robin Machcinski, Darrell King and Brett Heckman designed the jacket.

Publisher's Note: The original financial and economic analysis in *Conquer the Crash* remains intact as it was presented in March 2002. The updated analysis begins on page 281.

Contents

Foreword

"Look out! Look out! Look out! Look out!"
— Barry, Greenwich and Morton,
via The Shangri-Las

My first book, *Elliott Wave Principle*, which I wrote with A.J. Frost, was very bullish. It came out in November 1978, with the Dow at 790. Today the outlook is much different. Now is not the time to take financial risks. It's time to batten the hatches so you can emerge safe from the storm.

As you can see by this book's title, I am once again calling for events that few expect. But this time, I feel more trepidation about doing so. Deflation and depression are exceedingly rare. Sustained deflation hasn't occurred for 70 years, and the last one was so brief that it lasted less than 3 years. During the past two centuries, there have been just two periods that historians unanimously identify as depressions. The 19th century had one, and the 20th century had one. Predicting such extraordinary events is a complex and challenging task. Everyone who has tried it in the past fifty years has failed. Amidst today's social psychology, merely addressing the ideas of deflation and depression is considered something akin to heresy or lunacy. Survey after survey shows that most economists believe that depression and deflation, considered together or separately, are utterly impossible now if not *ever*. Most believe that the U.S. economy is in a rising trend of perpetual prosperity with moderate inflation and that if any interruptions do happen along the way, they will be mild and brief.

Despite this overwhelming consensus, I am resolute. Book One tells you why, and Book Two tells you what to do if you agree with my conclusions.

If by some bizarre circumstance you are already convinced that preparing for deflation and depression is your desired course of action, you can turn to Book Two right now. If not, then you need Book One. Before you can take steps to protect yourself against a deflationary crash and depression, you have to understand what they are, believe that they are possible, and then agree that they are *likely*. Guiding you to that point is Book One's goal. After you assimilate those ideas, you will be primed to act confidently to insure your survival and prosperity, as outlined in Book Two.

Warning

I've been wrong before. The biggest mistake of my career was in the stock market. After identifying the start of the great bull market and later forecasting, "Investor mass psychology should reach manic proportions," even I never imagined that the stock mania would last as long or go as high as it did. So I jumped off the train too early. Regardless, I think my *basic interpretation* of the long-term financial picture, which we will explore in Chapter 4, is correct. It has never been a matter of *whether* we would experience a tremendous bull market followed by a historic bear, only a matter of timing and extent.

The reason that I remain willing to express my unconventional view is that I believe that my ideas of finance and macroeconomics are correct and the conventional ones are wrong. True, wave analysts make mistakes, but they also make stunningly accurate long-term forecasts. In contrast, those who do not understand waves can't make any useful social predictions at all.

It may seem to you that the prospect of taking actions that are contrary to the beliefs of a vast array of experts is a big risk to take. But a practical point virtually eliminates that risk: If you follow the advice in this book and no financial crisis occurs, *you cannot get hurt.* In fact, you should profit nicely from most of these suggestions. Even if my outlook proves incorrect, the worst case is that your money will earn less than it otherwise may have. Compare these outcomes to the opposing scenario: If conventional economists, who in the aggregate have a perfect record of failing to predict economic contractions, are wrong again, you will lose everything that you have worked so hard to obtain. You will also blow the chance to make a fortune beginning at the next major bottom.

Here's a bonus: If you end up missing out on some of the investment profits that a decade of prosperity can provide, I hereby truly apologize; I know what it feels like to miss an opportunity, and I will regret that I influenced you to do so. By contrast, if you get destroyed financially by following the bullish advice of economists, money managers, brokers, media experts and the like, they will not apologize. They will claim that the future was unforeseeable, so *the rock-hard convictions and platitudes that they cavalierly expressed, the ones that you relied upon to plan your financial future,* were wrong through no fault of their own.

There is one catch: I refuse to offer you an excuse to disclaim all responsibility. If you lose your money, your house, your income and your pension in a deflation and depression, at least you can blame the experts for it. You can cry, "I did what *they* all told me to do!" If you take action after reading this book, I insist that you do so because you *agree* with my case, not because you are blindly following my conclusions. To be successful in life, or at least to learn something along the way, you have to think for yourself.

—*Robert Prechter, March 2002*

BOOK ONE

WHY A STOCK MARKET CRASH, MONETARY DEFLATION AND ECONOMIC DEPRESSION ARE LIKELY TO OCCUR SOON

PART I

THE CASE FOR CRASH AND DEPRESSION

Uncomfortable woman in car: "I'm sitting on something!"
W.C. Fields: "I lost mine in the stock market."
                                   —*International House* (1933)

Chapter 1:

A Myth Exposed

How many times over the past decade have you heard glowing reports about the "New Economy"? Hundreds, maybe thousands of times, right? Those of you who have been living on a desert island or who are reading this book fifty years from now can experience the same thing vicariously through Figure 1-1, which displays the accelerating frequency with which the global media have been referring to the "New Economy" year after year. It's been everywhere. Economists celebrate the broadening "service economy" and proclaim that economic growth in the new Information Age has been "unprecedented" in its vibrancy, resilience and scope. Rhetoric is cheap. Evidence is something else.

What would you say if you discovered that *we have not had anything near a New Economy*, that all that talk is a lie? This chapter is going to show you that the vaunted economic expansion of recent decades in the world's leading economic power, the United States — much less the rest of the world — is far less impressive than you are being led to believe.

First take a look at Figure 1-2, which depicts the U.S. stock market from its low in 1932 during the Great Depression all the way to the present. This graph delineates five phases — or "waves" — of rise and fall.

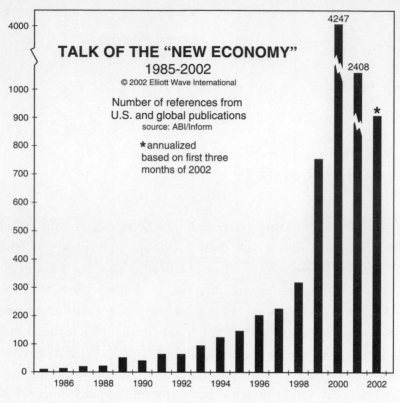

Figure 1-1

The notes on the chart summarize a shocking fact: The economic expansion during the latest phase, wave V, which lasted from 1974 to 2000, was demonstrably weaker than that during the preceding rising phase, wave III, which lasted from 1942 to 1966. Both periods sported a persistent bull market in stocks that lasted about a quarter century, so in that sense, they are quite similar. One noticeable difference is that the DJIA gained only 971 percent during wave III but a remarkable 1930 percent during wave V, *twice the amount.* This tremendous bull market in stocks in wave V is the great "boom" that people feel in their bones. Yet as you are about to see, the economic vigor and financial health

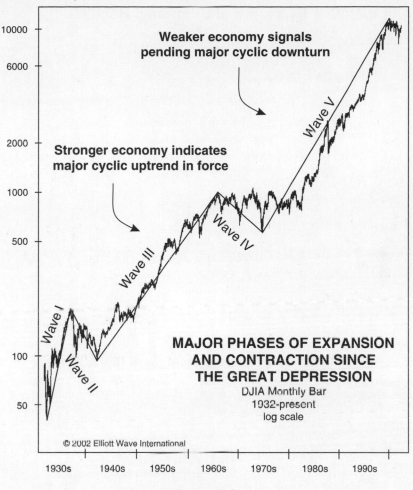

Figure 1-2

of wave V, the one that has received so much radiant press, failed
to measure up to those of wave III by every meaningful
comparison.

   Please go through the following citations one by one.
(Economists do not have all the data from the 1940s, so in some
cases, our data for wave III begin later.) After you absorb this
information, we will set to the task of finding out what it means.

Comparative Measures of Economic Health

(see Figure 1-3)

Gross Domestic Product

> • In wave III, from 1942 to 1966, the average annual real
> GDP growth rate was **4.5** percent.

> • In wave V, from 1975 through 1999, it was only **3.2**
> percent.

Industrial Production

> • In wave III, the average annual gain in industrial pro-
> duction was **5.3** percent.

> • In wave V, it was only **3.4** percent.

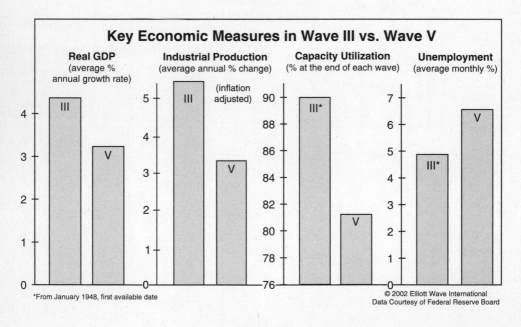

Figure 1-3

Combining GDP and industrial production figures, we may generalize from the reported data that the economic power of wave V was one-third less than that of wave III.

Capacity Utilization

Factories' capacity utilization depicts the energy of an economic expansion compared to the infrastructure's ability to handle it.

• In wave III from 1948 (when figures became available), capacity utilization rose 22 percent to **91.5** percent in June 1966 and stayed high through the late 1960s.

• In wave V, capacity utilization was net flat, peaking in January 1995 at **84.4** percent. U.S. plants were producing at only 82.7 percent of capacity at the ensuing peak in June 2000.

Unemployment Rate

This is an economic measure of *ill* health.
• In wave III from 1948 (when data became available), the monthly average of the unemployment rate was **4.9** percent.

• In wave V, it was **6.6** percent.

Comparative Measures of Debt, Deficits and Liquidity

(see Figure 1-4)

To grasp the full measure of the underlying weakness of wave V's "fundamentals," one must look beyond economic figures to the corporate, household and government balance sheets that underlie those results.

Balance Sheet Items at the End of Wave III vs. Wave V
(scales at left)

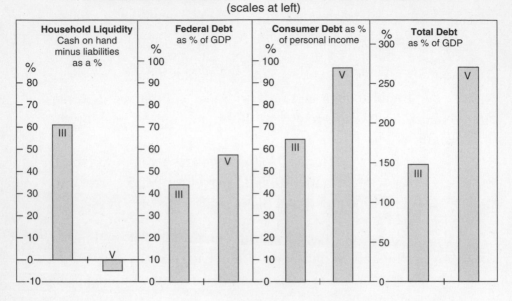

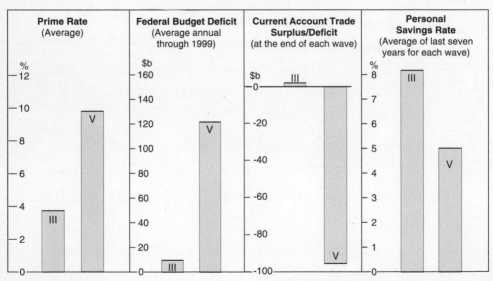

© 2002 Elliott Wave International
Data Courtesy of Ned Davis Research and Federal Reserve Board

Figure 1-4

Households' Liquid Assets

- At the end of wave III, households' liquid assets were **161** percent of liabilities.

- At the end of wave V, households' liquid assets were **93** percent of liabilities, meaning that they had *less cash on hand than they had liabilities.*

Federal Debt

- At the end of wave III, federal debt was **43.9** percent of GDP.

- At the end of wave V, it was **58.6** percent.

Consumer Debt

- At the end of wave III, consumer debt was **64** percent of annual disposable personal income.

- At the end of wave V, it was **97** percent.

Total Debt as a Percent of GDP

- During wave III, from 1949 to 1966, total credit market debt as a percentage of GDP slipped slightly from **151** percent to **148** percent.

- In wave V, it rose from **172** percent to **269** percent.

Prime Rate

- In wave III, the prime rate of interest, the cost of money for the highest quality corporate borrowers, averaged **3.74** percent.

- In wave V, it averaged **9.66** percent, nearly three times as high.

Federal Budget Deficit

> • In wave III, federal budget deficits were not sustained. The only consecutive years of deficits were in the war years of 1942-1946. The average annual federal deficit was less than **$9** billion.

> • In wave V, the annual federal deficit averaged **$127** billion, which is far greater even when adjusted for inflation.

Current Account Trade Figures

> • At the end of wave III, the U.S. showed a net Current Account trade *surplus* of **$1.3** billion.

> • At the end of wave V, the Current Account showed a record *deficit* of **$96.2** billion.

Personal Savings Rate

> • In wave III, the personal savings rate followed a fairly flat trend, bottoming at **6.5** percent of disposable personal income in February 1969.

> • In wave V, the personal savings rate dropped persistently, falling to a record low of **0.5** percent in March 2000.

U.S. Balance Sheet (not shown)

> • At the end of wave III, the U.S. was a net **creditor**.

> • At the end of wave V, the U.S. was a net **debtor**, owing a record $2 trillion more to foreigners than it is owed.

These figures, dramatic as they are, do not reveal the full extent of wave V's inferior relative performance because both the government's economic reports and corporate accounting methods changed during wave V in such a way as to overstate wave V's economic vigor. If we adjusted for those cosmetic alterations, most of these figures would reveal an even greater dichotomy between the two periods. If we begin wave V's figures in 1982 to put the expansion in the best possible light, they change little and in a few cases are worse. If the Dow were to manage a new high in coming months, we would have to add the weak economic and financial figures of the past two years to wave V's average performance, which would drag it down even more. So you see, *it has not been a New Economy after all* but rather a comparatively lackluster one.

Economic Deterioration During the Final Decade of Wave V

The economic expansion waned not only on a long-term basis but also on a near-term basis, *within* wave V. While real GDP stayed fairly steady throughout the bull market, some measures showed a subtle but persistent slowdown in economic vibrancy. For example, average annual corporate profit growth fell from **10.8** percent in the first 15 years of the bull market to **8.8** percent in the 1990s, a decline of about **20** percent. From the stock market's low in September/October 1998 through the third quarter of 2000 (the peak of economic performance for that period), profit growth averaged only **4.6** percent, revealing further slowing as wave V crested.

Portent of Reversal?

Collectively, these statistics reveal that the economic advance in the United States has been slowing *at multiple degrees of scale*, a trend that is still manifest today. A continuation of this trend will mean that the expansion that resumed in October 2001 will be the briefest and weakest yet.

The persistent deceleration in the U.S. economy is vitally important because, in my opinion, it portends a major reversal from economic expansion to economic contraction. Chapter 5 will expand upon the reasons for this conclusion. As we are about to see, though, we need not rely on hypothesis alone. The 20th century provides two great precursors to the current situation.

The U.S. in the 1920s

If you recall your economic history, you know that a phrase in vogue in the 1920s was that the economy had entered a "New Era." Economists of the day, as President Hoover ruefully recalled in his memoirs, gushed over the wonderful economy, just as they are doing today. Were the Roaring 'Twenties truly a New Era, or was such talk a spate of hype spurred by the good feelings associated with a soaring stock market?

According to data from Professor Mark Siegler of Williams College (MA), from 1872 through 1880, the annual inflation-adjusted Gross National Product of the United States rose from $98 billion to $172 billion, a **68** percent gain. From 1898 to 1906, real GNP rose from $228.8 billion to $403.7 billion, a **56** percent gain. In contrast, from 1921 through 1929, during the Roaring 'Twenties, GNP in the supposed "New Era" rose from $554.8 billion to $822.2 billion, only a **48** percent gain. This latter performance was particularly poor given that the *stock market* enjoyed a greater percentage rise from 1921 to 1929 than it had done in any equivalent time in U.S. history.

Similarly to today, the economy of that time failed to keep pace with the advance in stock prices *and* under-performed the prior expansion. The aftermath was the Great Depression.

The Japanese Experience and Its Implications

If you are over 20 years old, you surely remember the "Japanese Miracle" of the 1980s. The country's products were the best in the world. Its corporate managers lectured and wrote books on how they did it, and the world's CEOs flocked to emulate their style. The Japanese Nikkei stock average soared, and foreign investors poured into the "sure thing." Was the Japanese economy truly miraculous, or once again were economists ignoring economic statistics and simply expressing the good feelings associated with its stampeding stock market?

Figure 1-5 shows real GDP growth in Japan from 1955 to the present. Notice that Japan's growth from 1955 through 1973 was extremely powerful, averaging **9.4** percent per year. But its economic growth from 1975 through 1989 averaged only **4.0**

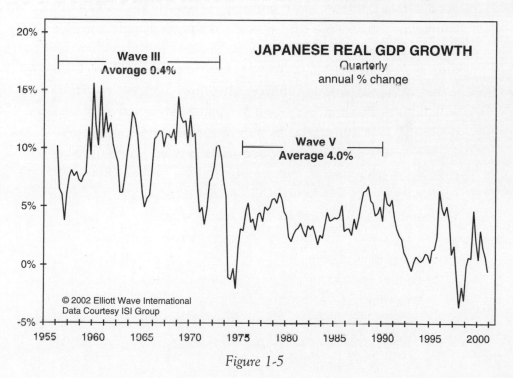

Figure 1-5

percent per year. This relatively poor economic performance coincided with a record-breaking stock market boom. Just as in the
U.S. in the 1920s, the economy in Japan's celebrated years failed
to keep pace with the advance in its Nikkei stock index *and* under-performed the prior expansion. This double dichotomy signaled
an approaching reversal of multi-decade importance in both stock
prices and the economy. Since the top of its own "wave V," the
Nikkei stock index has plunged 70 percent, the economy has had
three recessions in a dozen years, and the banking system has become deeply stressed. As we will see in Chapter 8, this downtrend
isn't over yet.

A Naked Emperor

The "New Era" of the 1920s ended in a bust. The "Japanese Miracle" of the 1980s ended in a bust. Is that what will
happen to today's "New Economy"? We have already gotten a
hint of the answer. The next seven chapters will provide a definitive reply to that question.

When historians return to this time, I suspect that they
will discover the slow but persistent regression in both U.S. and
worldwide growth over the decades in the latter half of the twentieth century and wonder why so few recognized it as a signal of
the coming change.

Chapter 2:

When Do Depressions Occur?

Depressions are not just an academic matter. In the Great Depression of 1929-1933, many people lost their investments, their homes, their retirement plans, their bank balances, their businesses — in short, their fortunes. Revered financial professionals lost their reputations, and some businessmen and speculators even took their own lives. The next depression will have the same effects. To avoid any such experience, you need to be able to foresee depression. Let's see if such a thing is possible.

Defining Depression

An economic contraction begins with a deficiency of total demand for goods and services in relation to their total production, valued at current prices. When such a deficiency develops, prices for goods and services fall. Falling prices are a signal to producers to cut back production. In response, total production declines.

Economic contractions come in different sizes. Economists specify only two, which they label "recession" and "depression."

Based on how economists have applied these labels in the past, we may conclude that a recession is a moderate decline in total production lasting from a few months to two years. A depression is a decline in total production that is too deep or prolonged to be labeled merely a recession. As you can see, these terms are quantitative yet utterly imprecise. They cannot be made precise, either, despite misguided attempts to do so (more on that later).

For the purposes of this book, all you need to know is that the degree of the economic contraction that I anticipate is far too large to be labeled a "recession" such as our economy has experienced eleven times since 1933. If my outlook is correct, by the time the contraction is over, no economist will hesitate to call it a depression.

Depressions and the Stock Market

Our investigation into the question of forecasting begins with a key observation: *Major stock market declines lead directly to depressions*. Figure 2-1 displays the entire available history of aggregate English and American stock price records, which go back over 300 years. It shows that depression has accompanied every stock market decline that is deep enough to stand out on this long-term graph. There are three such declines, which occurred from 1720 to 1784, 1835 to 1842 and 1929 to 1932.

To begin to orient you to my way of thinking, I would like to explain Figure 2-1's title. The stock market is modern society's most sensitive meter of social mood. An increasingly optimistic populace buys stocks and increases its productive endeavors. An increasingly pessimistic populace sells stocks and reduces its productive endeavors. Economic trends lag stock market trends because the consequences of economic decisions made at the peaks and nadirs of social mood take some time to play out. The Great Depression, for example, bottomed in February 1933, seven months after the stock market low of July 1932. So psychological trends create economic trends. This causal relationship between psychology and the economy is the opposite of what virtually everyone presumes, so do not be alarmed if you find it counter-intuitive. Chapter 3 will elaborate on this theme.

If you study Figure 2-1, you will see that the largest stock-market collapses appear *not* after lengthy periods of market deterioration indicating a slow process of long-term change but quite suddenly after long periods of rising stock prices and economic expansion. A depression begins, then, with the seemingly unpredictable reversal of a persistently, indeed often rapidly, rising stock market. The abrupt change from increasing optimism to increasing pessimism initiates the economic contraction.

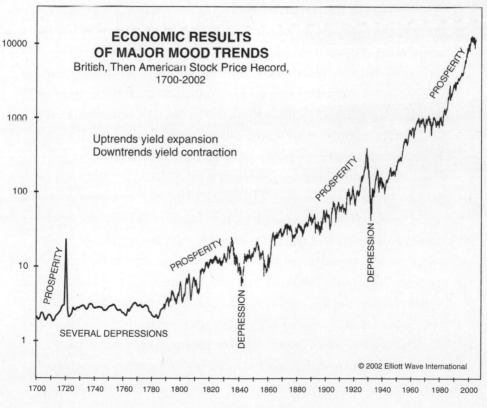

Figure 2-1

The graph shows that these reversals do not appear after every period of rising stock prices but only after some of them. If you are guessing that maybe one of the hints of reversal is a slowing economy in the face of such advances, you're right. We'll learn even more about this factor in Chapters 3 and 5.

Hierarchy in Finance and Economics

You might be interested to know that almost every smaller stock market decline observable in Figure 2-1 also led to an economic contraction. The severity of each contraction is related to the size of the associated stock market decline.

Unfortunately, this hierarchy in economic trends is difficult to display because conventional quantitative definitions of recession get in the way. Sometimes the economy just fails to breach the arbitrary definition of "official recession" that economists use, so their graphs show no recession when in fact the economy contracts, corporate earnings fall, and economic indicators weaken. In some cases of brief or small stock market declines, the economy simply slows down without actually having a "negative" month or quarter, but an effect occurs nevertheless.

Modern attempts to quantify the term "recession" by absolute size are flawed. It would be as if botanists decided to define "branch" or "twig" by length and width. The result may denote an "official" branch or twig, but the definition would obscure the actual continuum of sizes attending parts of trees. Likewise, attempted quantifications of the term "recession" derive from and foster misunderstanding with respect to the hierarchical nature of economic expansion and contraction. It would be far better for economists to adopt the perspective of the Wave Principle, a model of hierarchically patterned financial market change, which we are about to encounter in the next chapter.

All We Need

Such discussions aside, Figure 2-1 is all we need for our purposes. It shows that the biggest stock market declines follow long periods of advance of like degree. They lead to economic contractions so dramatic that nothing gets in the way of their being noticed and recorded as "depressions." Now let's see if we have the means to anticipate their arrival.

Chapter 3:

When Do Stock Markets Turn from Up to Down?

We see that depressions accompany major stock market declines. So if we can predict those rare and dramatic bear markets, we can predict depressions. Can we do that?

The Stock Market Is Patterned

In a series of books and articles published from 1938 to 1946 (available in *R.N. Elliott's Masterworks*, 1994), Ralph Nelson Elliott described the stock market as a fractal. A fractal is an object that is similarly shaped at different scales.

A classic example of a self-identical fractal is nested squares. One square is surrounded by eight squares of the same size, which forms a larger square, which is surrounded by eight squares of that larger size, and so on.

A classic example of an indefinite self-similar fractal is the line that delineates a seacoast. When viewed from space, a seacoast has certain irregularity of contour. If we were to drop to ten miles above the earth, we would see only a portion of the seacoast, but the irregularity of contour of that portion would resemble that of the whole. From a hundred feet up in a balloon, the same thing would be true. These ideas are elucidated in Benoit Mandelbrot's *The Fractal Geometry of Nature* (1982) and numerous publications since.

Scientists recognize financial markets' price records as fractals, but they presume them to be of the indefinite variety. Elliott undertook a meticulous investigation of financial market behavior and found something different. He described the record of stock market prices as a *specifically patterned* fractal yet with variances in its quantitative expression. I call this type of fractal — which has properties of both self-identical and indefinite fractals — a "robust fractal." Robust fractals permeate life forms. Trees, for example, are branching robust fractals, as are animals' circulatory systems, bronchial systems and nervous systems. The stock market record belongs in the category of life forms since it is a product of human social interaction.

How Is the Stock Market Patterned?

Figure 3-1 shows Elliott's idea of how the stock market is patterned. If you study this depiction, you will see that each component, or "wave," within the overall structure subdivides in a specific way. If the wave is heading in the *same* direction as the wave of one larger degree, then it subdivides into *five* waves. If the wave is heading in the *opposite* direction as the wave of one larger degree, then it subdivides into *three* waves (or a variation). Each of these waves adheres to specific traits and tendencies of construction, as described in *Elliott Wave Principle* (1978).

Waves subdivide this way down to the smallest observable scale, and the entire process continues to develop larger and larger waves as time progresses. Each wave's degree may be identified numerically by relative size on a sort of social Richter scale, but to keep things simple, this book's brief references to specific degrees use their traditional names.

Figure 3-2 shows a rising wave in a manner more consistent with Elliott's detailed observations about typical real-world development. Observe, for example, that waves 2 and 4 in each case take a slightly different shape.

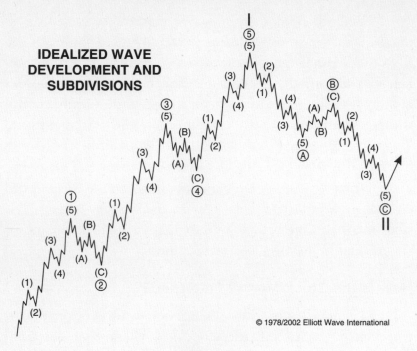

IDEALIZED WAVE DEVELOPMENT AND SUBDIVISIONS

© 1978/2002 Elliott Wave International

Figure 3-1

A MORE REALISTIC WAVE DEPICTION

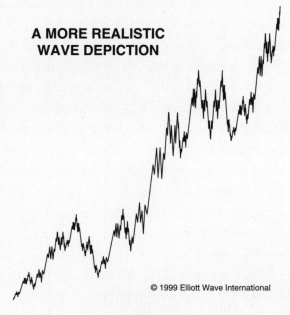

© 1999 Elliott Wave International

Figure 3-2

Understanding how the market progresses at all degrees of trend gives you an invaluable perspective. No longer do you have to sift through the latest economic data as if they were tea leaves. You gain a condensed view of the whole panorama of essential trends in human social mood and activity, as far back as the data can take you.

Why Is the Stock Market Patterned?

For the most part, consumers judge prices for bread and shoes consciously and reasonably according to their needs and means. When human beings value financial assets, they must contend with a debilitating lack of knowledge and feelings of uncertainty. They contend with these obstacles to a great degree by forming judgments in sympathy with or in reaction to the opinions and behavior of others. This surrender of responsibility makes them participants in a collective, which is not a reasoning entity. The fact that price changes are patterned proves that the collective's net valuations are not reasoned, but it also shows that they are not random, either. The remaining option is that they are unconsciously determined. Indeed, shared mood trends and collective behavior appear to derive from a herding impulse governed by the phylogenetically ancient, pre-reasoning portions of the brain. This emotionally charged mental drive developed through evolution to help animals survive, but it is maladaptive to forming successful expectations concerning future financial valuation. The only way for an individual to temper the consequences of the herding impulse and to gain independence from it is to understand that it exists. For some evidence of these conclusions, please see *The Wave Principle of Human Social Behavior* (1999).

Examples of Real-World Waves

Figures 3-3 through 3-6 display advancing waves in various financial markets. As you can see, they all sport five waves

SAMPLE ELLIOTT WAVES

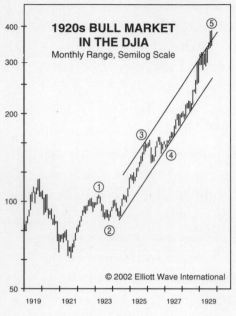

Figure 3-3

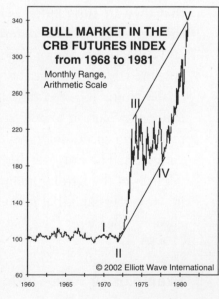

Figure 3-4

Figure 3-5

Figure 3-6

up. These five-wave patterns proceeded relentlessly, ignoring news of every imaginable variety, including Prohibition, a crash in Florida land values, Roosevelt's seizure of Americans' gold, Hitler's rise to power and the end of the Vietnam war.

I chose these examples because they display one of Elliott's guidelines, which is that bull market waves often end after reaching the upper parallel line of a trend channel. In most cases, the market creates channels in which the lower line touches the bottom of waves 2 and 4, while the upper line touches the top of wave 3 and, later, wave 5.

A Quiz

OK, now you try it. Figure 3-7 shows an actual price record. Does this record depict two, three, four or five completed waves? Based on your answer, what would you call for next?

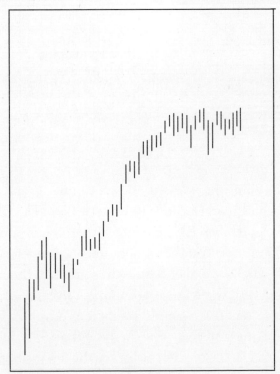

Figure 3-7

"Surveying all the market's action over the past 200
years, it is comforting to know exactly where you are
in the wave count."

— *The Elliott Wave Theorist*, November 8, 1982

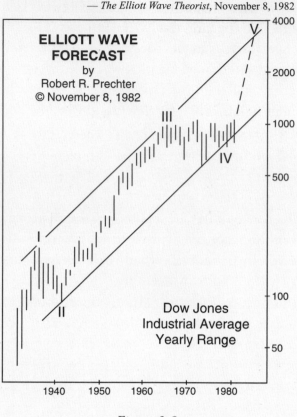

Figure 3-8

Let's compare your answer with mine. From the simple
idea that a bull market comprises five waves, *The Elliott Wave
Theorist* in September 1982 called for the Dow to quintuple to
nearly 4000 and on October 6 announced, "Super bull market
underway!" The November 8 issue then graphed the forecast for
the expected fifth wave up, as you can see in Figure 3-8.

I have kept this example as simple as possible. To view the
detailed labeling and real-time analysis that fully justified the
prediction made in Figure 3-8, please see the discussions attending
the Appendix and Figures 5-5 and 8-3 in *Elliott Wave Principle*.

As you can see, Elliott waves are clear not only in retrospect. They are often — particularly at turning points — quite clear in prospect. I could fill a book describing other triumphs (and failures) of applying the Wave Principle, but I hope this one example conveys its occasionally immense value for forecasting.

What Are the Signs of a Topping Stock Market?

Simply stated, a stock market uptrend ends when five waves of a specific construction are complete. The larger the degree of those five waves, the larger will be the ensuing partial retracement of their progress.

The real world is not as tidy as an idealized depiction of a wave, just as real trees are not as tidy as any single summary depiction of a tree in general. Often third waves are long, with distinct subdivisions. Sometimes first or fifth waves extend in the same manner. Using price patterns alone, there can often be some doubt as to whether one is accurately identifying a fifth wave or whether it might be part of another wave's extension.

To help overcome difficulty in real-world application, I recorded certain traits that waves seem always to display. Figure 3-9 illustrates some of these traits.

For the purposes of this book, the most crucial description is the one attending wave 5: "Market breadth and the economy improve, *but not to the levels of wave 3*. Optimism creates lofty valuation." These observations, which I formulated in 1980 after studying myriad fifth waves, tell us four things to look for any time we presume that the stock market is in a major *fifth* wave rather than a first or third wave:

(1) A fifth wave must have narrower "breadth" than the corresponding third wave, i.e., there must be fewer stocks advancing on the average day in a fifth wave than in the preceding third wave of the same degree.

Elliott Wave Characteristics
© 1980/2002 Elliott Wave International

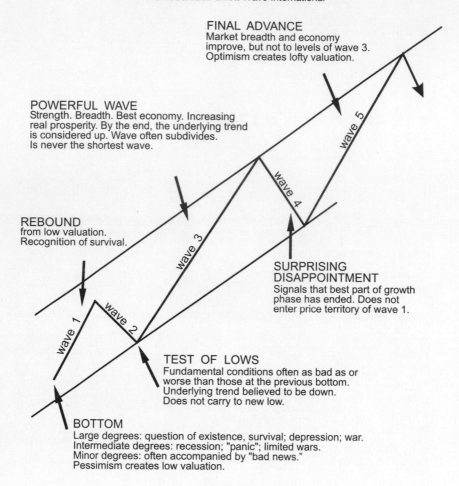

FINAL ADVANCE
Market breadth and economy
improve, but not to levels of wave 3.
Optimism creates lofty valuation.

POWERFUL WAVE
Strength. Breadth. Best economy. Increasing
real prosperity. By the end, the underlying trend
is considered up. Wave often subdivides.
Is never the shortest wave.

REBOUND
from low valuation.
Recognition of survival.

**SURPRISING
DISAPPOINTMENT**
Signals that best part of growth
phase has ended. Does not
enter price territory of wave 1.

TEST OF LOWS
Fundamental conditions often as bad as or
worse than those at the previous bottom.
Underlying trend believed to be down.
Does not carry to new low.

BOTTOM
Large degrees: question of existence, survival; depression; war.
Intermediate degrees: recession; "panic"; limited wars.
Minor degrees: often accompanied by "bad news."
Pessimism creates low valuation.

Figure 3-9

(2) In a fifth wave, there must be a lesser expansion in the
economy and weaker financial conditions than occurred
during the corresponding third wave.

(3) Stocks must attain high valuations based on their historic relationship to related data.

(4) There must be evidence of optimism among investors.

While we have already learned something along these lines in Chapter 1, Chapters 5 through 7 will discuss each of these aspects in detail, one at a time, with respect to today's stock market.

These distinctions, helpful though they are, do not eliminate uncertainty in interpretation. For example, sometimes fifth waves are quite brief, and other times they go on and on. Their own five-wave subdivisions will in turn display the proper characteristics of waves, of course, helping us to assess the picture. But because these wave characteristics are *relative*, there can always be more development that still reflects these guidelines even after the market has already met the minimum criteria.

That being said, we can often be certain of important things. For example, using the above criteria, we can *know* that a certain wave is — or is not — a fifth wave. The bigger it is, and the longer it has lasted, the more important that information becomes. Early in the process, we can anticipate the ultimate reversal; later in the process, we can begin to assert boldly that a downturn is imminent.

The reason that identifying the end of a fifth wave is so important is that when a fifth wave ends, a correspondingly large bear market ensues. That's what happened after each one of the bull markets shown in Figures 3-3 through 3-6. At this point, we have enough knowledge to figure out the position of the stock market in its wave pattern *right now*.

Chapter 4:

The Position of the Stock Market Today

Figures 4-1 through 4-3 display my interpretation of the stock market's wave position today at three degrees of trend. Once again, I am keeping these illustrations and explanations as simple as I can. Many fascinating nuances attend these structures, and you will be well rewarded for taking the time to study them via Elliott Wave International's publications if you are so inclined. Suffice it for now to say that the foregoing conclusions are consistent with the analysis of the main wave practitioners of the past century: R.N. Elliott (1871-1948), Charles J. Collins (1894-1982), A. Hamilton Bolton (1914-1967) and A.J. Frost (1908-1999). Their published works on the subject — along with my own — are available in their entirety (aside from a handful of Elliott's lost "market letters") for review at elliottwave.com/books.

Figure 4-1 shows the uptrend of a postulated "Grand Supercycle" wave ③ from 1784 (plus or minus a decade; records are sketchy) to the present. As you can see, its broad strokes seem to trace out a five-wave structure. I have left the preceding bear market of 64 years in British stock prices on the chart to show that the advance arose from the ashes of a bear market of corresponding degree, wave ②.

Figure 4-2 shows the detail of the fifth wave from Figure 4-1, "Supercycle" wave (V), which was born in 1932 at the bottom of the biggest bear market since the 1700s. As you can see, it

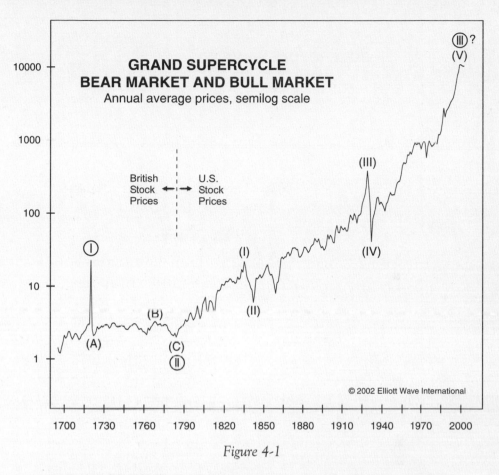

Figure 4-1

is easily identified as a five-wave structure, which emerged from the ashes of a bear market of corresponding degree, wave (IV). As Chapters 5 through 7 will show, this labeling is definitive.

Figure 4-3 shows the detail of the fifth wave from Figure 4-2, "Cycle" wave V, which began in 1974 at the bottom of wave IV, the biggest bear market since the one that ended in 1942. As you can see, the rise can be labeled as five completed waves, and in this case, they form a trend channel. Although I would like to be able to assert that Figure 4-3 is definitive, certain nuances of wave identification allow a slight chance that the Dow could make another new high within Cycle wave V. In that case, the final rally, currently underway, will be brief and short.

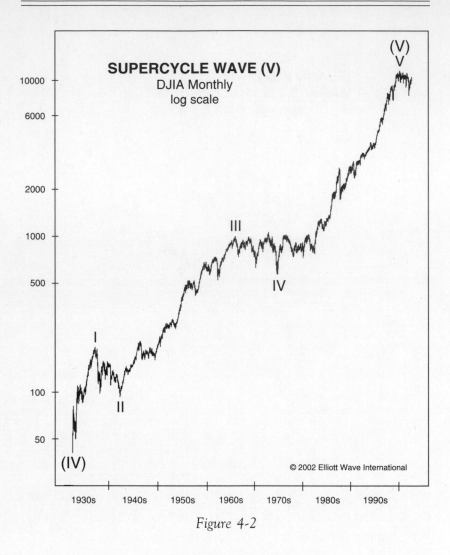

Figure 4-2

My summary of these pictures, then, is that the uptrend from around 1784 is *probably* five waves, the uptrend from 1932 is *definitely* five waves, and the uptrend from 1974 is *very probably* a completed five waves. To conclude, then, here is what we have: A bull market that has endured since the time of the Great Depression is definitely ending, and its termination could well mark the end of an uptrend of one degree larger, which has endured since the founding of the Republic.

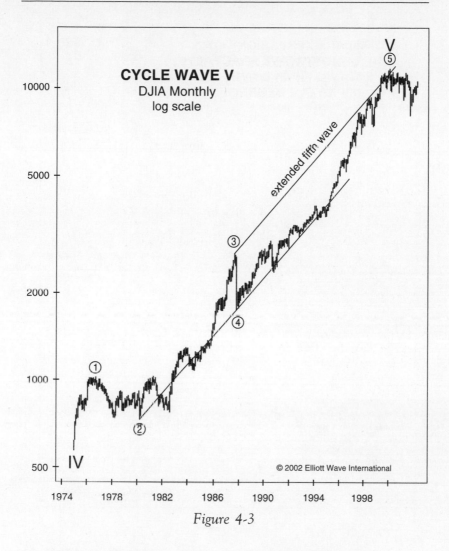

Figure 4-3

Specific Renditions of the Stock Market Fractal

The last time that the stock market formed a fifth wave of Cycle degree was in the 1920s. That's why Elliott-wave forecasts from November 1978 and September 1982 specifically called for the emerging bull market to "parallel the 1920s." (See *Elliott Wave Principle*, Chapter 8 and Appendix.) Although the two waves in Figure 4-4 are quite different quantitatively in terms of both duration (8.05 vs. 25.1 years) and extent (596.5% vs.

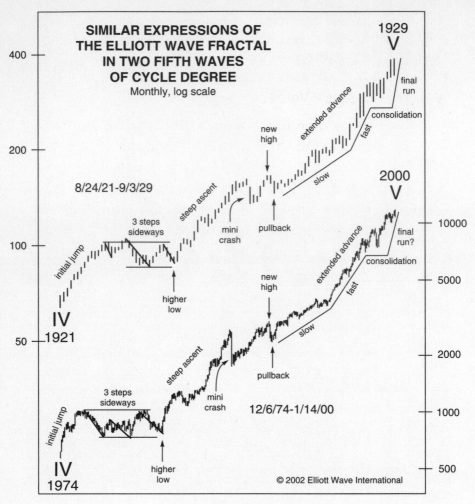

Figure 4-4

1929.6%), you can see that their *forms* are strikingly similar. If you apply your calculator to the figures just quoted, you will also discover that the lower graph rises 3.2 times the percentage gain of the upper graph in 3.1 times the time. In other words, their overall rates of ascent are essentially identical. If someone had showed you these two data series — unmarked — under the guise that they were concurrent, wouldn't you agree that they were correlated? In my opinion, the similarities between the two advances are not coincidental. This form is an expression of how mass psy-

chology progresses in Cycle degree fifth waves that contain extended fifth sub-waves, apparently an ideal setting for an
investment mania.

Worldwide Stock Values

The long-term Elliott wave position and outlook are
hardly confined to the United States. The World Stock Index,
which reflects the total value of stocks worldwide, also shows
five waves up from 1974 and portends a major decline. The wave
labeling in Figure 4-5 is slightly more detailed, showing Intermediate and Primary degree subdivisions.

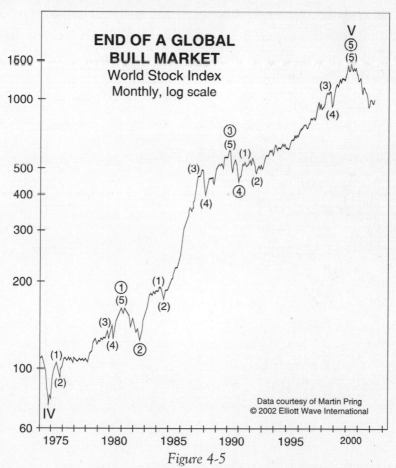

Figure 4-5

A Final Selling Opportunity in the Making

Immediately after the terrorist attack of September 11, 2001, the U.S. stock market was shut down. The entire country, not just the investment community, was in a panic. That day, my publication, *The Elliott Wave Theorist*, issued a forecast diagram of the Standard & Poor's 500 Composite Index. It called for the index to fall just a bit further and then begin the largest rally since it topped in March 2000. Six trading days later, the stock market bottomed and turned up.

You can see in Figure 4-6 why I made that forecast. In September 2001, the S&P Composite (along with the Wilshire 5000 and other indexes) was clearly finishing *five waves down*. If you re-examine Figure 3-1, you will see that a pattern of five waves down from a bull-market high always calls for a bear-market rally in an up-down-up pattern and then a resumption of the larger downtrend. The S&P's five waves down, then, called for a

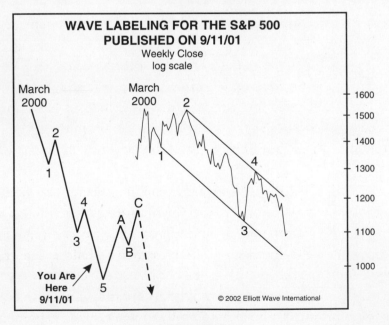

Figure 4-6

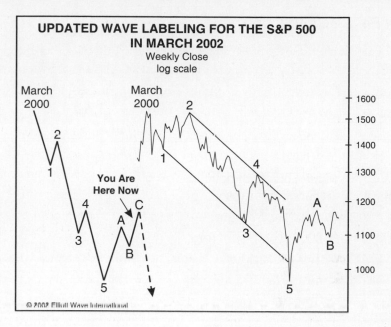

Figure 4-7

corresponding three-wave rally, which began on September 21, six days after the market re-opened.

Most segments of the market are still advancing here near the end of the first quarter of 2002 as I put the final touches on this book. The S&P and the Wilshire 5000 indexes have continued to follow the expected path, as you can see in the updated graph of the S&P in Figure 4-7, and the Dow has climbed back above 10,000.

This rally has been strong enough in selected secondary issues to propel two stock averages, which are constructed so as to reflect this bias, to new all-time highs, as you can see in Figure 4-8. While the first quarter of 2000 presented a whale of a selling opportunity for the S&P and the NASDAQ, the current rally is creating one just as good for many sectors of the market. Releasing this book into the heat of this rally should provide maximum benefit to you.

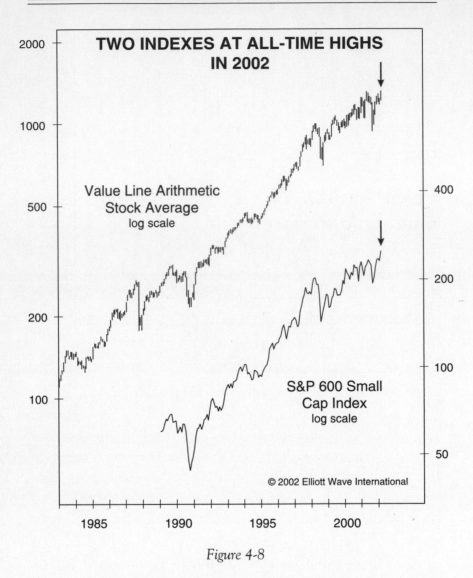

Figure 4-8

Further upside potential is nothing more than a near-term consideration. What you need to care about is the major reversal that is about to impact your financial health dramatically. The following three chapters demonstrate the extremely high probability that the larger advancing wave depicted in Figure 4-2 — the one that began seven decades ago — has run its course.

Chapter 5:

Evidence from Stock Participation and Economic Performance

Now let's conduct two key investigations to help answer the question of whether the advance from 1974 was truly a fifth wave. First we will examine the breadth of the market, and then we will confirm the value of our economic analysis in Chapter 1.

Stock Selectivity in Wave V

Elliott Wave Principle notes, "Fifth waves in stocks are always less dynamic than third waves in terms of breadth." In other words, if the advance from 1974 to 2000 is truly a *fifth* wave, then it must have been more selective than the third wave in terms of the number of stocks participating in the uptrend. Let's find out if wave V performed as expected compared to wave III.

Figure 5-1 shows the entire available history of what market analysts call the "advance-decline line." It is a cumulative sum of the daily ratio of the number of stocks advancing minus the number declining, the net then divided by the total number of changed issues. The resulting graph, for which the data begins in 1926, shows the tendency for all stocks traded to advance or decline on a daily basis. As you can see by the trend of this line, for most of waves I, III and V, when the overall trend of the Dow

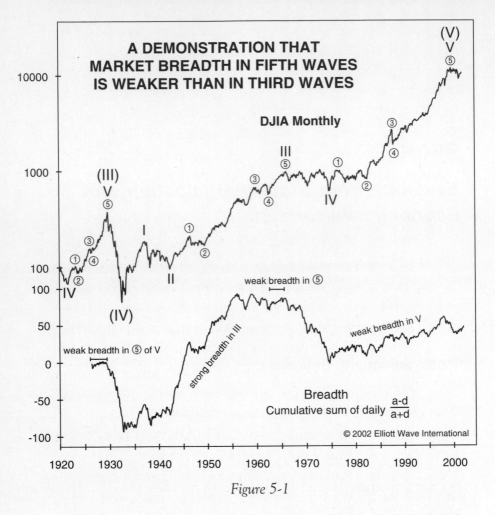

Figure 5-1

was up, more stocks advanced on the average day than declined, and for most of waves II and IV, when the overall trend of the Dow was down or sideways, more stocks declined on the average day than advanced.

Look more closely at the details of the line. Notice that during the stock market advance from 1926 to 1929, which was a fifth wave within a fifth wave, the advance-decline line made almost no upside progress. Observe that near the end of wave III, when subwave ⑤ was in force, the advance-decline line was not rising as dynamically as it was during the earlier wave ③. This is the breadth guideline of Figure 3-9 in action.

Now look at the dramatic difference between the behavior of this line from 1974 to 2000 and how it performed from 1942 to 1966. Despite what pundits myopically call "the greatest bull market in history," the advance-decline line over 26 long years of bull market was so weak that it could not even retrace what it lost in the bear market of 1966-1974, a mere eight years!

Anecdotal evidence dramatizes the difference. Here is R.N. Elliott's 1946 description of one stunning consequence of the overwhelming breadth of wave ① of III:

> The first wave, from 1942 to 1945, disclosed inflationary characteristics. Low-priced stocks of questionable value surged ahead at the expense of the "blue chips." *The New York Sun* selected ninety-six stocks that advanced phenomenally. Every stock started at some figure below $2 per share. The highest rate of advance was 13,300 percent. The lowest rate of advance was 433 percent. The average for the group was 2,776 percent.

Contrast that performance with the briar patch of the 1990s. In *The Wall Street Journal*'s stock-picking contests, for example, the pros beat the Dow only a little over half the time. Here are sample reports from some of the rougher periods:

July 13, 1994: **Darts Beat Pros but Losses Are the Rule**
> Four stocks chosen by a random throw of darts fell an average 8.7 percent between Jan. 10 and June 30, compared with an average loss of 13 percent for stocks selected by a team of four investment professionals. The Dow Jones Industrial Average, meanwhile, declined 6.2 percent.

July 10, 1996: **Pros Lose Out to Chance, Industrials**

The stocks chosen by the four pros declined an average 9.2 percent, while four stocks selected by flinging darts at the stock tables fell 5.3 percent. But the industrial average rose a tidy 10.2 percent.

February 11, 1997: **Investment Pros Defeat Darts, but Can't Top Surging Market**

Four investment professionals' stock picks posted an average gain of 7.7 percent in just under six months as of Jan. 31, 1997, a full three percentage points better than the Wall Street Journal staffers' dart board choices. However, the Dow's gain for the period was 19.6 percent.

April 9, 1997: **Pros Beat Darts, but in a Losing Contest**

Four stocks selected by the pros all lost money in the period from last Oct. 8 through March 31, declining an average 10 percent. They still did better than the forces of chance. Four stocks chosen by flinging darts at the stock tables dropped an average 16.9 percent. The Dow Jones Industrial Average, meanwhile, rose 9.6 percent during the same period.

May 13, 1998: **Pros Beat Darts, but Picks Trail Dow Jones Industrials**

Investment professionals walloped the [darts] but still couldn't keep up with the surging Dow Jones Industrial Average. The four pros racked up a 17.4 percent gain in the period from Nov. 12, 1997 to April 30, compared with an average loss of 10.5 percent for four stocks selected by Wall Street Journal staffers flinging darts at the stock tables. Meanwhile, the industrial average gained 22.5 percent.

November 5, 1998: ***Darts Draw Blood as Pro Losses Far Exceed Those of Industrials***

If you have been having trouble picking winning stocks in recent months, you aren't alone. A team of four investment professionals posted an average investment loss of 23.6 percent in this column's latest stock-picking contest, from May 12 through Friday. A portfolio of four stocks chosen by Wall Street Journal staffers flinging darts at the stock tables did only slightly better, with an average loss of 21.5 percent in the period. The Dow Jones Industrial Average slid 6.2 percent.

Stock market investors in the early 1940s, rare though they were in the beginning years of the wave (V) uptrend, must have felt like geniuses. Whatever method they used to pick stocks would have worked. Fund managers and stockbrokers in the 1980s and 1990s had no such luxury. Every other month, their clients would demand to know why their selections were not keeping up with the Dow, S&P and NASDAQ indexes. As the averages were soaring skyward in 1998, one brokerage firm manager confided to me, "I'm more depressed than I have ever been in my whole life." The key to his misery is that aside from a breathtaking "Internet stock" frenzy in 1999, the blue-chip components of the Dow, S&P and NASDAQ were the heart of the mania. Few stock pickers, money managers or stockbrokers could outperform them because the number of other stocks participating in the bull market was relatively small.

The Wave Principle not only provides a basis for *understanding* this breadth dichotomy but also a model for *predicting* it. The observation in Figure 3-9 and the simple labels "IV" and "V" in Figure 3-8 portended relative selectivity in the forecasted bull market, which is exactly what we got.

It is crucial to observe that *all* fifth waves feature a sharp deterioration in breadth. At stock market tops, when the "fifth of the fifth" wave is in force, the advance/decline line is typically already heading down. For example, in wave V of the 1920s, the advance-decline line peaked in May 1928, 16 months before the final high in the Dow. It trended down while the Dow traced out its final wave (5) of ⑤. Similarly, in the latest wave V, the advance-decline line peaked in April 1998, 21 months before the Dow's high in January 2000. During wave (5) of ⑤, which began in late 1998, breadth was so weak that the advance-decline line went down not only as the Dow and S&P market averages went to a new high but also as the NASDAQ nearly quadrupled! This is one reason why I am fairly confident that the labeling of the sub-waves in Figures 4-3 and 4-5 is correct, which means that the time is right to undertake the safeguards outlined in the second half of this book.

Economic Weakness in Wave V

As noted in Figure 3-9, if the advance from 1974 is truly a fifth and final wave, then it must also display weaker economic performance and financial conditions than did the preceding third wave, the one that lasted from 1942 to 1966. As you saw in Chapter 1, that's exactly what it did, by every pertinent measure. Chapter 1 also described two precedents, the U.S. experience of the 1920s and the Japanese experience of 1974-1989, in which economic performance seriously lagged both the stock market and the economic expansion of the previous comparable period. Now we see that the Elliott wave model both supports the implication of these analogies to the current situation *and explains them*: All three cases involve a major fifth wave; in fact, they were all of Cycle degree, labeled wave V under the Wave Principle.

Observe the similarity between the trends of the economic data summarized in Figure 1-2 and the advance/decline line of Figure 5-1. Both sets of statistics show weakness in wave V relative to wave III as well as deterioration in the latter portion of wave V as compared to the earlier portion. These two sets of data reveal a parallelism between the "technical" and "fundamental" aspects of waves, i.e., the psychology of waves and their product.

The Value of Knowing the Difference

Economists do not even *comment* upon the blatant long-term deterioration in economic performance over the last half-century. Now you know that there is an approach to macro-economic forecasting that actually *predicted* it.

In fact, the idea that there is a difference between economic performance during a *third* wave and that during a *fifth* wave has been a part of the Wave Principle for over twenty years. Frost's and my 1978 book *Elliott Wave Principle* describes third waves as "wonders to behold" as they bring about "increasingly favorable fundamentals." In contrast, "the fifth of the fifth [wave] will lack the dynamism that preceded it." By labeling the 1942 to 1966 bull market as "wave III," we established the economic growth rate of the 1950s and 1960s as a standard that the new bull market would not surpass. In an August 1983 report on the developing "Super Bull Market," *The Elliott Wave Theorist* reiterated the expected relationship between the two periods, adding, "This fifth wave will be built more on unfounded hopes than on soundly improving fundamentals such as the U.S. experienced in the 1950s and early 1960s."

These descriptions and forecasts were issued years before the data became available for wave V. Can you imagine any such perspective from conventional macroeconomics? I believe that wave analysts were able to anticipate the difference because we understand the dynamics that were set up to produce it.

Furthermore, we did not wait for recession to be in force before presenting this crucial data to business people who had to plan well ahead of the 2001 recession's arrival (which economists now date back to March 2001). In September 1998, five months after the top in the advance/decline line and 16 months before the top of wave V, we published "Wave V Fundamentals and Their Implications," which laid out the case (reprinted in *View from the Top of the Grand Supercycle* and re-capped here in Chapter 1) for an approaching major reversal in the economy. Anyone who read that article was given the opportunity to begin positioning his business dealings for the approaching trend change while everyone else was becoming overly extended speculating on the New Economy. The good news is that there is still time to take advantage of the opportunity, well before anyone else knows what's happening.

The Reason for Narrowness and Deceleration

Why does stock participation narrow and why does the economy expand more slowly in fifth waves? The simple answer to this question is that stock market advances and economic cycles must get weaker before they reverse. The final rise is where that weakness must be evident. Advances come in five waves, so the fifth wave is where the relative weakness manifests.

The mechanism of that difference, I believe, is the immense optimism of major fifth waves, which encourages the populace to engage in financial speculation. Third waves are built upon muscle and brains. Fifth waves are built upon cleverness and dreams. During third waves, people focus on production to get rich. During fifth waves, they focus on finance to get rich. Manipulating money is not very productive. The entire enterprise costs a fortune in transaction costs, personnel and time. Extensive borrowing for speculation also requires extensive interest payments, and the rising cost of interest burdens the entire process of production. In a production-oriented economy, most enterprises benefit. In a finance-oriented economy, comparatively few entities benefit. These differences show up blatantly in the advance/decline line and more subtly in overall economic performance figures.

A prime symbol of the deterioration in wave (V) of ⓘ (for orientation, see Figure 4-1) is the Federal Reserve System. Its manipulation of money and credit for the past 89 years (see Chapter 10) has been so destabilizing that it has transformed America from a production powerhouse into a society obsessed with dodging inflation and manipulating money and credit. These preoccupations have so burdened the productive capacity of the United States that even the major expansion of the 20th century, wave (V), has experienced a slowing in the rate of real growth relative to the major expansion of the 19th century, wave (III).

A prime symbol of the deterioration in wave V of (V) is General Electric, the oldest name in the Dow Jones Industrial Average. Through wave III ending in 1966, GE was one of the finest engineering and manufacturing concerns in the world. Its goods lasted for decades. In wave V, accountants took over the company and transformed it from a manufacturing concern into a financial concern. Today, its manufactured goods are often mediocre and its vaunted company a cardboard edifice of credit services. It is the United States in microcosm.

It's a Fifth Wave

The latter half of the last sixty years has seen deterioration both in the breadth of stock participation in the market's advance and in the long-term rate of economic progress. The degree of slowing — covering decades — confirms that the advance since 1974 is a *fifth wave*, which supports the wave labeling of Figure 4-2.

Chapter 6:

The Significance of Historically High Stock Market Valuation

Recall that fifth waves produce "lofty valuation" for stocks. The evidence that wave V in the global bull market has produced historically high valuations for corporate shares could fill two books. Let's look at the primary data for U.S. valuations to verify this point.

Dividend Yield

The "yield" of the Dow Jones Industrial Average is the annual dividends that the 30 companies listed in the Dow pay out to shareholders as a percentage of their stock prices. If you study Figure 6-1, you will see that investors accept low dividends at market tops and demand high dividends at market bottoms. It is easy to understand why. At tops, they believe that stocks will go up much more, providing a huge capital gain, so who needs dividends? At bottoms, they believe that stocks will fall much more, providing a capital loss, so they demand high dividends to offset their perceived risk.

Of course, this thinking is backwards and makes investors lose money. It nevertheless must be this way because if they acted otherwise, markets would not be continually forming tops and bottoms.

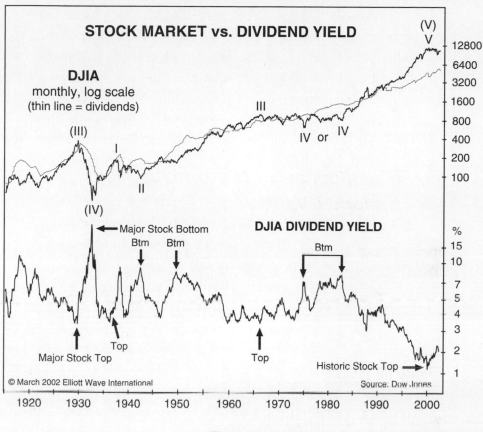

Figure 6-1

Observe that the DJIA's dividend yield tends to be around 6.5 percent near moderate bear market bottoms. It went far higher at the bottom of the Great Depression. Conversely, the dividend yield has tended to be around 3 percent at major tops, including the historic top of 1929.

In 2000, the Dow's dividend yield did something that it had never done before. It reached 1.5 percent. A larger index of industrial stocks, the Standard & Poor's 400 Industrials, yielded only 1 percent. This is historically high valuation.

It takes about 1 percent of the value of a stock for an investor to buy and then sell it. The dividend payout in the year 2000, then, was enough to cover transactions costs *if* you were to buy and sell no more than once a year. If you own shares of a mutual fund, the managers take 1 percent annually for fees. At 1 percent, then, stocks effectively have no yield. What's more, the DJIA represents the best of the country's blue-chip stocks. Most companies listed on the NASDAQ exchange pay no dividends at all. Throw in transaction costs or management fees, and they have a negative yield.

Today, optimists argue that dividends "don't matter." They claim that "investors want companies to plow money back into the company" so that the company will be more profitable and the stock price will go up more. These are excuses and rationalizations. If no dividend is ever paid, of what value is a share of stock? Do you really want to own a share of a super-successful enterprise that handsomely pays everyone involved in it except you, an owner?

The few optimists who still think that dividends matter declare that stock prices need not fall because our "unprecedented economy" eventually will generate enough corporate income to pay those higher dividends. Yet after two decades of nearly uninterrupted economic growth, it hasn't happened. Given the evidence in this book, it isn't about to happen, either. The economy will be unprecedented, all right, but in the other direction.

The inevitable fluctuations of mass psychology assure that at some time in the future, the dividend yields on the Dow and other major stock indexes will be far higher than they are today. Unfortunately, the change is not going to come about with a simple adjustment downward in stock prices. The reason is that when stock prices fall substantially, the result is almost always a weaker economy. The degree of the currently developing down-turn is so large that the economy will undoubtedly become extremely weak, and that trend in turn will put pressure on companies to *decrease* dividends. Falling dividends will follow falling stock prices, and falling stock prices will chase falling dividends, making it difficult for the stock market to return to an attractive yield typical of major bottoms. Stock indexes have a *long way down to go* before their yields return to levels that reflect investor pessimism.

Book Value

If a company has to value itself for liquidation, it does so on the basis of the market value of its assets. A company's "book value" comes close to reflecting that value.

As we are about to see, stock prices today reflect the most expensive valuation of corporate assets in recorded history. Today's stock prices are not just historically high compared to book values; they are amazingly, outrageously high.

How did they get that way? One of investors' requirements for buying expensive stock during the 1990s was that the associated company continually report higher earnings per share. Such an achievement is meaningless in isolation, because the real question is what are the earnings *relative to the size of the company* and *relative to the price of the stock*, questions no one has been asking. As you can see, we are not dealing with reason here but with rationalization. The last time investors adopted this guideline was the late 1920s. (For more on that point, see Graham & Dodd's comments in Chapter 14 of *Market Analysis for the New Millennium*, 2002.) Because investors adopted this guideline, "aggressive" accounting methods sprang up during wave V to help companies repeatedly perform the feat of reporting higher earnings per share. Achieving that goal often meant diluting the *true* underlying value of the company, for example by using company assets to buy back the company's own shares. As we will see in a moment, today's book values reflect this dilution.

A Composite Measure of Valuation

A low dividend yield might be acceptable if there were no other yields available, but there are. They come from bonds, and investors can choose between the two sources. To compare their

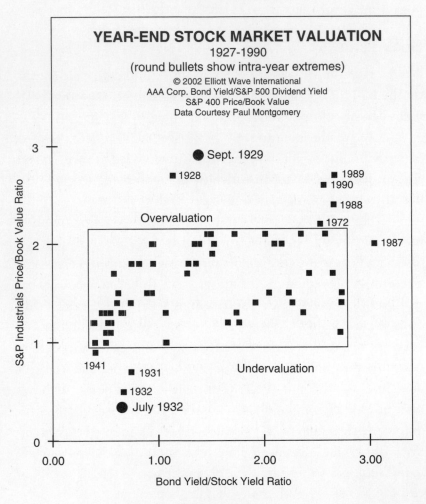

Figure 6-2

valuations, we must ask, what is the relative yield between the best stocks and the best bonds?

Figure 6-2 combines two of our benchmarks. The vertical axis reports the price-to-book value of the S&P 400 Industrials index. The horizontal axis reports the yield from top-grade corporate bonds relative to the yield of top-grade S&P 500 stocks. The rectangular box on the chart delineates the range of values that has held for most of the 20th century. Additional figures from prior years show that year-end bond yield/stock yield ratios were well to the left side of this box at least back to 1870.

Until 1987, only five years since 1927 (where our graph begins) ended with values outside that box, and only two of those were on the high-valuation side. These five readings indicated historic extremes of either pessimism or optimism and therefore a likely major turning point in the stock market.

Do you see anything missing from Figure 6-2? If you look closely, you will see that it is lacking a crucial set of data points, namely, all of the year-end values for the past 11 years!

Now look at Figure 6-3, which includes the year-end valuations from 1991 to the present. The bullet denoting valuations in March 2000 looks like Pluto in a picture of our solar system, doesn't it?

You do not need to investigate the worth of any argument that purports to justify these stock values. All you need is eyes.

The squares representing values at the end of 2000 and 2001 indicate that the trend has reversed. Rest assured that sometime soon, annual valuations will be back in that box. In fact, if investors follow their usual pattern, the decline will not end until there is at least one bullet below and/or to the left of the box.

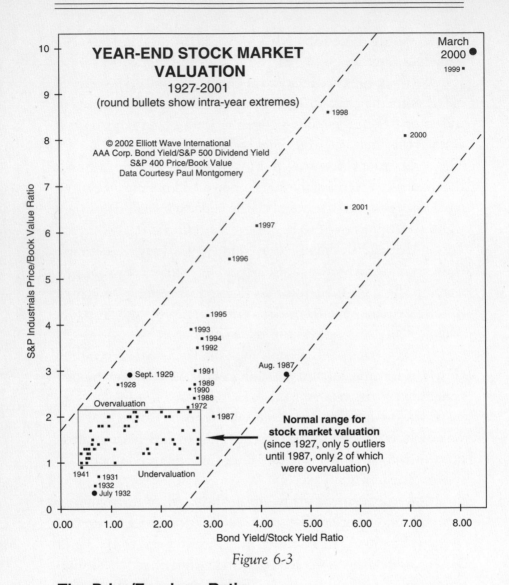

Figure 6-3

The Price/Earnings Ratio

The price/earnings ratio is the only popular market valuation indicator on Wall Street. It is also the least valuable except in rare cases.

The P/E is the ratio between the price of stocks and the value of their associated companies' annual earnings per share.

Sometimes the ratio's compilers use *projected* earnings, which is what brokerage house analysts think that earnings *will* be. Needless to say, earnings estimators are repeatedly too pessimistic at bottoms and too optimistic at tops, just when you most need the indicator to tell the truth. Therefore, our graph will compare stock prices to *actual* earnings for the preceding year.

Corporate earnings cycle with the stock market but with a 2-month to 2-year lag. Earnings do not begin to rise until well after stock prices have turned up from a bottom, and they do not begin to fall until well after stock prices turn down from a top. For this reason, the two trends often oppose each other. In contrast, book values and dividend payouts tend to be much steadier, cycling only on a very long-term basis with the largest economic trends, therefore providing a steady benchmark against which to compare stock prices to obtain a reliable relative valuation measure. There usually is little point in comparing stock prices to corporate earnings because the two opposing cycles push and pull on the ratio in such a way as to render most current readings nearly meaningless for market timing purposes. Most of the time, you could divide stock prices by the price of pickles and have a more reliable indicator.

There is one exception to this general objection. *After* the stock market has made a turn of *major* import, the earnings cycle comes into play with investor psychology in a most interesting way.

Usually, investors (erroneously) welcome rising earnings as bullish. There is one time that they don't, which (naturally) makes them wrong again.

Go back to Figure 3-9 and note the characteristics of "wave 2." That's when people believe fervently that the larger trend is down, *even though it isn't*. An excellent example of this proclivity is the fact that a New York Stock Exchange survey

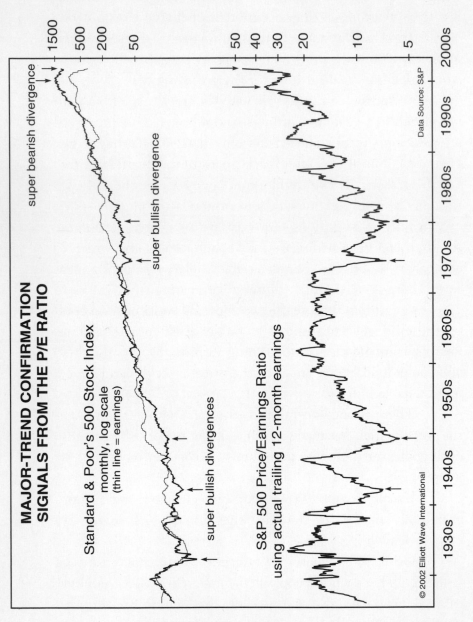

**MAJOR-TREND CONFIRMATION
SIGNALS FROM THE P/E RATIO**

Standard & Poor's 500 Stock Index
monthly, log scale
(thin line = earnings)

super bearish divergence

super bullish divergence

super bullish divergences

S&P 500 Price/Earnings Ratio
using actual trailing 12-month earnings

© 2002 Elliott Wave International

Data Source: S&P

1500
500
200
50

50
40
30
20

10

5

1930s   1940s   1950s   1960s   1970s   1980s   1990s   2000s

Figure 6-4

conducted in 1952 found that a paltry 4 percent of eligible Americans owned stocks! The other 96 percent apparently believed that holding stock was foolish and risky. Of course, the market was in the early years of a multi-decade uptrend; that's when people think this way.

Figure 6-4 displays the P/E ratio for the S&P 500 Composite index from the mid-1920s to the present. Study the first set of arrows toward the left of the graph. Generally speaking, earnings were dutifully following the stock market upward after the major bottom of 1932. Nevertheless, in 1942 and again in 1949, investors' pessimism was so strong that it pushed the P/E ratio *below its level at the preceding lower stock market bottom.* These readings indicated *deep pessimism in the face of rising stock prices and an expanding economy* and therefore an immense psychological potential to drive stock prices higher. The middle set of arrows marks a second occurrence of this phenomenon in 1980, when stocks had a lower P/E ratio than they did at the preceding lower stock market bottom in 1974. In each of these cases, stocks had already launched a huge long-term advance, and most of it lay ahead.

Today, for the first time in the history of the figures, we have the opposite situation, with the opposite implication. When stock prices decline from a major top, commercial activity decreases, and lower earnings follow. Last year, earnings fell faster than the S&P did, so the P/E ratio rose despite lower stock prices. It fact, it rose so strongly that the P/E ratio at the end of December was 46, the highest *ever*. The P/E ratio on the S&P 400 Industrials was 53. P/E ratios for the S&P 500 have ranged from around 7 at bear market bottoms to the low-to-mid 20s at bull market tops. So the S&P's P/E ratio today is twice what it is at a typical bull-market top and *six to seven times* what it is at a typical bear-market bottom. In other words, the S&P would have to fall about 85 percent to get its P/E to normal bottom levels, *and that's if earnings fall no further*. Earnings *will* fall in a bear market that size, so today's P/E ratios portend the same stock price debacle that is implied by the stock market's wave structure, the low dividend payout, overpriced book values and the high bond yield/stock yield ratio.

Today's record P/E ratios alone are enough to command attention (the stock/pickles price ratio is near the highest ever, too), but what matters more is the P/E ratio *relative* to the action of the market and the economy. Examine the third set of arrows, toward the right of Figure 6-4. Although earnings have been dutifully following the stock market downward since shortly after the top in the first quarter of 2000, investors' optimism remains so strong that it has pushed the P/E ratio to *above its level at the preceding higher stock market top*. This dramatic rise to an all-time record indicates *entrenched optimism in the face of falling stock prices and a weakening economy* and therefore an immense psychological potential to drive stock prices lower. The implication of this divergence is that blue-chip stocks have already launched a bear market with much more ahead of it than lies behind.

Why does this phenomenon occur? Early in major uptrends, investors remain deeply scarred psychologically by their experiences in the preceding bear market and economic contraction. Though the downtrends and contractions are over, the fear of them remains. The P/E ratio reaches an extreme low because people believe that the rise in earnings is temporary and that the economy will collapse back downward, justifying low stock valuations. The second arrow in the final set (marked "NOW") reflects investors' diametrically opposing attitudes today. Though the trend of stocks has been sideways to down for two years and the economy has receded, the presumption that the old uptrend and expansion are the natural order of things remains as firm as ever. Investors anticipate — directly opposing their counterparts of the 1940s — more glory days ahead. People think that earnings will begin rising again, and they want to own as much stock as they can before that happens.

The first problem with this idea is that investors have priced stocks so high that to get them bear-market cheap again, earnings would have to soar 600 percent, and that's if the S&P does not budge a single point higher than it is today! The second problem is that the extended economic expansion that so many expect almost certainly is not going to happen. If my interpretation of the P/E disparity is accurate, it has not been a stock market "correction" in the S&P; it's a bear market, which means that the economic contraction is not merely a "mild, brief recession," it's the first contraction in a developing depression.

Obfuscation and Rationalization

As I write this chapter, the "watchdog" of earnings, Standard & Poor's, has just bowed to pressure to change the basis of its earnings reports to "operating earnings" rather than total company earnings. As a result, the reported P/E ratio has suddenly changed to about half of what it really is. Analysts are expected to tack these ratios onto the old ratio's eighty-year history as if they are the same thing. Operating earnings omit several items, the main one being "non-recurring expenses." *Hello!* All expenses affect a company's performance. A creative accountant can drive a truck through that loophole and manipulate operating expenses to almost any desired level. Yet another proposal, to report only "core earnings," will exclude gains or losses due to companies' pension fund obligations. If my outlook is right, these obligations will soon be killing the profitability of industry. Leaving potentially massive drains on capital out of the earnings calculation is like leaving torture equipment out of a description of a dungeon. Real investors want real numbers, and these changes provide the opposite. The desperation within the financial world to avoid reporting "bad news" (i.e., the truth) is obviously immense.

How do so many public and professional investors justify holding such expensive stocks today? The latest issue of *Money* magazine (March 2002) quotes a manager at one of the largest stock mutual funds in the world: "You have to trust them. To some degree they become faith stocks." *Money* concurs, "Investors must rely as much on gut instinct as on objective analysis. Sometimes an extra-large helping of hope is required." One could hardly utter a worse guide to life, much less to the assumption of financial risk. Those of us dedicated to objective financial analysis aren't always right. But those who rely on extra-large helpings of trust, faith, hope and "gut instinct" always regret it.

Chapter 7:

The Significance of Historically Optimistic Psychology

The engine of high stock market valuation is widely shared *optimism*. The greater the degree of the advance that is ending, the greater the optimism at its peak. Optimism also tends to remain strong in the early stages of a bear market (waves "A" down and "B" up, in wave parlance). Bull markets, they say, climb a "Wall of Worry." I like to add, "and bear markets slide down a Slope of Hope."

Today, are investors optimistic or pessimistic, and to what degree? The answer is that measures of optimism in early 2000 reached awesome, historic levels, and they remain just below — and in some cases even above — those levels today. As you are about to see, psychology is a long way from the shared deep pessimism that produces a buying opportunity.

Psychology of Academics

In about 1997, professors, PhDs and decorated economists at universities and think-tanks began peppering the media with articles that essentially put before the public the idea that macroeconomic science has lent its sanction to the historic extremes in stock values generated by the great asset mania of the 1980s and 1990s. In *The Wall Street Journal* alone, we have read bullish essays and learned of bullish studies by two Nobel laureates, a former Fed Governor and scholars at the American Enterprise Institute, the University of Pennsylvania, the Massachusetts Institute of Technology, the Brookings Institution, the Wharton School, the University of Rochester, Princeton University, New York University, Bear Stearns, Credit Suisse First Boston, the Federal Reserve Banks of Dallas and Philadelphia, the Hoover Institution, the Discovery Institute and the Graduate School of Business of the University of Chicago, to list just the ones with the most prominent credentials. These articles were most abundant between March 1998 and April 2000, though they still appear today. Not one bases its conclusions on an analytical method that has any forecasting history at all, and others contradict ones that do. During the period that the quotations below appeared, only one academic made a passionate case for investor caution in the WSJ, in two articles published in April 1999 and March 2000.

As you look at the dates of the following quotes from some of these professorial essays, keep in mind that the Value Line Geometric stock average and the advance/decline line peaked in April 1998, the Dow and S&P in gold and commodity terms topped in July 1999, and the nominal highs in the S&P and NASDAQ (and probably the Dow as well) took place in the first quarter of 2000. Here is what the experts have told us:

•March 30, 1998: "Pundits who claim the market is overvalued are foolish."

•July 30, 1998: "This expansion will run forever."

•February 3, 1999: "We have at last arrived in a new-era economy."

•March 19, 1999: "A perfectly reasonable level for the Dow would be 36,000 — tomorrow, not 10 or 20 years from now. The risk premium is headed for its proper level: zero."

•August 30, 1999: "The recent dramatic upswing represents a rosy estimate about growth in future profits for the economy."

•September 18, 1999: "Researchers have found compelling evidence that conventional accounting understates the earning power of today's companies."

•January 1, 2000: "In much the way Albert Einstein's theory of relativity transformed the time-space grid of classical physics at the beginning of the twentieth century, the Einsteins of Internet communications are now transforming the time-space grid of the global economy."

•April 18, 2000: "Don't be fooled. Historical forces continue to point toward a Great Prosperity that could carry the Dow Jones Industrial Average to 35,000 by the end of the decade and 100,000 by 2020."

If this one-sided outpouring of scholarly judgment proves to be anything other than a manifestation of the prevailing optimistic mass psychology that crystallized after 7 decades of mostly rising stock prices and 2½ decades of dramatically rising stock prices, I will be mightily surprised.

Psychology of Economists

Two years ago, as most major U.S. stock indexes reached their all-time highs, *The Wall Street Journal* observed, "Economists are downright euphoric." Of 54 economists surveyed, all but two were bullish for 2000. One year later, when the Dow, S&P and NASDAQ were down 8 percent, 15 percent and 51 percent from their respective highs and the onset of recession was just weeks away, the consensus for continued growth was even stronger. Only one economist out of 54 surveyed called for a recession in 2001. On New Year's Day, January 2002, although the economy had been slumping for nearly a year, economists managed to achieve an even greater optimistic consensus, thanks surely to the Dow's rally back above 10,000. Not one of the 55 economists surveyed for *The Wall Street Journal*'s 2002 forecast expects the recent contraction to develop into a serious decline. All predict that the economy will expand this year and thereafter. The recent stock market rally — reflecting an improving social mood — has naturally led to a minor improvement in a number of economic indicators. These changes have induced economists to keep up the drumbeat. Here are just three excerpts out of hundreds:

The Atlanta Journal-Constitution, February 22, 2002: "Economists Optimistic: Survey Says Recession Likely Is Already Over"
> The U.S. recession has probably ended, according to a survey by the National Association for Business Economics that projects growth of at least 3.5 percent in the second half of 2002 and in 2003.

USA Today, February 28, 2002: "'Recessionette' Might Be at an End"
> Bank One's chief economist calls it a "recessionette," and the U.S. Chamber of Commerce's chief economist insists the current slump is no recession at all.

Fortune, March 18, 2002, adds that such is "the opinion of virtually every economic forecaster out there."

Obviously, economists of all stripes, from theoreticians to practitioners, have been bullish throughout the past two years, right past the top in most stocks, right past the onset of the 2001 recession (which may or may not be "officially" recognized) and right through today. You no longer need guess at the source of those "New Economy" quotes tallied in Figure 1-1.

Economists as a group have an unbroken record of failing to predict economic contraction. Most of the time, ill-timed optimism is harmless because most of the time, recessions are indeed mild and brief. The reason is that the fluctuations in the economy are a hierarchical fractal, as described in Chapter 3. Small, mild retrenchments occur more frequently than large ones, so forecasting errors are only mildly damaging. Yet rarity does not equate to impossibility. It is wrong to assume, after a long period of prosperity with only mild recessions, that the large economic contractions will never occur again. Yet that belief *invariably* materializes at such times. Why is that?

Economists' forecasts always seem to be little different from a description of the present, tempered or augmented by the forward-weighted trends of the past. That's how human nature works. People — including professionals who should know better — generally accept recent experience as "normal," no matter what it is. Economists would serve their clients much better if the trends and extremities of their opinions were the opposite of what they are.

Psychology of Brokerage Strategists

Professional brokerage-house equity-allocation strategists tend to recommend a heavy weighting in stocks just before the market falls and a lighter weighting just before the market ad-

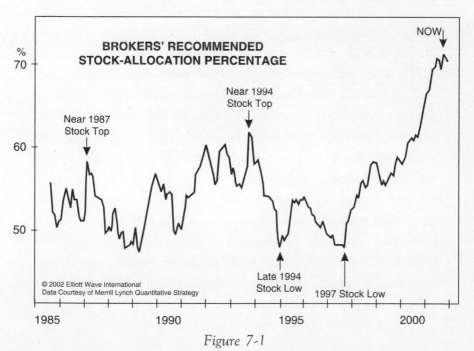

Figure 7-1

vances. This is normal behavior, which itself helps to set the market's highs and lows.

Figure 7-1 shows fifteen years of average weighting recommendations by brokers. Look at their current average opinion: a *record* high weighting recommendation of 71 percent! This is how advisors felt during the rally of early 1930, as well. Their advice was not profitable. Nor should it have been. A consensus this strong *means* that people are about as invested as they can get. It is bearish.

Psychology of Money Managers

In the aggregate, money managers are always most invested in stocks at tops and least invested at bottoms. Figure 7-2 shows how pension funds and insurance companies increased their percentage of stock holdings from 7 percent of total assets in 1952 to 53 percent on New Year's Day, 2000. Figure 7-3 shows the percentage of cash that stock mutual funds hold in their portfolios. Again, they usually hold lots of cash at bottoms and little at tops. Needless to say, it would benefit their clients if they did the opposite. Needless to say, it can be no different.

Managers' optimism today is stunningly one-sided not only in the U.S. but throughout the Western world. Canadian polling firm Towers Perrin reports that among 48 Canadian and 23 foreign investment firms, *not a single one* expects negative returns from their stock investments in 2002. Nor are they just mildly optimistic. As Toronto's *Globe and Mail* (1/10/02) summarizes the survey, "Money managers are looking for *double-digit returns* from Canadian, U.S. and international equity markets this year." Although the analysis in this book focuses primarily on the U.S. equity market, similar conditions attend all stock markets around the globe that have held near their highs.

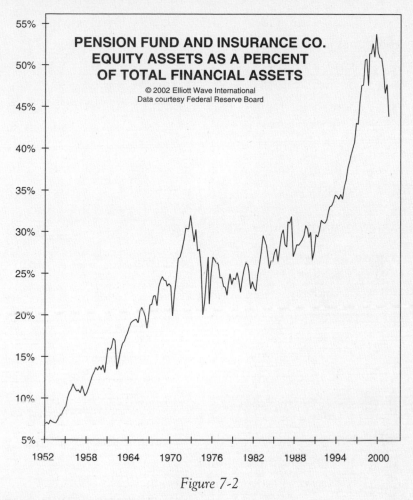

**PENSION FUND AND INSURANCE CO.
EQUITY ASSETS AS A PERCENT
OF TOTAL FINANCIAL ASSETS**

© 2002 Elliott Wave International
Data courtesy Federal Reserve Board

Figure 7-2

Psychology of the Public

The public agrees with the experts. Figure 7-4 shows that investors' margin debt, a paltry $3 billion in late 1974, topped $250 billion in early 2000. In just 25 years, investors multiplied *by over 80 times* the amount of money that they borrowed from brokers to buy stocks. Figures 7-5 and 7-6 are long-term measures of the public's attitude toward stocks. It took decades, but in the 1990s, the public became, by these measures, more bullish than it was at the two biggest tops of the past century: 1968 and 1929.

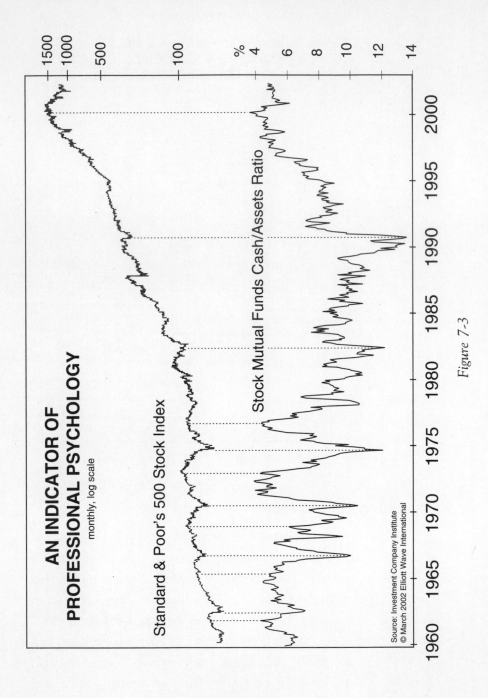

Figure 7-3

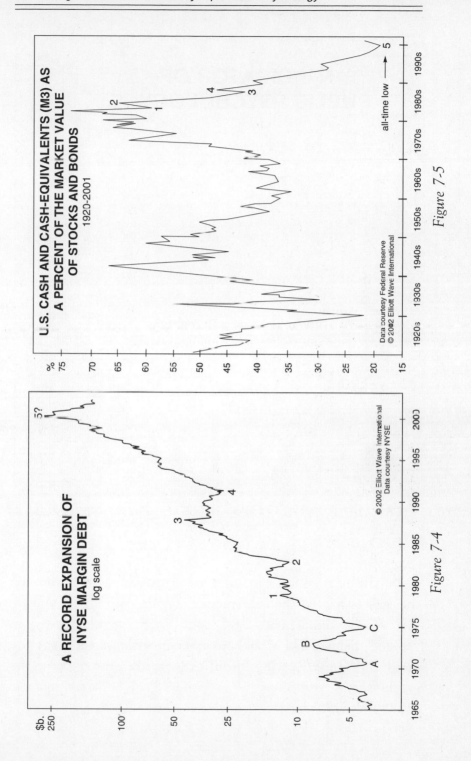

Figure 7-5

Figure 7-4

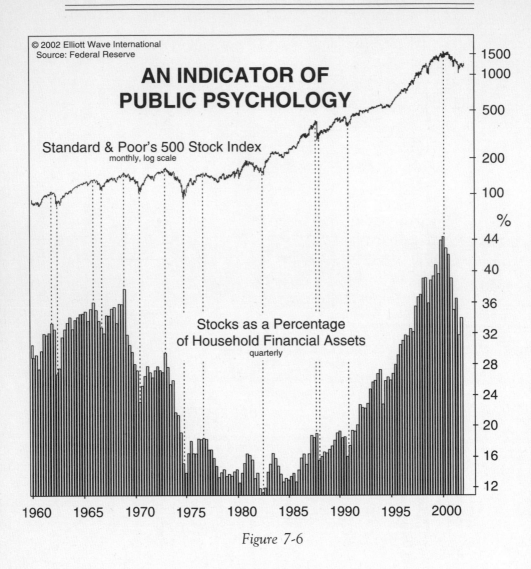

Figure 7-6

In utter contrast to their underinvested counterparts of the early 1950s, over half of American families, which must mean most families that actually have money to invest, are invested in the stock market. These readings make investors' level of excitement during the Roaring Twenties look like ennui. For more graphs of this type, please see Appendix D of At the Crest of the Tidal Wave (1995).

P/E ratios and brokerage strategists' allocations are not the only market psychology indicators at all-time highs. Here in the first quarter of 2002, the weekly survey of futures contract ownership shows that "small traders," i.e., the most naïve market players, have just reached an all-time record in their holdings of "long" futures contracts. The "commercials," i.e., the most sophisticated market players, have held record and near-record levels of *short*

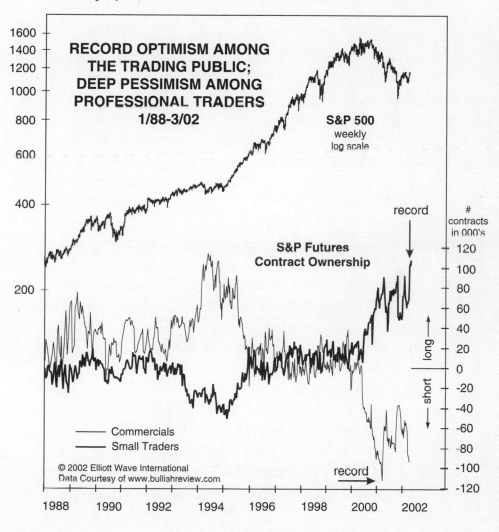

Figure 7-7

futures contracts since mid-2000. Figure 7-7 displays 13 years of history showing that commercials during that time were most bullish at the stock market bottoms of 1990 and 1994 and were most bearish recently; in other words, they tend to be right. Conversely, the public was most bearish in early 1995, as the market was blasting off for a record five-year run. As you can see, the public is generally wrong.

Becoming more bullish at lower prices is highly unusual behavior on the part of investors generally speaking, but, like the P/E phenomenon, *it is normal behavior shortly after a major top in stock prices.* As *Elliott Wave Principle* explained in 1978, "During the A wave of a bear market, the investment world is generally convinced that this reaction is just a pullback pursuant to the next leg of advance. The public surges to the buy side despite the first really technically damaging cracks in individual stock patterns." The B-wave rallies that follow exhibit "aggressive euphoria and denial." The past two years fit these descriptions. As with other indicators presented in this book, Figure 7-7 provides assurance that a major bear market is in force and that the bulk of it lies ahead.

The New York Times reports today (March 12) on a study of "newly optimistic" investor attitudes. It shows that an amazing 90 *percent* of individuals polled say that the stock market will continue to advance over the next 12 months. This revival of optimism is emerging *six months after* the proper time to have been near-term optimistic, six months after *The Elliott Wave Theorist* forecasted the largest rally in the S&P since the all-time high, six months after the bottom of wave A. The article concludes, "The optimism of individuals...suggests that the coming year could be a good one for stocks." This claim reflects a bizarre incognizance of the multi-decade history of stock market sentiment indicators.

Psychology of the Media

As you can see by the graphs in this chapter, there is no question that optimism is entrenched horizontally throughout the nation and vertically through all strata of expertise. This overwhelming consensus has engendered an outpouring of elation from the nation's magazine covers and newspapers' front pages here in the first quarter of 2002. "Positive Reports Hint at Swift Recovery," says *The New York Times*. "Better Times Coming," announces the Minneapolis *Star*. "Hope Soars in U.S." adds Denver's *Rocky Mountain News*. *The New York Post* enthuses, "Recovery at Last." *USA Today* announces, "Fed Chief Declares Recession at an End." *U.S. News and World Report* shows us "How to Cash In." The President himself assures us that 2002 will be a "Great Year."

The newspaper clippings on the following pages show that optimism permeates both local and national news reporting. (In case you can't see the one magazine cover clearly, that's Abraham Lincoln advising, "Buy!") Most of these headlines are from the cover of the magazine or page 1 of the newspaper in which they appeared, which means that editors deem the sentiments worthy of the strongest highlight. It's unfortunate, because such ideas expressed at the wrong time kill people financially and, in extreme cases, physically as well.

The Next Psychological Trend

When the stock market turns back down, academics, economists, advisors, money managers and media commentators will begin to turn bearish. Bad news will begin pouring out of the newspapers as a consequence of the emerging negative-mood trend. The more the market falls, the higher the number of bears will become, because enough time will go by that the trends not only of the present but also of the recent past will be down. The largest number of bears, public and professional, will be at the bottom.

Poll: Americans optimistic

Positive Reports Hint at Swift Recovery
—*New York Times*, December 29, 2001

President says 2002 will be 'a great year'

DECEMBER 31, 2001   BARRON'S

The Case for a "Super-V"

Three stimulating economic factors may come together in 2002

According to various surveys, strategists look for about a 9 percent gain by the Dow Jones industrial average next year, 12 percent for Standard & Poor's 500-stock index and 13 percent for the Nasdaq composite.

Forecast For Growth: Even More

Confidence in economy on the rise
—*The Atlanta Journal-Constitution*, December 29, 2001

Forecasters smell a recovery

STRONG RECOVERY FOR STOCKS
—*Financial Times*, Jan 2, 2002

As 2001 bows out, economy looks up

—*The Atlanta Journal-Constitution*, December 29, 2001

American consumers are ending a frightening year in a cheery mood, more confident about the future.

Consumer spending the key to forecasts for a rebound
—*The Atlanta Journal-Constitution*, December 29, 2001

BANKS FORECAST A STRONG RECOVERY

Economy shows signs of year-end comeback
Recession threatening North America is yesterday's story,' chief economist says
—*Globe and Mail*, December 29, 2001

ANNUAL FORECAST ISSUE

SmartMoney
THE WALL STREET JOURNAL MAGAZINE OF PERSONAL BUSINESS

THE Best Investments FOR 2002

Buy!

As our economy rebounds, these 10 stocks and 6 mutual funds will make you big money. Honest.

Consumer confidence hits unexpected high

Hope Soars in U.S.
—*Rocky Mountain News*, December 29, 2001

Yes, There Are Still Optimists in Japan
—*New York Times*, Dec 30, 2001

Market raises new year hopes

City optimistic after two years of sliding equities

Recession May Have Bottomed
Economy, consumer confidence, home sales and other indicators suggest early recovery.
—*Los Angles Times*, December 29, 2001

Factors seem in place to end market two-year losing streak

"It's clear that we've started the next leg-up."

Economists Declare Recovery
—*USA Today*

"Everything that could be going right for the recovery is going right." Indeed, from manufacturing and consumer spending to construction, almost every report for January and February has beaten expectations. Not only, in the words of one Federal Reserve insider, could the first half "be gangbusters," the momentum may well be sustainable.
—*BusinessWeek*, March 18, 2002

The upbeat trend had economists upwardly revising their quarterly growth forecasts and fund managers enthusiastically reinvesting in the equity markets.

What Recession?
—*Christian Science Monitor*, Mar 12, 2002

Officials Question if Recession Was Real
—*Reuters*, March 4, 2002

Rallying Cry from the US
The US Economy Is Greeting the Arrival of Spring With a Host Of Golden Indicators
—*Financial Times*, Mar 9, 2002

recent data shows that the econom is not only on the mend, but that expectations are also rising for a more robust recovery than previously thought.

GET READY FOR REBOUNDING PROFITS
—*Business Week*, March 25, 2002

Mood on Wall St. Is 'Euphoria'
—*The Record*, Mar 5, 2002

Traders say new buyers are stepping into the market because/no one wants to miss the next leg-up in the rally.

FOR MANY, RECESSION PROVED BARELY VISIBLE
—*Boston Globe*, Mar 11, 2002

With evidence now overwhelming that the recession has ended, some economists argue the decline in output was so mild it didn't qualify as a recession at all.
—*The Wall Street Journal*, March 11, 2002

Chapter 8:

Implications for the Stock Market and the Economy

If the analysis in the preceding chapters is correct, the U.S. stock market, and by extension most stock indexes world-wide, is rounding the cusp of a trend change of at least Supercycle degree. The DJIA has completed (or is completing) five waves up that will lead to a three-step partial retracement of corresponding degree. This means that the decline will not be a moderate setback such as the market has undergone from time to time since 1932. It will be at least large enough to complete the downside portion of Figure 3-1 if we label its start "1932" and its peak "2000." That is a large setback. We may even have to label its start "1784," in which case the bear market will be the largest since that of the 1700s. In other words, the stock market is embarking upon its biggest bear market assuredly since that of 1929-1932 and possibly since that of 1720-1784. If any such bear market occurs, then as we saw in Chapter 2, the economy will experience a depression.

How Far Will the Market Fall?

As implied in Figure 3-2, stock market corrections tend to bottom in the area of the fourth wave of the largest immediately preceding five-wave structure. Study the actual record, and you will see this guideline fulfilled often. Note, for example, in Figure 4-2, that wave II bottomed in the price area of the 1934 low, and wave IV bottomed in the price area of the 1962 low, which ended fourth waves within waves I and III respectively. Way back in 1978, *Elliott Wave Principle* said that when the great bull market expected for wave V was over, the DJIA would fall back to the area of the preceding fourth wave, which is *at least* to the 577 to 1051 range of wave IV (see Figure 4-2) and possibly down to the 41-381 range of wave (IV) (see Figure 4-1). To summarize, though my outlook may sound impossible, I am quite comfortable saying that the DJIA will fall from *quintuple* digits, where it is today, to *triple* digits, an unprecedented amount.

What I cannot say with quite as much conviction is which wave of the bear market will carry the Dow to that area. Odds are very strong that it will happen on the first major decline, a potential that the next section supports. Otherwise, it will do so on another decline decades hence. For more on such nuances, please see Chapter 5 of *At the Crest of the Tidal Wave*.

Studies of Manias Bear Out This Downside Potential

In 1997, I undertook a study of financial manias. Manias are episodes of relentless financial speculation that involve substantial infusions of credit, wide public participation, and which drive values to unprecedented levels. For the full study, please see the first essay in *View from the Top*.

A pertinent observation with respect to our current concern is that a mania is always followed by a collapse so severe that it brings values to *below* where they were when the mania began. The apparent reason for this outcome is that so many ordinary people entrust their fortunes to the mania that its reversal brings widespread financial distress, which feeds on itself to force an immense liquidation of investment media.

Famous Market Manias
And Their Aftermaths, 1600-2001

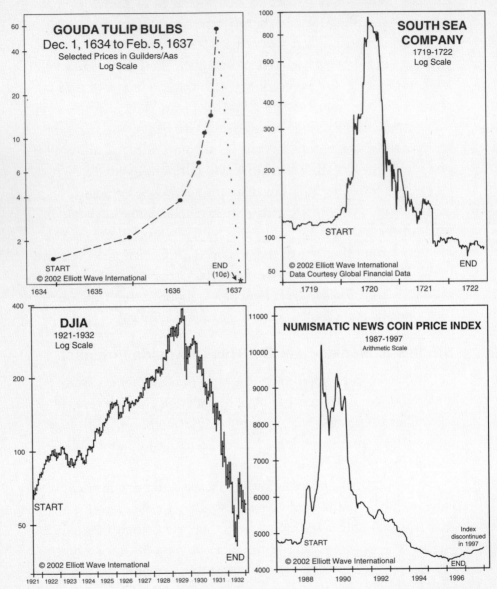

Figures 8-1 through 8-4

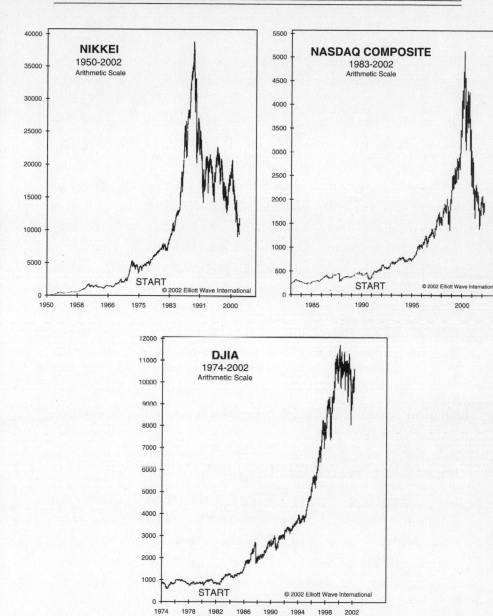

Figures 8-5 through 8-7

Figures 8-1 through 8-7 show the record to date of seven manias. The first four of them are far enough in the past to show the ultimate outcome in which values fell below what they were at the mania's start. The fifth graph is Japan's Nikkei stock index, which topped out on the last trading day of 1989. Its consequences have not fully played out yet, but the relentless fall has already wiped out 80 percent of the Nikkei's peak value and should, if the mania model holds, ultimately carry to or below the values of 1974. The sixth graph is the NASDAQ index, which topped in March 2000. It fell 75 percent into September 2001 and is recovering. Optimists believe that the bear market is over, but it has a long way down to go before erasing the entire mania. The final graph displays the U.S. blue-chip stock mania of the 1980s and 1990s as represented by the DJIA, which remains near its all-time high. If this index behaves like the others, the Dow should fall to below the starting point of its mania. That level is 777, the August 1982 low. So as you can see, the downside potential on this basis is compatible with that indicated by my interpretation of the market's position under the Wave Principle.

Implications for the Economy

If the stock market is going to fall far enough to retrace a substantial portion of the uptrend from at least 1932 and to retrace the price advance that it has undergone during its mania, then it will fall far enough to cause a significant contraction in the economy. How deep will the contraction ultimately become?

The termination of wave III in 1966/68 led to a string of four recessions between 1970 and 1982. Because wave V has had a weaker economic background, and because of the great imbalance between today's sky-high expectations and the decreasingly robust economy, the contraction resulting from this bear market will unquestionably be more severe than any of the contractions following wave III.

Re-examine Figures 2-1 and 4-1. Notice that the last two depressions marked on Figure 2-1 immediately followed the Supercycle degree labels (I) and (III), as shown in Figure 4-1. As you can see in Figure 4-1, we have a new label, wave (V), in place. Notice that the first depression marked on Figure 2-1 immediately followed the Grand Supercycle degree label Ⓘ in 1720. In Figure 4-1, we also tentatively have a label Ⓘ in place. These labels, if they are correct, are precursors of a tremendous stock-market crash and a deep depression.

The proper models for the developing economic experience are those that accompanied the stock market setbacks of 1720-1722 in England, 1835-1842 and 1929-1932 in the United States and from 1990 forward in Japan. In two of those cases (1720-1722 and 1929-1932), the contraction was a relentless, acute, brief, all-out depression. In the other two cases (1835-1842 and 1990 to date), the economy contracted over a longer period in two or more steps, with recoveries in between. Either style of progression could happen now.

Japan's retrenchment has been long and slow because most of the rest of the world's economies continued their investment manias and economic growth, allowing vigorous trade to provide support during the first decade of its economic decline. When the rest of the world's economies falter, they will lack a group of healthy trading partners to mitigate the speed of their contractions. For this reason, the developing contraction in the U.S. and around the globe will likely be far swifter than Japan's experience to date.

For the purposes of this book, these observations are all the evidence we need to form at least a general idea of the downside potential in the stock market and the economy in the U.S., and by extension, the rest of the world as well. If you would like more specifics on the details of how the bear market is likely to play out in terms of pattern, time and target levels, please read Chapter 5 of *At the Crest of the Tidal Wave*.

No Alternative Scenarios

Given the evidence, I think it would be financially suicidal to bet on an extension of the bull market and a requirement of even moderate prudence to prepare for a major reversal. Aside from a near-term nuance allowed for the Dow in Chapter 4, I have no other long-term interpretations of the wave status and the economy and *no alternative scenarios* at the three illustrated degrees. The evidence as I see it is too one-sided for me to be anything now but a one-armed economist. If I turn out wrong, so be it.

PART II

THE CASE FOR DEFLATION

"Pay no attention to that man behind the curtain."
—*The Wizard of Oz*

Chapter 9:

When Does Deflation Occur?

Defining Inflation and Deflation

Webster's says, "Inflation is an increase in the volume of money and credit relative to available goods," and "Deflation is a contraction in the volume of money and credit relative to available goods." To understand inflation and deflation, we have to understand the terms money and credit.

Defining Money and Credit

Money is a socially accepted medium of exchange, value storage and final payment. A specified amount of that medium also serves as a unit of account.

According to its two financial definitions, *credit* may be summarized as *a right to access money*. Credit can be held by the owner of the money, in the form of a warehouse receipt for a money deposit, which today is a checking account at a bank. Credit can also be *transferred* by the owner or by the owner's custodial institution to a borrower in exchange for a fee or fees — called interest — as specified in a repayment contract called a bond, note, bill or just plain IOU, which is *debt*. In today's economy, most credit is lent, so people often use the terms "credit" and "debt" interchangeably, as money lent by one entity is simultaneously money borrowed by another.

Price Effects of Inflation and Deflation

When the volume of money and credit *rises* relative to the volume of goods available, the relative value of each unit of money falls, making prices for goods generally rise. When the volume of money and credit *falls* relative to the volume of goods available, the relative value of each unit of money rises, making prices of goods generally fall. Though many people find it difficult to do, the proper way to conceive of these changes is that the value of units of *money* are rising and falling, not the values of goods.

The most common misunderstanding about inflation and deflation — echoed even by some renowned economists — is the idea that inflation is rising prices and deflation is falling prices. General price changes, though, are simply *effects*.

The price effects of inflation can occur in goods, which most people recognize as relating to inflation, or in investment assets, which people do not generally recognize as relating to inflation. The inflation of the 1970s induced dramatic price rises in gold, silver and commodities. The inflation of the 1980s and 1990s induced dramatic price rises in stock certificates and real estate. This difference in effect is due to differences in the social psychology that accompanies inflation and disinflation, respectively, as we will discuss briefly in Chapter 12.

The price effects of deflation are simpler. They tend to occur across the board, in goods and investment assets simultaneously.

The Primary Precondition of Deflation

Deflation requires a precondition: a major societal buildup in the extension of credit (and its flip side, the assumption of debt). Austrian economists Ludwig von Mises and Friedrich Hayek warned of the consequences of credit expansion, as have a handful of other economists, who today are mostly ignored. Bank credit and Elliott wave expert Hamilton Bolton, in a 1957 letter, summarized his observations this way:

> In reading a history of major depressions in the U.S. from 1830 on, I was impressed with the following:
>
> (a) All were set off by a deflation of excess credit. This was the one factor in common.
>
> (b) Sometimes the excess-of-credit situation seemed to last years before the bubble broke.
>
> (c) Some outside event, such as a major failure, brought the thing to a head, but the signs were visible many months, and in some cases years, in advance.
>
> (d) None was ever quite like the last, so that the public was always fooled thereby.
>
> (e) Some panics occurred under great government surpluses of revenue (1837, for instance) and some under great government deficits.
>
> (f) Credit is credit, whether non-self-liquidating or self-liquidating.
>
> (g) Deflation of non-self-liquidating credit usually produces the greater slumps.

Self-liquidating credit is a loan that is paid back, with interest, in a moderately short time from production. Production facilitated by the loan — for business start-up or expansion, for example — generates the financial return that makes repayment possible. The full transaction adds value to the economy.

Non-self-liquidating credit is a loan that is not tied to production and tends to stay in the system. When financial institutions lend for consumer purchases such as cars, boats or homes, or for speculations such as the purchase of stock certificates, no production effort is tied to the loan. Interest payments on such loans stress some other source of income. Contrary to

nearly ubiquitous belief, such lending is almost always counter-
productive; it adds *costs* to the economy, *not value*. If someone
needs a cheap car to get to work, then a loan to buy it adds value
to the economy; if someone wants a new SUV to consume, then
a loan to buy it does not add value to the economy. Advocates
claim that such loans "stimulate production," but they ignore
the cost of the required debt service, which burdens production.
They also ignore the subtle deterioration in the quality of spending choices due to the shift of buying power from people who
have demonstrated a superior ability to invest or produce (creditors) to those who have demonstrated primarily a superior ability
to consume (debtors).

Near the end of a major expansion, few creditors expect
default, which is why they lend freely to weak borrowers. Few
borrowers expect their fortunes to change, which is why they
borrow freely. Deflation involves a substantial amount of *invol-
untary* debt liquidation because almost no one expects deflation
before it starts.

What Triggers the Change to Deflation

A trend of credit expansion has two components: the
general *willingness* to lend and borrow and the general *ability* of
borrowers to pay interest and principal. These components depend respectively upon (1) the trend of people's confidence, i.e.,
whether both creditors and debtors *think* that debtors will be able
to pay, and (2) the trend of production, which makes it either
easier or harder *in actuality* for debtors to pay. So as long as confidence and production increase, the supply of credit tends to
expand. The expansion of credit ends when the desire or ability
to sustain the trend can no longer be maintained. As confidence
and production decrease, the supply of credit contracts.

The psychological aspect of deflation and depression cannot be overstated. When the social mood trend changes from

optimism to pessimism, creditors, debtors, producers and consumers change their primary orientation from *expansion* to *conservation*. As creditors become more conservative, they slow their lending. As debtors and potential debtors become more conservative, they borrow less or not at all. As producers become more conservative, they reduce expansion plans. As consumers become more conservative, they save more and spend less. These behaviors reduce the "velocity" of money, i.e., the speed with which it circulates to make purchases, thus putting downside pressure on prices. These forces reverse the former trend.

The structural aspect of deflation and depression is also crucial. The ability of the financial system to sustain increasing levels of credit rests upon a vibrant economy. At some point, a rising debt level requires so much energy to sustain — in terms of meeting interest payments, monitoring credit ratings, chasing delinquent borrowers and writing off bad loans — that it slows overall economic performance. A high-debt situation becomes unsustainable when the rate of economic growth falls beneath the prevailing rate of interest on money owed and creditors refuse to underwrite the interest payments with more credit.

When the burden becomes too great for the economy to support and the trend reverses, reductions in lending, spending and production cause debtors to earn less money with which to pay off their debts, so defaults rise. Default and fear of default exacerbate the new trend in psychology, which in turn causes creditors to reduce lending further. A downward "spiral" begins, feeding on pessimism just as the previous boom fed on optimism. The resulting cascade of debt liquidation is a deflationary crash. Debts are retired by paying them off, "restructuring" or default. In the first case, no value is lost; in the second, some value; in the third, all value. In desperately trying to raise cash to pay off loans, borrowers bring all kinds of assets to market, including stocks, bonds, commodities and real estate, causing their prices

to plummet. The process ends only after the supply of credit falls
to a level at which it is collateralized acceptably to the surviving
creditors.

Why Deflationary Crashes and Depressions Go Together

A deflationary crash is characterized in part by a persistent, sustained, deep, general decline in people's desire and ability to lend and borrow. A depression is characterized in part by a persistent, sustained, deep, general decline in production. Since a decline in production reduces debtors' means to repay and service debt, a depression supports deflation. Since a decline in credit reduces new investment in economic activity, deflation supports depression. Because both credit and production support prices for investment assets, their prices fall in a deflationary depression. As asset prices fall, people lose wealth, which reduces their ability to offer credit, service debt and support production. This mix of forces is self-reinforcing.

The U.S. has experienced two major deflationary depressions, which lasted from 1835 to 1842 and from 1929 to 1932 respectively. Each one followed a period of substantial credit expansion. Credit expansion schemes have always ended in bust. The credit expansion scheme fostered by worldwide central banking (see Chapter 10) is the greatest ever. The bust, however long it takes, will be commensurate. If my outlook is correct, the deflationary crash that lies ahead will be even bigger than the two largest such episodes of the past 200 years.

Financial Values Can Disappear

People seem to take for granted that financial values can be created endlessly seemingly out of nowhere and pile up to the moon. Turn the direction around and mention that financial values can disappear into nowhere, and they insist that it is not possible. "The money has to go *somewhere*...It just moves from stocks to bonds to money funds...It never goes away...For every buyer, there is a seller, so the money just changes hands." That *is* true of the money, just as it was all the way up, but it's not true of the *values*, which *changed* all the way up.

Asset prices rise not because of "buying" *per se*, because indeed for every buyer, there is a seller. They rise because those transacting agree that their prices should be higher. All that everyone else — including those who own some of that asset and those who do not — need do is *nothing*. Conversely, for prices of assets to fall, it takes only *one* seller and *one* buyer who agree that the former value of an asset was too high. If no other bids are competing with that buyer's, then the value of the asset falls, *and it falls for everyone who owns it*. If a million other people own it, then their net worth goes down even though they did nothing. Two investors made it happen by transacting, and the rest of the investors made it happen by choosing not to disagree with their price. Financial values can disappear through a decrease in prices for any type of investment asset, including bonds, stocks and land.

Anyone who watches the stock or commodity markets closely has seen this phenomenon on a small scale many times. Whenever a market "gaps" up or down on an opening, it simply registers a new value *on the first trade*, which can be conducted by as few as two people. It did not take everyone's action to make it happen, just most people's *inaction* on the other side. In financial market "explosions" and panics, there are prices at which assets do not trade at all as they cascade from one trade to the next in great leaps.

A similar dynamic holds in the creation and destruction of credit. Let's suppose that a lender starts with a million dollars and the borrower starts with zero. Upon extending the loan, the borrower possesses the million dollars, yet the lender feels that he still owns the million dollars that he lent out. If anyone asks the lender what he is worth, he says, "a million dollars," and shows the note to prove it. Because of this conviction, there is, in the minds of the debtor and the creditor combined, two million dollars worth of value where before there was only one. When the lender calls in the debt and the borrower pays it, he gets back his million dollars. If the borrower can't pay it, the value of the note goes to zero. Either way, the extra value disappears. If the original lender sold his note for cash, then someone else down the line loses. In an actively traded bond market, the result of a sudden default is like a game of "hot potato": whoever holds it last loses. When the volume of credit is large, investors can perceive vast sums of money and value where in fact there are only repayment contracts, which are financial assets dependent upon consensus valuation and the ability of debtors to pay. IOUs can be issued indefinitely, but they have value only as long as their debtors can live up to them and only to the extent that people believe that they will.

The dynamics of value expansion and contraction explain why a bear market can bankrupt millions of people. At the peak of a credit expansion or a bull market, assets have been valued upward, and all participants are wealthy — both the people who sold the assets and the people who hold the assets. The latter group is far larger than the former, because the total supply of money has been relatively stable while the total value of financial assets has ballooned. When the market turns down, the dynamic goes into reverse. Only a very few owners of a collapsing financial asset trade it for money at 90 percent of peak value. Some others may get out at 80 percent, 50 percent or 30 percent of peak value. In each case, sellers are simply transforming the remaining future value losses to someone else. In a bear market, the vast, vast majority does nothing and gets stuck holding assets with low or non-existent valuations. The "million dollars" that a wealthy investor might have thought he had in his bond portfolio or at a stock's peak value can quite rapidly become $50,000 or $5000 or $50. *The rest of it just disappears.* You see, he never really had a million dollars; all he had was IOUs or stock certificates. The idea that it had a certain *financial value* was in his head and the heads of others who agreed. When the point of agreement changed, so did the value. Poof! Gone in a flash of aggregated neurons. This is exactly what happens to most investment assets in a period of deflation.

A Global Story

The next four chapters present a discussion that will allow you to understand today's money and credit situation and why deflation is due. I have chosen to focus on the history and conditions of the United States because (1) I have more knowledge of them, (2) the U.S. provides the world's reserve currency, making its story the most important, (3) the U.S. has issued more credit than any other nation and is the world's biggest debtor, and (4) to discuss other countries' financial details would be superfluous. If you understand one country's currency, banking and credit history, to a significant degree you understand them all. Make no mistake about it: It's a global story. Wherever you live, you will benefit from this knowledge.

Chapter 10:

Money, Credit and the Federal Reserve Banking System

An argument for deflation is not to be offered lightly because, given the nature of today's money, certain aspects of money and credit creation cannot be forecast, only surmised. Before we can discuss these issues, we have to understand how money and credit come into being. This is a difficult chapter, but if you can assimilate what it says, you will have knowledge of the banking system that not one person in 10,000 has.

The Origin of Intangible Money

Originally, money was a *tangible good* freely chosen by society. For millennia, gold or silver provided this function, although sometimes other tangible goods (such as copper, brass and seashells) did. Originally, credit was the right to access that tangible money, whether by an ownership certificate or by borrowing.

Today, almost all money is *intangible*. It is not, nor does it even represent, a physical good. How it got that way is a long, complicated, disturbing story, which would take a full book to relate properly. It began about 300 years ago, when an English financier conceived the idea of a national central bank. Governments have often outlawed free-market determinations of what constitutes money and imposed their own versions upon society by law, but earlier schemes usually involved coinage. Under central banking, a government forces its citizens to accept its *debt* as the only form of legal tender. The Federal Reserve System assumed this monopoly role in the United States in 1913.

What Is a Dollar?

Originally, a dollar was defined as a certain amount of gold. Dollar bills and notes were promises to pay lawful money, which was gold. Anyone could present dollars to a bank and receive gold in exchange, and banks could get gold from the U.S. Treasury for dollar bills.

In 1933, President Roosevelt and Congress outlawed U.S. gold ownership and nullified and prohibited all domestic contracts denoted in gold, making Federal Reserve notes the legal tender of the land. In 1971, President Nixon halted gold payments from the U.S. Treasury to foreigners in exchange for dollars. Today, the Treasury will not give anyone anything tangible in exchange for a dollar. Even though Federal Reserve notes are defined as "obligations of the United States," they are not obligations to *do* anything. Although a dollar is labeled a "note," which means a debt contract, it is not a note *for* anything.

Congress claims that the dollar is "legally" 1/42.22 of an ounce of gold. Can you buy gold for $42.22 an ounce? No. This definition is bogus, and everyone knows it. If you bring a dollar to the U.S. Treasury, you will not collect any tangible good, much less 1/42.22 of an ounce of gold. You will be sent home.

Some authorities were quietly amazed that when the government progressively removed the tangible backing for the dollar, the currency continued to function. If you bring a dollar to the marketplace, you can still buy goods with it because the government says (by "fiat") that it is money and because its long history of use has lulled people into accepting it as such. The volume of goods you can buy with it fluctuates according to the total volume of dollars — in both cash and credit — and their holders' level of confidence that those values will remain intact.

Exactly what a dollar *is* and what *backs* it are difficult questions to answer because no official entity will provide a satisfying answer. It has *no simultaneous actuality and definition*. It may be defined as 1/42.22 of an ounce of gold, but it is not *actually* that. Whatever it actually is (if anything) may not be definable. To the extent that its physical backing, if any, may be officially definable in actuality, no one is talking.

Let's attempt to define what gives the dollar objective value. As we will see in the next section, the dollar is "backed" primarily by government bonds, which are promises to pay dollars. So today, *the dollar is a promise backed by a promise to pay an identical promise*. What is the nature of each promise? If the Treasury will not give you anything tangible for your dollar, then the dollar is a promise to pay *nothing*. The Treasury should have no trouble keeping this promise.

In Chapter 9, I called the dollar "money." By the definition given there, it is. I used that definition and explanation because it makes the whole picture comprehensible. But the truth is that since the dollar is backed by *debt*, it is actually a *credit*, not money. It is a credit against what the government owes, denoted in dollars and backed by nothing. So although we may use the term "money" in referring to dollars, there is no longer any real money in the U.S. financial system; there is nothing but credit and debt.

As you can see, defining the dollar, and therefore the terms money, credit, inflation and deflation, today is a challenge, to say the least. Despite that challenge, we can still use these terms because people's minds have conferred meaning and value upon these ethereal concepts. Understanding this fact, we will now proceed with a discussion of how money and credit expand in today's financial system.

How the Federal Reserve System Manufactures Money

Over the years, the Federal Reserve Bank has transferred purchasing power from all other dollar holders primarily to the U.S. Treasury by a complex series of machinations. The U.S. Treasury borrows money by selling bonds in the open market. The Fed is said to "buy" the Treasury's bonds from banks and other financial institutions, but in actuality, it is allowed by law simply to fabricate a new checking account for the seller in exchange for the bonds. It holds the Treasury's bonds as assets against — as "backing" for — that new money. Now the seller is whole (he was just a middleman), the Fed has the bonds, and the Treasury has the new money. This transactional train is a long route to a simple alchemy (called "monetizing" the debt) in which the Fed turns government bonds into money. The net result is as if the government had simply fabricated its own checking account, although it pays the Fed a portion of the bonds' interest for providing the service surreptitiously. To date, the Fed has monetized about $600 billion worth of Treasury obligations. This process expands the supply of *money*.

In 1980, Congress gave the Fed the legal authority to monetize any agency's debt. In other words, it can exchange the bonds of a government, bank or other institution for a checking account denominated in dollars. This mechanism gives the President, through the Treasury, a mechanism for "bailing out" debt-troubled governments, banks or other institutions that can no longer get financing anywhere else. Such decisions are made for political reasons, and the Fed can go along or refuse, at least as the relationship currently stands. Today, the Fed has about $36 billion worth of foreign debt on its books. The power to grant or refuse such largesse is unprecedented.

Each new Fed account denominated in dollars is new money, but contrary to common inference, it is not new value.

The new account *has* value, but that value comes from a *reduction* in the value of all other outstanding accounts denominated in dollars. That reduction takes place as the favored institution spends the newly credited dollars, driving up the dollar-denominated demand for goods and thus their prices. All other dollar holders still hold the same *number* of dollars, but now there are more dollars in circulation, and each one purchases less in the way of goods and services. The old dollars *lose* value to the extent that the new account *gains* value. The net result is a transfer of value to the receiver's account from those of all other dollar holders. This fact is not readily obvious because the *unit of account* throughout the financial system does not change even though its *value* changes.

It is important to understand exactly what the Fed has the power to do in this context: It has legal permission to transfer wealth from dollar savers to certain debtors *without the permission of the savers*. The effect on the money supply is exactly the same as if the money had been counterfeited and slipped into circulation.

In the old days, governments would inflate the money supply by diluting their coins with base metal or printing notes directly. Now the same old game is much less obvious. On the other hand, there is also far more to it. This section has described the Fed's *secondary* role. The Fed's main occupation is not creating money but *facilitating credit*. This crucial difference will eventually bring us to why deflation is possible.

How the Federal Reserve Has Encouraged the Growth of Credit

Congress authorized the Fed not only to create money for the government but also to "smooth out" the economy by manipulating credit (which also happens to be a re-election tool for incumbents). Politics being what they are, this manipulation has been almost exclusively in the direction of making credit easy to obtain. The Fed used to make more credit available to the banking system by monetizing federal debt, that is, by creating money. Under the structure of our "fractional reserve" system, banks were authorized to employ that new money as "reserves" against which they could make new loans. Thus, new money meant new credit.

It meant a *lot* of new credit because banks were allowed by regulation to lend out 90 percent of their deposits, which meant that banks had to keep 10 percent of deposits on hand ("in reserve") to cover withdrawals. When the Fed increased a bank's reserves, that bank could lend 90 percent of those new dollars. Those dollars, in turn, would make their way to other banks as new deposits. Those other banks could lend 90 percent of *those* deposits, and so on. The expansion of reserves and deposits throughout the banking system this way is called the "multiplier effect." This process expanded the supply of *credit* well beyond the supply of money.

Because of competition from money market funds, banks began using fancy financial manipulation to get around reserve requirements. In the early 1990s, the Federal Reserve Board under Chairman Alan Greenspan took a controversial step and removed banks' reserve requirements almost entirely. To do so, it first lowered to zero the reserve requirement on all accounts other than checking accounts. Then it let banks pretend that they have almost no checking account balances by allowing them to "sweep" those deposits into various savings accounts and money market funds at the end of each business day. Magically, when monitors check the banks' balances at night, they find the value of checking accounts artificially understated by hundreds of billions of dollars. The net result is that banks today conveniently meet their nominally required reserves (currently about $45b.) with the cash in their vaults that they need to hold for everyday transactions anyway.

By this change in regulation, the Fed essentially removed itself from the businesses of requiring banks to hold reserves and of manipulating the level of those reserves. This move took place during a recession and while S&P earnings per share were undergoing their biggest drop since the 1940s. The temporary cure for that economic contraction was the ultimate in "easy money."

We still have a fractional reserve system on the books, but we do not have one in actuality. Now banks can lend out virtually all of their deposits. In fact, they can lend out *more* than all of their deposits, because banks' parent companies can issue stock, bonds, commercial paper or any financial instrument and lend the proceeds to their subsidiary banks, upon which assets the banks can make new loans. In other words, to a limited degree, banks can arrange to create their own new money for lending purposes. Today, U.S. banks have extended 25 percent more total credit than they have in total deposits ($5.4 trillion vs. $4.3 trillion). Since all banks do not engage in this practice, others must be quite aggressive at it. For more on this theme, see Chapter 19.

Recall that when banks lend money, it gets deposited in other banks, which can lend it out again. Without a reserve requirement, the multiplier effect is no longer restricted to ten times deposits; it is virtually unlimited. Every new dollar deposited can be lent over and over throughout the system: A deposit becomes a loan becomes a deposit becomes a loan, and so on.

As you can see, the fiat money system has encouraged inflation via both money creation and the expansion of credit. This dual growth has been the monetary engine of the historic uptrend of stock prices in wave (V) from 1932. The stupendous growth in bank credit since 1975 (see graphs in Chapter 11) has provided the monetary fuel for its final advance, wave V. The effective elimination of reserve requirements a decade ago extended that trend to one of historic proportion.

The Net Effect of Monetization

Although the Fed has almost wholly withdrawn from the role of holding book-entry reserves for banks, it has not retired its holdings of Treasury bonds. Because the Fed is legally bound to back its notes (greenback currency) with government securities, today almost all of the Fed's Treasury bond assets are held as reserves against a nearly equal dollar value of Federal Reserve notes in circulation around the world. Thus, the net result of the Fed's 89 years of money inflating is that the Fed has turned $600 billion worth of U.S. Treasury and foreign obligations into Federal Reserve notes.

Today the Fed's production of currency is passive, in response to orders from domestic and foreign banks, which in turn respond to demand from the public. Under current policy, banks must pay for that currency with any remaining reserve balances. If they don't have any, they borrow to cover the cost and pay back that loan as they collect interest on their own loans. Thus, as things stand, the Fed no longer considers itself in the business of "printing money" for the government. Rather, it facilitates the expansion of credit to satisfy the lending policies of government and banks.

If banks and the Treasury were to become strapped for cash in a monetary crisis, policies could change. The unencumbered production of banknotes could become deliberate Fed or government policy, as we have seen happen in other countries throughout history. At this point, there is no indication that the Fed has entertained any such policy. Nevertheless, Chapters 13 and 22 address this possibility.

For Information

There is much information available on the Fed's activities, but nowhere have I found a concise summary such as presented in this chapter. If you would like to learn more, I can start you off on your search. For a positive spin on the Fed's value, contact the Fed itself or any conventional economist. For a less rosy view, contact the Foundation for the Advancement of Monetary Education or join the Ludwig von Mises Institute and order a copy of their 150-page paperback, *The Case Against the Fed*, by Murray N. Rothbard, which is just $5 plus shipping from www.mises.org/catalog.asp. The most knowledgeable source that I have found with respect to the workings of the Federal Reserve System is Lou Crandall of Wrightson Associates, publisher of *The Money Market Observer*, a service for traders. Contact information is as follows:

> *The Money Market Observer*
> Wrightson Associates
> Website: www.wrightson.com
> Email: sales@wrightson.com
> Address: 560 Washington St., New York, NY 10014
> Phone: 212-815-6540
> Fax: 212-341-9253
>
> Federal Reserve
> Website: www.federalreserve.gov
> Phone: 202-452-3819
>
> Ludwig von Mises Institute
> Website: www.mises.org
> Email: mail@mises.org
> Address: 518 West Magnolia Avenue, Auburn, AL 36832
> Phone: 334-321-2100
> Fax: 334-321-2119
>
> Foundation for Advancement of Monetary Education
> Website: www.fame.org
> Email: info@fame.org
> Address: Box 625, FDR Station, New York, NY 10150
> Phone: (212) 818-1206
> Fax: (212) 818-1197

Chapter 11:

What Makes Deflation Likely Today?

Following the Great Depression, the Fed and the U.S. government embarked on a program, sometimes consciously and sometimes not, both of increasing the creation of new money and credit and of fostering the confidence of lenders and borrowers so as to facilitate the expansion of credit. These policies both accommodated and encouraged the expansionary trend of the 'Teens and 1920s, which ended in bust, and the far larger expansionary trend that began in 1932 and which has accelerated over the past half-century.

Other governments and central banks have followed similar policies. The International Monetary Fund, the World Bank and similar institutions, funded mostly by the U.S. taxpayer, have extended immense credit around the globe. Their policies have supported nearly continuous worldwide inflation, particularly over the past thirty years. As a result, the global financial system is gorged with non-self-liquidating credit.

Conventional economists excuse and praise this system under the erroneous belief that expanding money and credit promotes economic growth, which is terribly false. It appears to do so for a while, but in the long run, the swollen mass of debt collapses of its own weight, which is deflation, and destroys the economy. Only the Austrian school understands this fact. A devastated economy, moreover, encourages radical politics, which is even worse. We will address this topic in Chapter 26.

A House of (Credit) Cards

The value of credit that has been extended worldwide is unprecedented. *At the Crest of the Tidal Wave* reported in 1995 that United States entities of all types owed a total of $17.1 trillion dollars. I thought it was a big number. That figure has soared to $29.5 trillion at the end of 2001, so it should be $30 trillion by the time this book is printed. That figure represents three times the annual Gross Domestic Product, the highest ratio ever.

Worse, most of this debt is the non-self-liquidating type. Much of it comprises loans to governments, investment loans for buying stock and real estate, and loans for everyday consumer items and services, none of which has any production tied to it. Even a lot of corporate debt is non-self-liquidating, since so much of corporate activity these days is related to finance rather than production. The Fed's aggressive easy-money policy of recent months has cruelly enticed even more marginal borrowers into the ring, particularly in the area of mortgages.

This $30 trillion figure, moreover, does not include government guarantees such as bank deposit insurance, unfunded Social Security obligations, and so on, which could add another $20 trillion or so to that figure, depending upon what estimates we accept. It also does not take into account U.S. banks' holdings of $50 trillion worth of derivatives at representative value (equaling five full years' worth of U.S. GDP), which could turn into IOUs for more money than their issuers imagine. Then there is the problem of major corporations' unfunded pension plan liabilities. Companies have promised billions of dollars in fixed-income pensions, but their plan assets will fall so much in value that they will have to fund those pensions from their operating budgets. How much of those liabilities will turn into debt is unknown, but the risk is large and real. Is it not appropriate that you are now reading Chapter 11?

Figures 11-1 through 11-4, along with Figure 7-6, show some aspects of both the amazing *growth* in credit — as much as

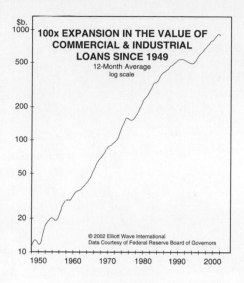

Figure 11-1

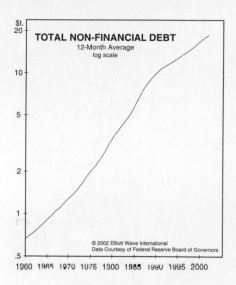

Figure 11-2

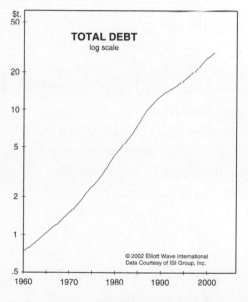

Figure 11-3

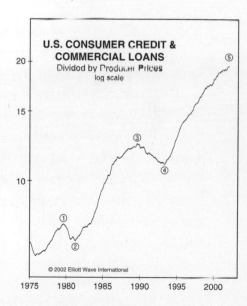

Figure 11-4

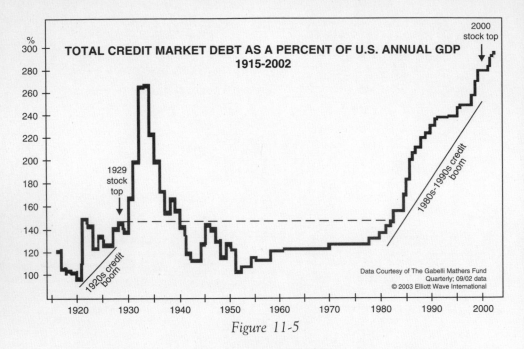

Figure 11-5

100 fold since 1949 — and the astonishing *extent* of indebtedness today among corporations, governments and the public, both in terms of total dollars' worth and as a percent of GDP. There are so many measures revealing how extended debtors have become that I could dedicate a whole book to that topic alone.

Runaway credit expansion is a characteristic of major fifth waves. Waxing optimism supports not only the investment boom but also a credit expansion, which in turn fuels the investment boom. Figure 11-5 is a stunning picture of the credit expansion of wave V of the 1920s (beginning the year that Congress authorized the Fed), which ended in a bust, and of wave V in the 1980s-1990s, which is even bigger.

I have heard economists understate the debt risk of the United States by focusing on the level of its net debt to foreigners, which is just above $2 trillion, as if all other debt we just "owe to ourselves." But every loan involves a creditor and a debtor, who are separate entities. No one owes a debt to himself. Creditors in other countries who have lent trillions to the U.S. and their own fellow citizens have added to the ocean of worldwide debt, not reduced it. So not only has there been an expansion of credit, but it has been the biggest credit expansion in history by a huge margin. Likewise, not only is there a threat of deflation, but there is also the threat of the biggest deflation in history by a huge margin.

Broader Ideas of Money

It is a good thing that deflation is defined as a reduction in the relative volume of money *and* credit, so we are not forced to distinguish too specifically between the two things in today's world. Exactly what paper and which book entries should be designated as "money" in a fiat-enforced debt-based paper currency system with an overwhelming volume of credit is open to debate.

Many people believe that when they hold stock certificates or someone's IOUs (in the form of bills, notes and bonds), they still have money. "I have my money in the stock market" or "in municipal bonds" are common phrases. In truth, they own not money but financial assets, in the form of corporate shares or repayment contracts. As we will see in Chapter 19, even "money in the bank" in the modern system is nothing but a call on the bank's loans, which means that it is an IOU.

There is no universally accepted definition of what constitutes "the money supply," just an array of arguments over where to draw the line. The most conservative definition limits money to the value of circulating cash currency and checking accounts. As we have seen, though, even they have an origin in debt. Broader definitions of money include the short-term debt of strong issuers. They earn the description "money equivalents" and are often available in "money market funds." Today, there are several accepted definitions of the "money supply," each with its own designation, such as M1, M2 and M3.

The mental quality of modern money extends the limits of what people *think* is money. For example, a futures contract is

an IOU for goods at a certain price. Is that money? Many companies use stock options as payment for services. Is that money?
Over the past fifteen years, a vast portion of the population has
come to believe the oft-repeated phrase, "Owning shares of a
stock fund is just like having money in the bank, only better."
They have put their life's savings into stock funds under the assumption that they have the equivalent of a money account *on
deposit* there. But is it money? The answer to all these questions
is no, but people have come to think of such things as money.
They spend their actual money and take on debt in accordance
with that belief. Because the idea of money is so highly psychological today, the line between what is money and what is not
has become blurred, at least in people's minds, and that is where
it matters when it comes to understanding the psychology of deflation. Today the vast volume of what people consider to be
money has ballooned the psychological potential for deflation
far beyond even the immense monetary potential for deflation
implied in Figures 11-1 through 11-5.

A Reversal in the Making

No tree grows to the sky. No shared mental state, including confidence, holds forever. The exceptional volume of credit
extended throughout the world has been precarious for some time.
As Bolton observed, though, such conditions can maintain for
years. If the trend toward increasing confidence were to reverse,
the supply of credit, and therefore the supply of money, would
shrink, producing deflation. Of course, that is a big "if," because
for half a century, those wary of credit growth in the U.S. have
sounded warnings of collapse, and it has not happened. This is
where wave analysis comes in.

Recall that two things are required to produce an expansionary trend in credit. The first is expansionary psychology, and
the second is the ability to pay interest. Chapter 4 of this book
makes the case that after nearly seven decades of a positive trend,

confidence has probably reached its limit. Chapter 1 demonstrates a multi-decade deceleration in the U.S. economy that will soon stress debtors' *ability to pay*. These dual forces should serve to usher in a credit contraction very soon.

Wave analysis can also be useful when applied directly to the realm of credit growth. Figure 11-4 is a plot of consumer credit and commercial loans divided by the Producer Price Index to reflect loan values in constant dollars. It shows that the uptrend in real credit value extended to consumers and businesses has traced out five waves since the major bottom of 1974. This is nearly the same picture that we see in stock market margin debt (Figure 7-4). Plots of the credit expansion's rate of change show that the growth in credit is running out of steam at multiple degrees of trend, which is what the analysis in Chapter 1 reveals about the economy. The downturn, it appears, is imminent if not already upon us.

If borrowers begin paying back enough of their debt relative to the amount of new loans issued, or if borrowers default on enough of their loans, or if the economy cannot support the aggregate cost of interest payments and the promise to return principal, or if enough banks and investors become sufficiently reluctant to lend, the "multiplier effect" will go into reverse. Total *credit* will contract, so bank deposits will contract, so the supply of *money* will contract, *all with the same degree of leverage with which they were initially expanded.* The immense reverse credit leverage of zero-reserve (actually *negative*-reserve) banking, then, is the primary fuel for a deflationary crash.

Japan's deflation and its march into depression began in 1990. Southeast Asia's began in 1997. Argentina's has just made headlines. The U.S. and the rest of the nations that have so far escaped are next in line. When the lines in Figures 11-1 through 11-5 turn down (the first one may already have done so), the game will be up.

How Big a Deflation?

Today, under what is left of bank reserves, there are $11 billion on reserve at the Fed plus $44 billion in cash on hand in banks' vaults. This $55 billion total covers the entire stock of bank credit issued in the United States. This amount equates to 1/100 of M2, valued today at $5.5 trillion, and 1/550 of all U.S. debt outstanding, valued today at $30 trillion. If we generously designate the U.S. money supply to include all Federal Reserve notes worldwide, totaling just under $600 billion, these ratios are 1/10 and 1/55.

Of course, since the dollar itself is just a credit, there is no tangible commodity backing the debt that is outstanding to-day. Real collateral underlies many loans, but its total value may be as little as a few cents on the dollar, euro or yen of total credit. I say "real" collateral because although one can borrow against the value of stocks, for example, they are just paper certificates, inflated well beyond the liquidating value of the underlying company's assets. One can also borrow against the value of bonds, which is an amazing trick: using debt to finance debt. As a result of widespread loans made on such bases, the discrepancy between the value of total debt outstanding and the value of its real un-derlying collateral is huge. It is anyone's guess how much of that gap ultimately will have to close to satisfy the credit markets in a deflationary depression. For our purposes, it is enough to say that the gap itself, and therefore the deflationary potential, is histori-cally large.

Although the United States is the world leader in fiat money and credit creation, a version of the story told in this and the preceding chapter has happened in every country in the world with a central bank. As a result, we risk overwhelming deflation in every corner of the globe.

Chapter 12:

Timing Deflations: The Kondratieff Cycle

I believe I have a leg to stand on with respect to forecasting monetary trends. In November 1979, right in the culminating heat of a hard-money panic following 30 years of accelerating inflation, *The Elliott Wave Theorist* reasoned, "The incredible conjunction of 'fives' in different markets [gold, silver, interest rates, bonds and commodities] all seem to point to the same conclusion: *The world is about to begin a phase of general disinflation.*" That is exactly what began the following month and has been in force ever since. For the story behind this prediction, please see Chapter 14 of *At the Crest of the Tidal Wave*.

As this example shows, Elliott waves provide an excellent tool for anticipating the nuances of inflation and deflation. However, a particular cycle of social activity has also proved useful in the effort.

Nikolai Kondratieff, a Russian economist, proposed in a 1926 paper that industrial economies followed a repeating cycle of change in prices and production. Actually, this cycle is primarily one of liquidity, not price, so rising and declining trends in prices for money, labor and goods are an effect of the cycle, not a cause. Although this cycle has averaged 54 years in duration, cyclic periodicities can expand and contract and are therefore inherently unreliable for precise timing. But the sequence of events within the Kondratieff cycle may be an immutable social process, regardless of how many decades it takes to play out. The presence of an inflating mechanism exacerbates the extremes of the cycle's manifestations.

Although the precise sequence and interplay of events can be different depending upon the position of the major Elliott waves, here is how recent Kondratieff cycles have played out: As liquidity expands in the initial phase of the cycle, commodity prices rise to reflect increasing business activity and (in most cases) inflation. As business activity and inflation accelerate, speculators begin to bid up commodity prices so as to reflect their increasing fear that inflation will *continue* to accelerate. After the *rate* of inflation peaks and begins to fall, the "acceleration premium" is removed from prices. Thus, commodity prices begin to fall despite continued but slowing inflation, a trend called disinflation. At the same time, a change in psychology away from fear and toward feelings of relief and hope induces people to channel the excess purchasing media created during disinflation into bidding up the prices of investment assets such as stocks. Because inflation continues, the wholesale prices that manufacturers charge for finished products, the retail prices that stores charge for goods and the level of wages that employers pay for labor all continue to rise but at a continuously lesser rate, following the rising but slowing trend of business activity and inflation.

Near the end of the cycle, the rates of change in business activity and inflation slip to zero. When they fall *below* zero, deflation is in force. As liquidity contracts, commodity prices fall more rapidly, and prices for stocks, wages and wholesale and retail goods join in the decline. When deflation ends and prices reach bottom, the cycle begins again.

The position of the current Kondratieff cycle supports the case for deflation directly ahead. In the previous cycle, wholesale prices of commodities generally bottomed in 1932-33. But many important prices, such as those for rent and corporate earnings (see Figure 6-4), bottomed as late as 1949, 53 years after the

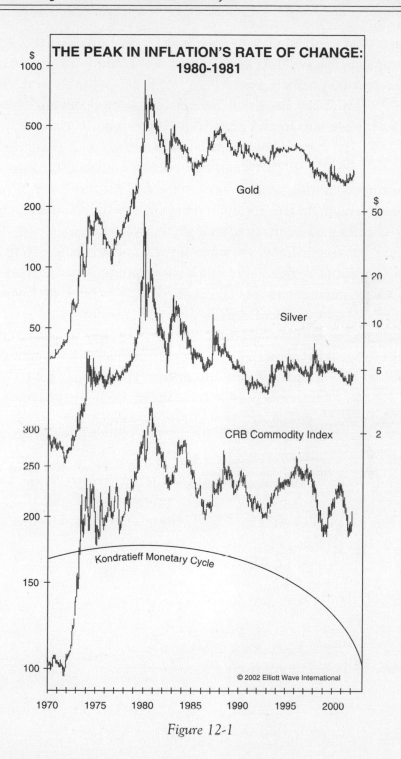

Figure 12-1

preceding Kondratieff cycle bottom in 1896. You can see this influence in Figure 11-5, which shows that credit extension as a percent of GDP also bottomed in 1949. Figure 3-1 in *At the Crest of the Tidal Wave* shows that PPI-adjusted stock prices ended an Elliott wave bear market pattern in 1949 as well.

The rise in liquidity after 1949 was the upside portion of a new cycle. Figure 12-1 shows that prices for monetary and agricultural commodities generally peaked in 1980-1981 and have been trending lower ever since. That top marked the transition to disinflation and the downside of the cycle.

You can also see evidence of the Kondratieff cycle in the price of money extended to reliable borrowers. Since total borrowing contracts during deflation, prime interest rates fall. Figure 12-2 shows most of four cycles. As you can see, long-term interest rates last bottomed in the 1940s as well. They topped again in 1981 at the peak of the current cycle and have been trending down ever since, as it heads into its low. This cycle is not to be taken as assurance that rates specifically on U.S. Treasury bonds

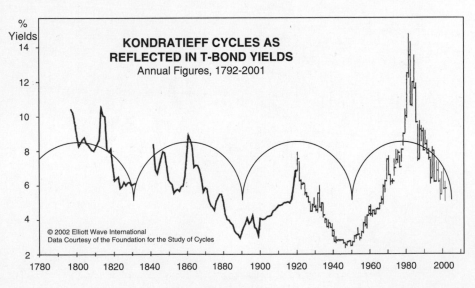

Figure 12-2

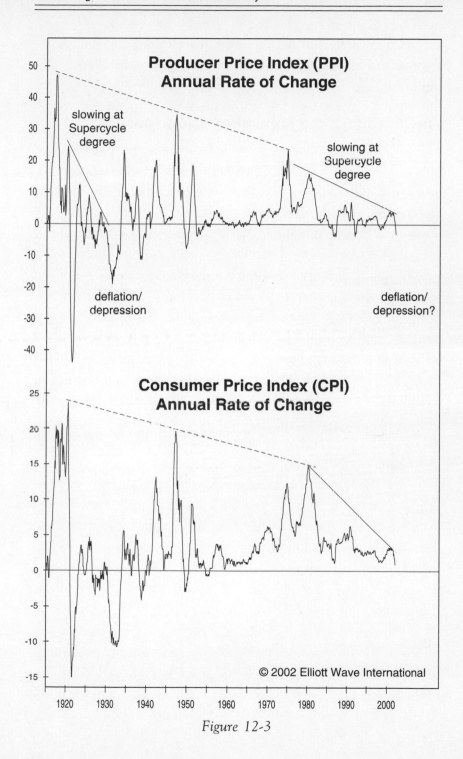

Figure 12-3

will necessarily fall further. As we will see in Chapter 15, rates fall only on the highest quality debt, which may or may not include long-term U.S. Treasuries in the current cycle.

The Position of the Kondratieff Cycle Today

Disinflation has been in force for over twenty years, since 1980-1981. During this time, wholesale and retail prices continued to rise but at a progressively lesser rate, following the slowing trend of disinflation. Today, the rate of upside change in both of these sets of prices combined has reached zero, as you can see in Figure 12-3.

In recent years, economists have been applauding the Fed for engineering a perfect world of economic growth with low inflation. We thus possess "the holy grail sought by most central bankers," as a national business magazine puts it. Are you shocked to learn that this is the same situation that economists applauded in 1929? In both cases, the uptrend in goods prices that the Fed fostered for years through credit expansion slowed due to the drag of interest payments on the consumer's capacity to spend. As in 1930-1932, today's "perfect world" will soon be revealed as something quite different.

If the Kondratieff cycle performs normally, the combined rate of change for the PPI and CPI will soon go negative. Whatever the cycle's timing may be, its *sequence* calls for several more years of declining commodity prices, a few years of newly declining wholesale and retail prices and a sharp decline in industrial production. These trends will end when the deflation ends, at the bottom of the cycle.

If the duration of recent past cycles is to repeat, then the falling portion of the current economic cycle would last another two years, and the depression would reach bottom in 2004. If the cycle lasts as long as the longest cycle of the past three centuries, the depression would end in 2011. For our current purposes, these numbers are guides, not predictions, primarily indicating that we are talking a matter of years, not forever. As happened during the late 1700s and in 1835-1842 in the U.S., and as has been happening over the past twelve years in Japan, the economy could experience multiple contractions with intervening recoveries. In fact, since the initial stock market decline should take an A-B-C shape, I lean toward expecting two depressions with an intervening recovery. Regardless, as of today, the process of society-wide debt liquidation lies ahead. Given the long-term five-wave patterns in several debt series (see Figures 7-4 and 11-4), the near-term three-wave rallies in stock averages (see Figure 4-7), the CRB index (see Figure 21-10), gold and silver, the fall to a zero rate of change in the combined PPI and CPI (see Figure 12-3), the sharp drop in interest rates last year and the fact that house prices are scaling new heights all alone (a technical condition called a "bearish non-confirmation"), I conclude that deflation — a contraction in the total volume of money and credit — is probably due to begin just about now.

A Minority View

In the interest of full disclosure, I should warn you that most of today's economists dismiss the Kondratieff cycle as a fantasy. When markets and the economy oscillate violently, as they did during the 1840s and 1850s, the 1930s and 1940s and the 1970s, cycles are a popular topic. Harvard professor Dr. Joseph Schumpeter wrote in the 1930s, "The Kondratieff Wave is the single-most important tool in economic forecasting." By contrast, when investment markets and the economic trend have been up for a long time, the very idea of cycles is generally dismissed out of hand. Here at the peak of a two-centuries-long uptrend, what can cycles be other than a subject of derision? Ironically, this oscillating psychology toward the idea of cycles is exactly what allows cycles to exist.

More striking in my opinion is the fact that most of the rare believers in the Kondratieff cycle think it has already bottomed. Some say it bottomed in the early 1980s, an idea that is as contrary to Kondratieff's cycle as it could possibly be. Others were arguing that it bottomed in 1997 or 1998, which did not fit the degree of retrenchment required by the cycle at all. These interpreters have been calling for more decades of expansion, in fact an *acceleration* of growth.

I am convinced that the explanation for such opinions is that these analysts feel optimistic and have to rationalize why. I am aware of only two other writers who see the cycle performing in its typical way and with its normal timing. Ian Gordon, who in 1998 began publishing *The Long Wave Analyst*, is an astute historian and student of the subject. If you would like to pursue this subject further, you may request copies of his publication through the following means:

> *The Long Wave Analyst*
> Email: ian_gordon@canaccord.com
> Address: Canaccord Capital, Suite 1200, 595 Burrard St.,
>   Vancouver, BC, V7X 1J1 Canada
> Phone: 604-643-0280
> Fax: 604-643-0152
> Editor: Ian Gordon

The stock market and the economy weave around the Kondratieff cycle in interesting ways. For a depiction of the Kondratieff cycle's operation over the past 300 years as reflected in stock prices, please see Appendix B of *At the Crest of the Tidal Wave*.

Chapter 13:

Can the Fed Stop Deflation?

Consensus Opinion Concerning Deflation

Seventy years of nearly continuous inflation have made most people utterly confident of its permanence. If the majority of economists have any monetary fear at all, it is fear of inflation, which is the opposite of deflation. Two of the world's most renowned economists have reiterated this fear in recent months in *The Wall Street Journal*, predicting an immediate acceleration of inflation.

As for the very idea of deflation, one economist a few years ago told a national newspaper that deflation had a "1 in 10,000" chance of occurring. The Chairman of Carnegie Mellon's business school calls the notion of deflation "utter nonsense." A professor of economics at Pepperdine University states flatly, "Rising stock prices will inevitably lead to rising prices in the rest of the economy." The publication of an economic think-tank insists, "Anyone who asserts that deflation is imminent or already underway ignores the rationale for fiat currency — that is, to facilitate the manipulation of economic activity." A financial writer explains, "Deflation…is totally a function of the Federal Reserve's management of monetary policy. It has nothing to do with the business cycle, productivity, taxes, booms and busts or anything else." Concurring, an adviser writes in a national magazine, "U.S. deflation would be simple to stop today. The Federal Reserve could just print more money, ending the price slide in its tracks." Yet another sneers, "Get real," and likens anyone concerned about deflation to "small children." One maverick economist whose model accommodates deflation and who actually *expects* a period of deflation is nevertheless convinced that it will be a "good deflation" and "nothing to fear." On financial television, another analyst (who apparently defines deflation as falling prices) quips, "Don't worry about deflation. All it does is pad profits." A banker calls any episode of falling oil prices "a positive catalyst [that] will put more money in consumers' pockets. It will benefit companies that are powered by energy and oil, and it will benefit the overall economy." Others excitedly welcome recently falling commodity prices as an economic stimulus "equivalent to a massive tax cut." A national business magazine guarantees, "That's not deflation ahead, just slower inflation. Put your deflation worries away." The senior economist with Deutsche Bank in New York estimates, "The chance of deflation is at most one in 50" (apparently up from the 1 in 10,000 of a couple of years ago). The President of the San Francisco Fed says, "The idea that we are launching into a prolonged period of declining prices I don't think has substance." A former government economist jokes that deflation is "57th on my list of worries, right after the 56th — fear of being eaten by piranhas." These comments about deflation represent entrenched professional opinion.

As you can see, anyone challenging virtually the entire army of financial and economic thinkers, from academic to professional, from liberal to conservative, from Keynesian socialist to Objectivist free-market, from Monetarist technocratic even to many vocal proponents of the Austrian school, must respond to their belief that inflation is virtually inevitable and deflation impossible.

"Potent Directors"

The primary basis for today's belief in perpetual prosperity and inflation with *perhaps* an occasional recession is what I call the "potent directors" fallacy. It is nearly impossible to find a treatise on macroeconomics today that does not assert or assume that the Federal Reserve Board has learned to control both our money and our economy. Many believe that it also possesses immense power to manipulate the stock market.

The very idea that it *can* do these things is false. Last October, before the House and Senate Joint Economic committee, Chairman Alan Greenspan himself called the idea that the Fed could prevent recessions a "puzzling" notion, chalking up such events to exactly what causes them: "human psychology." In August 1999, he even more specifically described the stock market as being driven by "waves of optimism and pessimism." He's right on this point, but no one is listening.

The Chairman also expresses the view that the Fed has the power to temper economic swings for the better. Is that what it does? Politicians and most economists assert that a central bank is necessary for maximum growth. Is that the case?

This is not the place for a treatise on the subject, but a brief dose of reality should serve. Real economic growth in the U.S. was greater in the nineteenth century without a central bank than it has been in the twentieth century with one. Real economic growth in Hong Kong during the latter half of the twentieth century outstripped that of every other country in the entire world, and it had no central bank. Anyone who advocates a causal connection between central banking and economic performance must conclude that a central bank is harmful to economic growth. For recent examples of the failure of the idea of efficacious economic directors, just look around. Since Japan's boom ended in 1990, its regulators have been using every presumed macroeconomic "tool" to get the Land of the Sinking Sun

rising again, as yet to no avail. The World Bank, the IMF, local
central banks and government officials were "wisely managing"
Southeast Asia's boom until it collapsed spectacularly in 1997.
Prevent the bust? They expressed profound dismay that it even
happened. As I write this paragraph, Argentina's economy has
just crashed despite the machinations of its own presumed "potent directors." I say "despite," but the truth is that directors,
whether they are Argentina's, Japan's or America's, *cannot* make
things better and have *always* made things worse. It is a principle
that meddling in the free market can only disable it. People think
that the Fed has "managed" the economy brilliantly in the 1980s
and 1990s. Most financial professionals believe that the only
potential culprit of a deviation from the path to ever greater prosperity would be current-time central bank actions so flagrantly
stupid as to be beyond the realm of possibility. But the deep flaws
in the Fed's manipulation of the banking system to induce and
facilitate the extension of credit will bear bitter fruit in the next
depression. Economists who do not believe that a prolonged expansionary credit policy has consequences will soon be blasting
the Fed for "mistakes" in the present, whereas the errors that
matter most reside in the past. Regardless of whether this truth
comes to light, the populace will disrespect the Fed and other
central banks mightily by the time the depression is over. For
many people, the single biggest financial shock and surprise over
the next decade will be the revelation that the Fed has never
really known what on earth it was doing. The spectacle of U.S.
officials in recent weeks lecturing Japan on how to contain deflation will be revealed as the grossest hubris. Make sure that you
avoid the disillusion and financial devastation that will afflict
those who harbor a misguided faith in the world's central bankers and the idea that they can manage our money, our credit or
our economy.

The Fed's Final Card

The Fed used to have two sources of power to expand the total amount of bank credit: It could lower reserve requirements or lower the discount rate, the rate at which it lends money to banks. In shepherding reserve requirements down to zero, it has expended all the power of the first source. In 2001, the Fed lowered its discount rate from 6 percent to 1.25 percent, an unprecedented amount in such a short time. By doing so, it has expended much of the power residing in the second source. What will it do if the economy resumes its contraction, lower interest rates to zero? *Then what?*

Why the Fed Cannot Stop Deflation

Countless people say that deflation is impossible because the Federal Reserve Bank can just *print money* to stave off deflation. If the Fed's main jobs were simply establishing new checking accounts and grinding out banknotes, that's what it might do. But in terms of *volume*, that has not been the Fed's primary function, which for 89 years has been in fact to foster the *expansion of credit*. Printed fiat currency depends almost entirely upon the whims of the issuer, but credit is another matter entirely.

What the Fed does is to set or influence certain very short-term interbank loan rates. It sets the discount rate, which is the Fed's nominal near-term lending rate to banks. This action is primarily a "signal" of the Fed's posture because banks almost never borrow from the Fed, as doing so implies desperation. (Whether they will do so more in coming years under duress is another question.) More actively, the Fed buys and sells overnight "repurchase agreements," which are collateralized loans among banks and dealers, to defend its chosen rate, called the "federal funds" rate. In stable times, the lower the rate at which banks can borrow short-term funds, the lower the rate at which they

can offer long-term loans to the public. Thus, though the Fed
undertakes its operations to influence bank borrowing, its ultimate
goal is to influence public borrowing from banks. Observe that
the Fed makes bank credit more available or less available to two
sets of *willing borrowers*.

During social-mood uptrends, this strategy appears to
work, because the borrowers – i.e., banks and their customers —
are confident, eager participants in the process. During monetary
crises, the Fed's attempts to target interest rates don't appear to
work because in such environments, the demands of creditors
overwhelm the Fed's desires. In the inflationary 1970s to early
1980s, rates of interest soared to 16 percent, and the Fed was
forced to follow, not because it *wanted* that interest rate but
because debt investors demanded it.

Regardless of the federal funds rate, banks set their own
lending rates to customers. During economic contractions, banks
can become fearful to make long-term loans even with cheap
short-term money. In that case, they raise their loan rates to make
up for the perceived risk of loss. In particularly scary times, banks
have been known virtually to cease new commercial and
consumer lending altogether. Thus, the ultimate success of the
Fed's attempts to influence the total amount of credit outstanding
depends not only upon willing borrowers but also upon the banks
as *willing creditors*.

Economists hint at the Fed's occasional impotence in fostering credit expansion when they describe an ineffective monetary strategy, i.e., a drop in the Fed's target rates that does not
stimulate borrowing, as "pushing on a string." At such times, low
Fed-influenced rates cannot overcome creditors' disinclination
to lend and/or customers' unwillingness or inability to borrow.
That's what has been happening in Japan for over a decade, where
rates have fallen effectively to zero but the volume of credit is
still contracting. Unfortunately for would-be credit manipula-

tors, the leeway in interest-rate manipulation stops at zero percent. When prices for goods fall rapidly during deflation, the
value of money rises, so even a zero interest rate imposes a heavy
real cost on borrowers, who are obligated to return more valuable dollars at a later date. No one with money wants to pay
someone else to borrow it, so interest rates cannot go negative.
(Some people have proposed various pay-to-borrow schemes for
central banks to employ in combating deflation, but it is doubt-
ful that the real world would accommodate any of them.)

When banks and investors are reluctant to lend, then
only *higher* interest rates can induce them to do so. In deflationary
times, the market accommodates this pressure with falling bond
prices and higher lending rates for all but the most pristine debtors.
But wait; it's not that simple, because higher interest rates do not
serve only to *attract* capital; they can also make it flee. Once
again, the determinant of the difference is market psychology:
Creditors in a defensive frame of mind can perceive a borrower's
willingness to pay high rates as desperation, in which case, the
higher the offer, the more repelled is the creditor. In a deflationary
crash, rising interest rates on bonds mean that creditors fear
default.

A defensive credit market can scuttle the Fed's efforts to
get lenders and borrowers to agree to transact at all, much less at
some desired target rate. If people and corporations are unwilling
to borrow or unable to finance debt, and if banks and investors
are disinclined to lend, central banks cannot force them to do
so. During deflation, they cannot even *induce* them to do so with
a zero interest rate.

Thus, regardless of assertions to the contrary, the Fed's
purported "control" of borrowing, lending and interest rates
ultimately depends upon an accommodating market psychology
and cannot be set by decree. So ultimately, the Fed does not
control either interest rates or the total supply of credit; the market
does.

There is an invisible group of lenders in the money game: *complacent depositors*, who — thanks to the FDIC (see Chapter 19) and general obliviousness — have been letting banks engage in whatever lending activities they like. Under pressure, bankers have occasionally testified that depositors might become highly skittish (if not horrified) if they knew how their money is being handled. During emotional times, the Fed will also have to try to maintain bank depositors' confidence by refraining from actions that appear to indicate panic. This balancing act will temper the Fed's potency and put it on the defensive yet further.

In contrast to the assumptions of conventional macroeconomic models, people are not machines. They get emotional. People become depressed, fearful, cautious and angry during depressions; that's essentially what causes them. A change in the population's mental state from a desire to expand to a desire to conserve is key to understanding why central bank machinations cannot avert deflation.

When ebullience makes people expansive, they often act on impulse, without full regard to reason. That's why, for example, consumers, corporations and governments can allow themselves to take on huge masses of debt, which they later regret. It is why creditors can be comfortable lending to weak borrowers, which they later regret. It is also why stocks can reach unprecedented valuations.

Conversely, when fear makes people defensive, they again often act on impulse, without full regard to reason. One example of action impelled by defensive psychology is governments' recurring drive toward protectionism during deflationary periods. Protectionism is correctly recognized among economists of all stripes as destructive, yet there is always a call for it when people's mental state changes to a defensive psychology. Voting blocs, whether corporate, union or regional, demand import tariffs and bans, and politicians provide them in order to get re-elected. If one country does not adopt protectionism, its trading partners will. Either way, the inevitable dampening effect on trade is inescapable. You will be reading about tariff wars in the newspapers before this cycle is over. Another example of defensive psychology is the increasing conservatism of bankers during a credit contraction. When lending officers become afraid, they call in loans and slow or stop their lending no matter how good their clients' credit may be in actuality. Instead of seeing opportunity, they see only danger. Ironically, much of the actual danger appears as a consequence of the reckless, impulsive decisions that they made in the preceding uptrend. In an environment of pessimism, corporations likewise reduce borrowing for expansion and acquisition, fearing the burden more than they believe in the opportunity. Consumers adopt a defensive strategy at such times by opting to save and conserve rather than to borrow, invest and spend. Anything the Fed does in such a climate will be seen through the lens of cynicism and fear. In such a mental state, people will interpret Fed actions differently from the way that they did when they were inclined toward confidence and hope.

With these thoughts in mind, let's return to the idea that the Fed could just print banknotes to stave off bank failures. One can imagine a scenario in which the Fed, beginning soon after the onset of deflation, trades banknotes for portfolios of bad loans, replacing a sea of bad debt with an equal ocean of banknotes, thus smoothly monetizing all defaults in the system without a ripple of protest, reaction or deflation. There are two problems with this scenario. One is that the Fed is a bank, and it would have no desire to go broke buying up worthless portfolios, debasing its own reserves to nothing. Only a government mandate triggered by crisis could compel such an action, which would come only *after* deflation had ravaged the system. Even in 1933, when the Fed agreed to monetize some banks' loans, it offered cash in exchange for only the very best loans in the banks' portfolios, not the precarious ones. Second, the smooth reflation scenario is an ivory-tower concoction that sounds plausible only by omitting human beings from it. While the Fed could embark on an aggressive plan to liquefy the banking system with cash in response to a developing credit crisis, that action itself ironically could serve to aggravate deflation, not relieve it. In a defensive emotional environment, evidence that the Fed or the government had decided to adopt a deliberate policy of inflating the currency could give bondholders an excuse, justified or not, to panic. It could be taken as evidence that the crisis is worse than they thought, which would make them fear defaults among weak borrowers, or that hyperinflation lay ahead, which could make them fear the depreciation of all dollar-denominated debt. Nervous holders of suspect debt that was near expiration could simply decline to exercise their option to repurchase it once the current holding term ran out. Fearful holders of suspect long-term debt far from expiration could dump their notes and bonds on the market, making prices collapse. If this were to happen, the net result of an attempt at inflating would be a system-wide reduction in the purchasing power of dollar-denominated debt, in other words, a drop in the dollar value of total credit extended, which is deflation.

The myth of Fed omnipotence has three main counter-vailing forces: the bond market, the gold market and the currency market. With today's full disclosure of central banks' activities, governments and central banks cannot hide their monetary decisions. Indications that the Fed had adopted an unwelcome policy would spread immediately around the world, and markets would adjust accordingly. Downward adjustments in bond prices could easily negate and even *outrun* the Fed's attempts at undesired money or credit expansion.

The problems that the Fed faces are due to the fact that the world is not so much awash in money as it is awash in *credit*. The amount of outstanding credit today dwarfs the quantity of money, so debt investors, who can always choose to sell bonds in large quantities, are now in the driver's seat with respect to interest rates, currency values and the total quantity of credit. So they, not the Fed, are also in charge of the prospects for inflation and deflation. The Fed has become a slave to trends that it has fostered for seventy years and to events that have already transpired. For the Fed, the mass of credit that it has nursed into the world is like having raised King Kong from babyhood as a pet. He might behave, but only if you can figure out what he wants and keep him satisfied.

In the context of our discussion, the Fed has four relevant tasks: to keep the banking system liquid, to maintain the public's confidence in banks, to maintain the market's faith in the value of Treasury securities, which constitute its own reserves, and to maintain the integrity of the dollar relative to other currencies, since dollars are the basis of the Fed's power. In a system-wide financial crisis, these goals will conflict. If the Fed chooses to favor any one of these goals, the others will be at least compromised, possibly doomed.

The Fed may have taken its steps to eliminate reserve requirements with these conflicts in mind, because whether by unintended consequence or design, that regulatory change transferred the full moral responsibility for depositors' money onto the banks. The Fed has thus excused itself from responsibility in a system-wide banking crisis, giving itself the option of defending the dollar or the Treasury's debt rather than your bank deposits. Indeed, from 1928 to 1933, the Fed raised its holdings of Treasury securities from 10.8 percent of its credit portfolio to 91.5 percent, effectively fleeing to "quality" right along with the rest of the market. What path the Fed will take under pressure is unknown,

but it is important to know that it is under no *obligation* to save
the banks, print money or pursue any other rescue. Its primary
legal obligation is to provide backing for the nation's currency,
which it could quite merrily fulfill no matter what happens to
the banking system.

Local Inflation by Repatriation?

Other countries hold Treasury securities in their central
banks as reserves, and their citizens keep dollar bills as a store of
value and medium of exchange. In fact, foreigners hold 45 percent of Treasury securities in the marketplace and 75 percent of
all $100 bills. Repatriation of those instruments, it has been pro-
posed, could cause a dramatic local inflation. If in fact investors
around the world were to panic over the quality of the Treasury's
debt, it would cause a price collapse in Treasury securities, which
would be deflationary. As for currency repatriation, if overall
money and credit were deflating in dollar terms, dollar bills would
be rising in value. Foreigners would want to hold onto those remaining dollar bills with both hands. Even if foreigners did return
their dollars, the Fed, as required by law, would offset returned
dollar currency with sales of Treasury bonds, thus neutralizing
the monetary effect.

Can Fiscal Policy Halt Deflation?

Can the government spend our way out of deflation and
depression? Governments sometimes employ aspects of "fiscal
policy," i.e., altering spending or taxing policies, to "pump up"
demand for goods and services. Raising taxes for any reason would
be harmful. Increasing government spending (with or without
raising taxes) simply transfers wealth from savers to spenders,
substituting a short-run stimulus for long-run financial deterioration. Japan has used this approach for twelve years, and it hasn't
worked. Slashing taxes absent government spending cuts would

be useless because the government would have to borrow the difference. Cutting government spending is a good thing, but politics will prevent its happening prior to a crisis.

The government's "tools" of macroeconomic manipulation are not mechanical levers on a machine, either. The very decision to use them is subject to psychology, as is the subsequent choice of methods and then the extent of their use. Have you noticed the government's increasing fiscal conservatism over the past decade? Even Democrats have been voicing the virtues of a balanced budget! This is a sea change in *thinking*, and that is what ultimately causes trends such as inflation and deflation.

Endgame

Prior excesses have resulted in a lack of solutions to the deflation problem. Like the discomfort of drug addiction withdrawal, the discomfort of credit addiction withdrawal cannot be avoided. The time to have thought about avoiding a system-wide deflation was years ago. Now it's too late.

It does not matter how it happens; in the right psychological environment, *deflation will win*, at least initially. People today, raised in the benign, expansive environment of Supercycle wave (V), love to quote the conventional wisdom, "Don't fight the Fed." Now that the environment is about to change, I think that the cry of the truly wise should be, *"Don't fight the waves."*

Currency Hyperinflation

Although I can discern no obvious forces that will counteract deflation, what comes *after* deflation is another matter. At the bottom, when there is little credit left to destroy, currency inflation, perhaps even hyperinflation, could well come into play. In fact, I think this outcome has a fairly high probability in the next Kondratieff cycle.

When a government embarks on a policy of currency hyperinflation, such as the Confederate States did in the 1860s, Germany did in the early 1920s or France did after World War II, the monetary path is utterly different from that of deflation, but ironically, the final result is about the same as that of a deflationary crash. At the end of hyperinflation, total bank accounts denominated in the hyperinflated currency are worth far less than they were, sometimes nothing at all. Total debts have shrunk or disappeared because the notes were denominated in depreciated money. In the severest cases, even the money disappears. In this sense, even with hyperinflation, the end result is the destruction of money and credit, which is deflation.

The Markets Will Signal Inflation

Despite my conclusions, I recognize that international money flows are massive, central bankers can be ingenious, and politics can be volatile. Perhaps there is some way that inflation, whether globally or locally, could accelerate in the immediate future. How can you tell if my forecast for deflation is wrong and that inflation or hyperinflation is taking place *instead of* deflation?

One way is to monitor the ebb and flow of the quantity of credit outstanding. As long as total system liquidity expands, deflation will remain at bay. When it contracts, you will know that deflation is in force. To stay informed, investigate a website called TrimTabs.com. Free trial subscriptions are available via the following avenues:

TrimTabs.com Investment Research
Website: www.trimtabs.com
Email: info@trimtabs.com
Address: 520 Mendocino Avenue, Suite 350,
    Santa Rosa, CA 95401

Phone: 707-874-9546
Fax: 707-525-1011
Director: Michael Alexander
Editor: Charles Biderman

You can anticipate major changes yourself by monitoring the two most sensitive barometers of monetary trends. One is the currency market. If the price of the dollar against other currencies begins to plummet, it *might* mean that the market fears dollar inflation. On the other hand, it might simply mean that credit denominated in other currencies is deflating faster than credit denominated in dollars or that foreign demand for dollars to buy U.S. stocks, property and products has waned. The other monetary barometer, which is more important, is the gold market. If gold begins to soar in dollar terms, then the market almost surely fears inflation. The bond market will not make the best barometer of inflation because much of it will fall under either scenario. I hope to recommend gold at lower prices near the bottom of the deflationary trend, but if gold were to move above $400 per ounce, I would probably be convinced that a major low had passed. The ideas in Chapters 18 and 22 will show you how to protect yourself simultaneously against deflation *and* a collapse in dollar value.

A High Degree of Complexity

Stocks are not registering a Supercycle top like that of 1929 but a *Grand* Supercycle top, per Figure 4-1. This means that the ultimate — if not the immediate — consequences will be more severe and more confounding than the consequences of the 1929-1932 crash. As Chapter 5 of *At the Crest of the Tidal Wave* explains, the entirety of Grand Supercycle wave Ⓘ should last a century and comprise two or three major bear markets with one or two intervening bull markets. This book addresses primarily the first bear market, although the two preceding sections attempt to outline some of the longer-term risks. Because in some ways the financial world is in uncharted waters, this book may not have all the answers.

BOOK TWO

HOW TO PROTECT YOURSELF AND PROFIT FROM DEFLATION AND DEPRESSION

"...but Philamis...followed his ould course...thinking that the tide would have no ebb, the tune would have no ende."
— Thomas Lodge, *Euphues' Shadowe* (1592)

For Your Safety

Every course of action discussed or recommended in this book is freely permitted in all Western-style democracies worldwide. If present or future laws pertaining to the reader prohibit any financial or other activity suggested in this book, the reader is advised to consider any contrary suggestion null and void and proceed according to applicable law. Neither the author nor the publisher acts as portfolio manager, securities advisor, commodity trading advisor, attorney, underwriter, solicitor or broker. At no time does the author or publisher advocate the reader's acquisition of any specific financial product or service. If you require personalized advice, you should seek the services of a competent professional.

Chapter 14:

Making Preparations and Taking Action

The ultimate effect of deflation is to reduce the supply of money and credit. Your goal is to make sure that it doesn't reduce the supply of *your* money and credit. The ultimate effect of depression is financial ruin. Your goal is to make sure that it doesn't ruin *you*.

Many investment advisors speak as if making money by investing is easy. It's not. What's easy is *losing* money, which is exactly what most investors do. They might make money for a while, but they lose eventually. Just keeping what you have over a lifetime of investing can be an achievement. That's what this book is designed to help you do, in perhaps the single most difficult financial environment that exists.

Protecting your liquid wealth against a deflationary crash and depression is pretty easy once you know what to do. Protecting your other assets and ensuring your livelihood can be serious challenges. Knowing how to proceed used to be the most difficult part of your task because almost no one writes about the issue. This book remedies that situation.

Preparing To Take the Right Actions

In a crash and depression, we will see stocks going down 90 percent and more, mutual funds collapsing, massive layoffs, high unemployment, corporate and municipal bankruptcies, bank and insurance company failures and ultimately financial and political crises. The average person, who has no inkling of the risks in the financial system, will be shocked that such things could happen, despite the fact that they have happened repeatedly throughout history.

Being unprepared will leave you vulnerable to a major disruption in your life. Being prepared will allow you to make exceptional profits both in the crash and in the ensuing recovery. For now, you should focus on making sure that you do not become a zombie-eyed victim of the depression.

The best news of all is that this depression should be relatively brief, though it will seem like an eternity while it is in force. The longest depression on record in the U.S. lasted three years and five months, from September 1929 to February 1933. The longest sustained stock market decline in U.S. history lasted seven years, from 1835 to 1842, and featured two depressions in close proximity. As the expected trend change is of one larger degree than those, it should be a commensurately large setback, but it should still be brief relative to the duration of the preceding advance.

Taking the Right Actions

Countless advisors have touted "stocks only," "gold only," "diversification," a "balanced portfolio" and other end-all solutions to the problem of attending to your investments. These approaches are usually delusions. As I try to make clear in the following pages, no investment strategy will provide stability *forever*. You will have to be nimble enough to see major trends coming and make changes accordingly. What follows is a good guide, I think, but it is only a guide.

The main goal of investing in a crash environment is *safety*. When deflation looms, almost every investment category becomes associated with immense risks. Most investors have no idea of these risks and will think you are a fool for taking precautions.

"What's THAT for?"

Many readers will object to taking certain prudent actions because of the presumed cost. For example: "I can't take a profit; I'll have to pay taxes!" My reply is, if you don't want to pay taxes, well, you'll get your wish; your profit will turn into a loss, and you won't have to pay any taxes. Or they say, "I can't sell my stocks for cash; interest rates are only 2 percent!" My reply is, if you can't abide a 2 percent annual gain, well, you'll get your wish there, too; you'll have a 30 percent annual loss instead. Others say, "I can't cash out my retirement plan; there's a penalty!" I reply, take your money out before there is none to get. Then there is the venerable, "I can't sell now; I'd be taking a loss!" I say no, you are recovering some capital that you can put to better use. My advice always is, make the right move, and the costs will take care of themselves.

If you are preoccupied with pedestrian concerns or blithely going along with mainstream opinions, you need to wake up now, while there is still time, and actively take charge of your personal finances. First you must make your capital, your person and your family safe. Then you can explore options for making money during the crash and especially after it's over.

As the subtitle implies, this book is designed as a guide for arranging your finances prior to any future deflationary depression, whether one occurs now, as I expect, or not. Although I want this book to have value beyond the present situation, some of the specifics of my suggestions are time-sensitive by nature. If you need to know today where you can find the few exceptionally sound banks, insurers and other essential service providers, if you want to locate the safest structures in the world for storing your wealth, whether in paper monetary instruments or physical assets such as precious metals, you will find the answers in these chapters. Yet over time, the best institutions and services today might be long gone, and others may have taken their place. For a few years at least, we will post free updates to this information at www.elliottwave.com/conquerthecrash. But if you read this book 50 years from now, you may have to do your own research to fit the investment options and service providers available at the time. Nevertheless, the general nature of your goals should be much as outlined herein.

Most people do not have the foggiest idea how to prepare their investments for a deflationary crash and depression, so the techniques are almost like secrets today. The following chapters show you a few steps that will make your finances secure despite almost anything that such an environment can throw at them.

Chapter 15:

Should You Invest in Bonds?

If there is one bit of conventional wisdom that we hear repeatedly with respect to investing for a deflationary depres-sion, it is that long-term bonds are the best possible investment. This assertion is wrong. Any bond issued by a borrower who can-not pay goes to *zero* in a depression. In the Great Depression, bonds of many companies, municipalities and foreign govern-ments were crushed. They became wallpaper as their issuers went bankrupt and defaulted. Bonds of *suspect* issuers also went way down, at least for a time. Understand that in a crash, no one knows its depth, and almost everyone becomes afraid. That makes investors sell bonds of any issuers that they fear could default. Even when people trust the bonds they own, they are sometimes forced to sell them to raise cash to live on. For this reason, even the safest bonds can go down, at least temporarily, as AAA bonds did in 1931 and 1932.

Figure 15-1 shows what happened to bonds of various grades in the last deflationary crash. Figure 15-2 shows what hap-pened to the Dow Jones 40-bond average, which lost 30 percent of its value in four years. Observe that the collapse of the early 1930s brought these bonds' prices *below* — and their interest rates above — where they were in 1920 near the peak in the intense inflation of the 'Teens. Figure 15-3 shows a comparable data series (the Bond Buyer 20-Bond average) in recent decades.

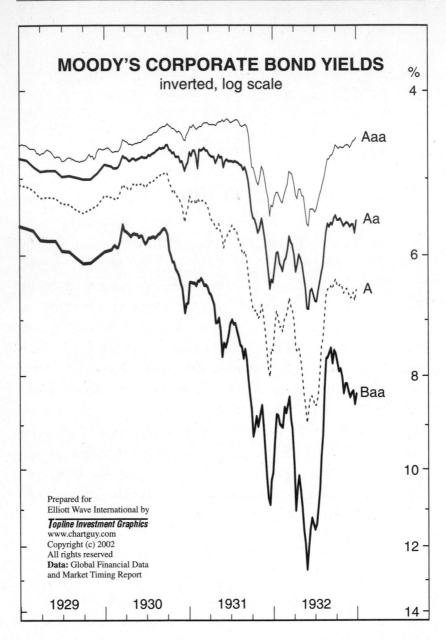

Figure 15-1

Notice how similar the pattern is to that of 1915-1928. If bonds follow the path that they did in the 1930s, their prices will fall *below the 1981 low, and their interest rates will exceed that year's peak of 13+ percent.*

Conventional analysts who have not studied the Great Depression or who expect bonds to move "contra-cyclically" to stocks are going to be shocked to see their bonds plummeting in value right along with the stock market. Ironically, economists will see the first wave down in bonds as a sign of inflation and recovery, when in fact, it will be the opposite.

The Specter of Downgrading

The main problem with even these cautionary graphs is that they do not show the full impact of *downgrades*. They show what bonds *of a certain quality* sold for at each data point. Bonds rated AAA or BBB at the start of a depression generally do not keep those ratings throughout it. Many go straight to D and then become de-listed because of default. Figure 15-1 does not take the price devastation of these issues into account. Like keepers of stock market averages who replace the companies that fail along the way, keepers of the bond averages of Figures 15-2 and 15-3 stand ready to replace component bonds whose ratings fall too far. As scary as they look, these graphs fail to depict the real misery that a depression inflicts upon bond investors.

High-Yield Bonds

When rating services rate bonds between BBB and AAA, they imply that they are considered safe investments. Anything rated BB or lower is considered speculative, implying that there is a risk that the borrower someday could default. The lower the rating, the greater that risk. Because of this risk, Wall Street, in a rare display of honesty, calls bonds rated BB or lower "junk." They appear to have "high yields," so people still buy them.

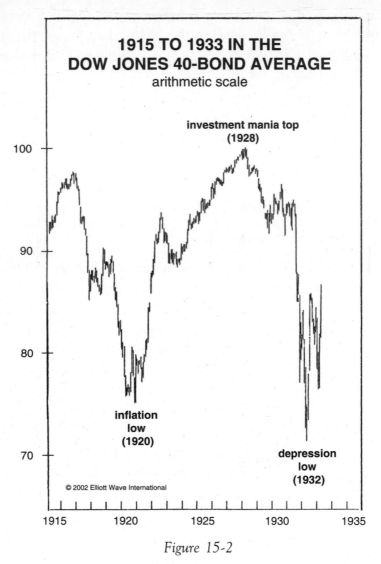

Figure 15-2

That very yield, though, compounds the risk to principal. In a bad economy, companies and municipalities that have issued bonds at high yields find it increasingly difficult to meet their interest payments. The prices of those bonds fall as investors perceive increased risk and sell them. The real result in such cases is a *low* yield or a *negative* yield, particularly if the issuer defaults and your principal is gone.

Figure 15-3

The converse is not necessarily true. We are *told* that in a good economy, high-yield bonds are safe because the economic expansion means good business conditions, which should support the company that issued the bond. Can you rely on this reasoning? Figure 15-4 shows what has been happening to junk bonds over the past 14 years. As you can see, they have been crashing in value *even though the economy was mostly expanding*

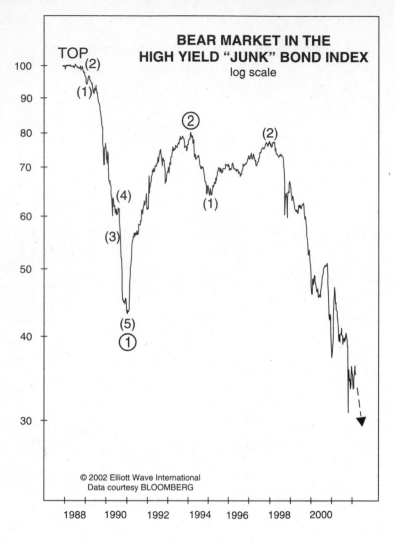

Figure 15-4

during that time. At least with respect to this debt class, the late Franz Pick, who used to call bonds "certificates of guaranteed confiscation," seems not to have been overly strident.

In recent weeks, advisors have been assuring readers that the recession is ending, so it is the "perfect time" to buy "depressed" junk bonds. The main entities that will be further greatly depressed in coming years besides these junk bonds are the suckers who buy them. Way back in 1988, I published a special analysis urging readers to avoid junk bonds entirely. I added, "If you can figure out a way to short junk bonds, do it." That's when they started down. Their "high yields" have been a chimera, as the bonds' prices have fallen 70 percent on average since then. Most of these issues are headed straight for default.

Today's "High-Grade" Bonds

Don't think that you will be safe buying bonds rated BBB or above. The unprecedented mass of vulnerable bonds extant today is on the verge of a waterfall of downgrading. Many bonds that are currently rated investment grade will be downgraded to junk status and then go into default. The downgrades will go hand-in-hand with falling prices, so you will not be afforded advance warning of loss. When the big slide begins, I doubt that the rating services will even be able to keep up with the downgrades at the rate that they will be required.

Owning government bonds also involves a political risk. Governments have a long record of stiffing their creditors in a crisis, and no government is immune from adopting that solution to its financial problems. A new regime especially may have little regard for previously squandered credit.

Today, millions of individuals and institutions own tax-exempt municipal bonds. While there are assuredly many exceptions, this class of bonds is the riskiest among popular government issues. In the United States, defaults on municipal bonds could occur at any moment after times get difficult. Politicians in many jurisdictions have borrowed and spent way more money than is likely ever to be paid back. Merely paying the interest on that debt in tough economic times will become an acute problem for many issuers. In such cases, default for many cities and counties will be inevitable. Even the debt of some higher-level government agencies is at serious risk of default in a worst-case scenario.

The Answer To Bond Selection

So if conventional wisdom is wrong, what is the correct way to frame the problem of investment opportunity and risk with respect to bonds in a deflationary depression? It is this: Any bond that is AAA at the start of the depression *and remains AAA throughout it* will be a satisfactory investment. The problem is, who can figure out which bonds those are? As we will see in Chapter 25, you cannot rely on bond rating services to guide you in a crunch.

If a crash and depression take place, some corporations whose products or services are important in that environment will become special situations, and their bonds will shine as viable investments. Unfortunately, I don't have the expertise to pick out the handful of long-term corporate bonds that will hold their value in a deflationary crash; I can only speculate on what will obviously be some of the worst. Since you can't short individual bonds, there's no point in making a list.

As debt prices fall, yields rise. If you're in long-term bonds, you're stuck with only the "falling prices" part of the equation. It's better to own short-term debt instruments, which can keep rolling over at ever-higher yields to compensate substantially for price losses. So, generally speaking, for safety, it is better to own high-quality *short-term* debt than long-term debt. We will explore that option in Chapter 18.

Chapter 16:

Should You Invest in Real Estate?

So bonds are risky. But we all know that property values never go down. Right?

After the stock experience of 2000-2001, people are saying, "Maybe stocks *can* come down for a few months from time to time, but real estate won't; real estate never has." They are saying it because real estate is the last thing still soaring at the top of the Great Asset Mania, but it, too, will fall in conjunction with a deflationary depression. Property values collapsed along with the depression of the 1930s. Few know that many values associated with property — such as rents — continued to fall through most of the 1940s, even after stocks had recovered substantially.

The worst thing about real estate is its *lack of liquidity* during a bear market. At least in the stock market, when your stock is down 60 percent and you realize you've made a horrendous mistake, you can call your broker and *get out* (unless you're a mutual fund, insurance company or other institution with millions of shares, in which case, you're stuck). With real estate, you can't pick up the phone and sell. You need to find a *buyer* for your house in order to sell it. In a depression, buyers just go away. Mom and Pop move in with the kids, or the kids move in with Mom and Pop. People start living in their offices or moving their offices into their living quarters. Businesses close down. In time, there is a massive glut of real estate.

In the initial stages of a depression, sellers cling to an illusion about what their property is really worth. They keep a high list price on their house, reflecting what it was worth *last year*. I know people who are doing that now. This stubbornness leads to a drop in sales volume. At some point, a few owners cave in and sell at much lower prices. Then others are forced to drop their prices, too. What is the potential *buyer's* psychology at that point? "Well, *gee*, property prices have been coming down. Why should I rush? I'll wait till they come down further." The further they come down, the more the buyer wants to wait. It's a downward spiral.

When Real Estate Falls

Real estate prices have always fallen hard when stock prices have fallen hard. Figure 16-1 displays this reliable relationship. We found that in some cases, the real estate peak was offset from the stock market peak by about two years. It is now two years since the major stock indexes topped, and the current real estate frenzy is giving signs of extremity. Property prices should be the last financial domino to peak out and fall.

The overwhelming evidence for a major stock market decline presented in Chapters 4 through 7 is enough by itself to portend a tumble in real estate prices. Usually the culprit behind these joint declines is a credit deflation. If there were ever a time we were poised for such a decline, it is now.

The Extension of Credit

What screams "bubble" — giant, historic bubble — in real estate today is the system-wide extension of *massive* amounts of credit to finance property purchases. As a result, a record percentage of Americans today are nominal "homeowners" via $7.6 trillion in mortgage debt. Two-thirds of them owe an average of

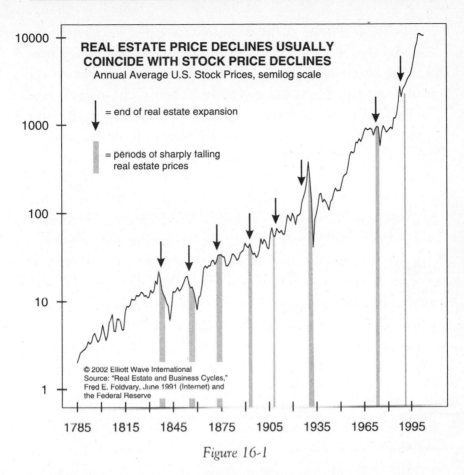

REAL ESTATE PRICE DECLINES USUALLY
COINCIDE WITH STOCK PRICE DECLINES
Annual Average U.S. Stock Prices, semilog scale

↓ = end of real estate expansion

= periods of sharply falling
real estate prices

© 2002 Elliott Wave International
Source: "Real Estate and Business Cycles,"
Fred E. Foldvary, June 1991 (Internet) and
the Federal Reserve

Figure 16-1

two-thirds of the value of their homes, plus interest, and both ratios have been increasing at a blistering pace.

People can buy a house with little or no down payment in many cases. They can refinance a house for its entire value. "How can this be?" you ask. "Isn't at least 20 percent homeowner equity required?" Well, sort of. Credit institutions are supposed to be penalized for lending more than 80 percent on an uninsured mortgage. But if they get it insured, which is generally not difficult, the limit can go up to 90 percent. With VA or FHA approval, it can go up to 95 percent. "Prime borrowers" can refinance for up to 125 percent of a home's appraised value.

What if none of these exceptions apply? Real estate in-siders on a quiet Saturday afternoon will tell you that many banks skirt the intent of laws aimed to ensure some homeowner equity in refinancing deals. For example, suppose the owner of a $500,000 home wants to refinance it at the full amount, but the bank is restricted to lending him only 80 percent of the value of the property, which is $400,000. If the homeowner wants the whole half-million anyway, the bank will send in an appraiser who magically discerns that the property is actually worth $625,000. Get it? 80 percent of $625,000 is $500,000. The home-owner has his 100 percent loan, the bank earns more interest, and the rules are satisfied. If you are creative, you can wangle even more than 100 percent out of a deal. The principle (and maybe later the principal) is out the window, and no one's the wiser, at least until a bear market imparts wisdom.

The problem with these schemes is that their success and continuation depend upon continuously rising property prices. Once the bank extends a loan of that size, it owns the house at full value. *Then, any drop in that value directly causes a drop in the value of the bank's capital.* By contrast, when the bank lends only half of the value of a home, its value can drop as much as half, and the bank can still get all of its depositors' money out of the deal by selling the house. With these latest methods of "creative financing," depositors' money is utterly unprotected from mar-ket risk.

Bank loans to home buyers are bad enough, but government-sponsored mortgage lenders — the Federal National Mortgage Corp. (Fannie Mae), the Federal Home Loan Mortgage Corp. (Freddie Mac) and the Federal Home Loan Bank — have extended $3 *trillion* worth of mortgage credit. Major financial institutions actually *invest* in huge packages of these mortgages, an investment that they and their clients (which may include *you*) will surely regret. *Money* magazine (December 2001) reports that the CEO of Fannie Mae "may be the most confident CEO in America." Certainly his stockholders, clients and mortgage-package investors had better share that feeling, because confidence is the only thing holding up this giant house of cards. When real estate prices begin to fall in a deflationary crash, lenders will experience a rising number of defaults on the mortgages they hold. My guess is that the Treasury will lose the $7 billion line of credit that it is required by law to extend to these quasi-government companies and even more if it attempts a bailout.

Another remarkable trend of recent years adds to the precarious nature of mortgage debt. Many people have been rushing to borrow the last pennies possible on their homes. They have been taking out home equity loans so they can buy stocks and TVs and cars and whatever else their hearts desire at the moment. This widespread practice is brewing a *terrible* disaster. Taking out a home equity loan is nothing but turning ownership of your home over to your bank in exchange for whatever other items you would like to own or consume. It's a reckless course, and it stems from the extreme confidence that accompanies a major top in social mood.

At the bottom of the depression, banks are going to own many, many homes, and their previous owners will be out in the street. That's not so bad; at least they got their money's worth from the TVs and cars. It will be a disaster for the banks' depositors, though, because there will be no one to buy the homes at mortgage-value prices. Depositors' money will be stuck in lifeless property deals, marked down 50 percent, 90 percent or (as happened in the Great Depression) even more.

Credit expansion has supported real estate prices, but it is late in the game. The dramatic tumble in interest rates in 2001 has spurred a record number of home sales because financing rates appear low. Marginal buyers, who had waited on the sidelines, are finally taking the plunge. People around the country are nearly unanimous in thinking that this is their last great opportunity to buy a house. Naturally, it is the opposite: It's your last chance to sell. The market is becoming as bought up as it can get, and there is little interest-rate ammunition left to win the battle for even more borrowers.

Some Things To Do

For more on the prospects for property values, please see Chapter 20 of *At the Crest of the Tidal Wave*. In the meantime, you can take the following steps:

- Make sure you avoid real estate investment trusts, which are perhaps the worst property-related investments during a bear market. Some REITs valued at $100 a share in the early 1970s fell to ¼ by late 1974, and most of them never recovered. REITs are sold to the public because the people who do the deals don't want to stick with them. The public falls for REITs cycle after cycle. These "investments" hold up in the best part of bull markets, but they are disasters in bear markets.

- If you are in the real estate business, wrap up any sales deals you are working and get out of all investment real estate holdings unless they are special situations about which you know much more than the market does. In general, wait for lower prices to re-invest.

- If you hold a big mortgage on expensive property that depends upon massive public patronage, such as an arena, playhouse, amusement park, arts center or other such facility, consider selling it or subleasing it insured.

- If you are a banker, sell off your largest-percentage mortgages and get into safer investments.

• If you rent your living or office space, make sure that your lease either allows you to leave on short notice or has a clause lowering your rent if like units are reduced in price to new renters.

• If you have a huge mortgage on a McMansion or condo that you cannot afford unless your current income maintains, sell it and move into something more reasonable. If at all possible, join the 1/3 of title-holding Americans who own their homes outright. Be willing to trade down to make it happen. See Chapter 29 for more on this topic.

• If you consider your home a consumption item, and you wish to keep it on that basis, fine. If you are just as happy renting your residence as owning, do so.

• At the bottom, buy the home, office building or business facility of your dreams for ten cents or less per dollar of its peak value.

Chapter 17:

Should You Invest in Collectibles?

Collecting for Investment

Collecting for investment purposes is almost always foolish. Never buy anything *marketed* as a collectible. The chances of losing money when collectibility is priced into an item are huge. Usually, collecting trends are fads. They might be short-run or long-run fads, but they eventually dissolve. The inflation of the 1970s pushed gold and silver higher, so rare coins got a free ride of new interest. What did coin rarity have to do with inflation? Nothing.

Except perhaps for certain enduring masters' works, the focus of art appreciation goes through cycles. So do prices, even for the best art. Japanese investors who bought paintings at record prices a decade ago have lost much of the value of their "investments."

There are times when collecting makes sense, but you have to be in on the ground floor. When I was a kid, I collected coins. You could find rare coins in everyday pocket change. In the 1950s, my grandmother persuaded the local parking meter collector to let her sort through the town's weekly take of coins and exchange them one for one. There was *no downside* to the hobby because the coins were always worth at least face value.

If you have speculated in rare coins or other collectibles that you do not want for their aesthetic or nostalgic value, sell them at today's prices, before they fall further in the crash. In depressions, people care about gold or silver content in coins, not rarity. One company that specializes in liquidating U.S. coin collections is American Federal, which can broker your coins or buy them outright. Be sure to compare prices with other dealers, some of which are listed in Chapter 22. Here is the contact information:

> American Federal Rare Coin & Bullion
> Website: americanfederal.com
> Email: info@americanfederal.com
> Address: 14602 North Cave Creek Rd., Ste. C, Phoenix,
> AZ 85022
> Phone: 1-800-221-7694 or 602-992-6857
> Fax: 602-493-8158
> CEO: Nick Grovich

Also taking a hard-nosed consumer-advocacy stance is the *Rosen Numismatic Advisory*, which has won many awards over its 27 years of publication. If you prefer handling your own financial dealings, this is a good source of buy-and-sell coin strategies, information and advice. Here's how to get in touch:

> *Rosen Numismatic Advisory*
> Numismatic Counseling, Inc.
> Email: mauricerosen@aol.com
> Address: P.O. Box 38, Plainview, NY 11803
> Phone: 516-433-5800
> Fax: 516-433-5801
> CEO: Maurice Rosen

Rock 'n' roll memorabilia and other baby-boomer collectibles are probably at an all-time top. Baby boomers who covet reminders of their youth will die off in the next 30 years, and most of their collectibles will be considered little more than curios.

For many supposed collectibles, such as Beanie Babies and such, it's already too late. Others, such as baseball cards, comic books and Barbie dolls, still have some value. If you want to sell your pedestrian collectibles, few venues are better than Ebay on the web, at www.ebay.com. For fine art sales, contact:

Christie's
Website: christies.com
Address: 20 Rockefeller Place, New York, NY 10020
Phone: 212-646-2000
Fax: 212-636-2399

Sotheby's
Website: sothebys.com
Address: 1334 York Ave, New York, NY 10021
Phone: 212-606-7000/541-312-5682
Fax: 212-606-7107/541-312-5684

For more on collectibles in a bear market, see Chapter 19 of *At the Crest of the Tidal Wave*.

Collecting for Pleasure

If you collect certain items for the love of them, you are about to be made very happy. Prices for art and collectibles, so outrageous today, will fall to joyously affordable levels in a depression. If you want to enhance your collection, keep your capital safe, wait until the bottom, and buy up all the items you want at pennies on today's dollar value.

Chapter 18:

Should You Invest in "Cash"?

The Wonder of Cash

For those among the public who have recently become concerned that being fully invested in one stock or stock fund is not risk-free, the analysts' battle cry is "diversification." They recommend having your assets spread out in numerous different *stocks*, numerous different stock *funds* and/or numerous different (foreign) stock *markets*. Advocates of junk bonds likewise counsel prospective investors that having lots of different issues will reduce risk.

This "strategy" is bogus. Why invest in anything unless you have a strong opinion about where it's going and a game plan for when to get out? Diversification is gospel today because investment assets of so many kinds have gone up for so long, but the future is another matter. Owning an array of investments is financial *suicide* during deflation. They all go down, and the logistics of getting out of them can be a nightmare. There can be weird exceptions to this rule, such as gold in the early 1930s when the government fixed the price, or perhaps some commodity that is crucial in a war, but otherwise, *all assets go down in price during deflation except one: cash.*

Today, few people give cash a thought. They sneer at the mere suggestion. "Cash is trash," goes the popular saying. Because interest rates are "too low," investors claim that they have

"no choice" but to invest in something with more "upside potential." Ironically but obviously necessarily, the last major interest-rate
cycle was perfectly aligned to convince people to do the wrong
thing. Two decades ago, when rates were high, people insisted
that stocks were not worth buying. Now that rates are low, they
insist that cash is not worth holding. It's a psychological trap keeping investors from doing the right thing: buying stocks at the bottom
(when rates were high) and selling them at the top (when rates
are low).

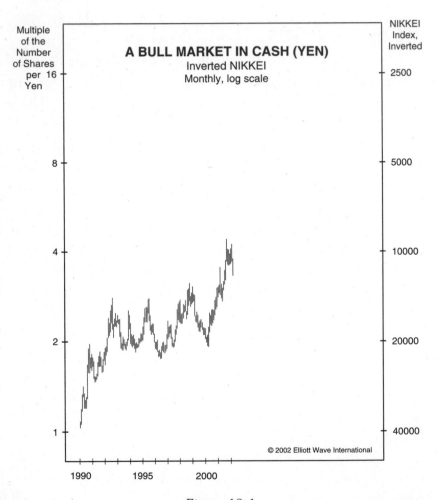

Figure 18-1

Now let's dispose of the idea that the return on cash is "low." How would you like to own an asset that goes up *four times in value* in eleven years? Figure 18-1 is a picture of the soaring value of cash in Japan from 1990 through 2001. Cash has appreciated 300 percent in eleven years in terms of how many shares of Japanese stocks it can buy. Figure 18-2 is one picture of the rising value of cash in the United States, which appreciated nearly 250 percent from March 2000 to the present in terms of how many

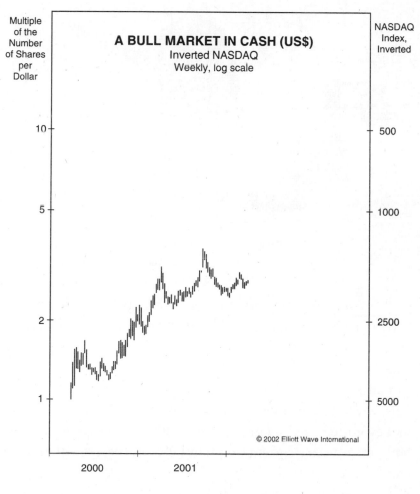

Figure 18-2

shares of the NASDAQ index it can buy. Wouldn't you like to enjoy this kind of performance, too? You can, if you move into cash before a major deflation. Then when the stock markets reach bottom, you can buy incredibly cheap shares that almost no one else can afford because they lost it all when their stocks collapsed.

"If I hadn't lost everything I'd definitely be buying right now."

reproduced by permission of Leo Cullum

Cash is the only asset that assuredly rises in value during deflation. One safe "parking place" for capital during a deflationary crash is cash notes — for example, $100 bills, £50 notes or the equivalent in your home currency — in a safe depository that you can always access. That way, you will have money if the bank fails, you will have money if credit collapses, and you will have money if the government defaults on its debt. I suggest that you have at least *some* currency on hand if you expect a deflationary crash.

Unfortunately, currency has no yield, it is destructible, and it cannot be transferred with a phone call. Carefully selected "cash equivalents" can solve those problems.

The Risk in Many "Cash Equivalents"

Cash equivalents are high-quality short-term debt. They are extremely attractive investments in a deflationary crash. Choosing them, however, can be tricky. You must own *safe* instruments stored in a *safe* facility.

Most cautious investors think that their capital is safe, and the yield guaranteed, in any money market fund. Do not fall for this illusion. Money market funds are *relatively* safe, but they are still nothing but portfolios of debt, short-term debt to be sure, but debt nonetheless. When a company or government goes bankrupt, it stops paying interest on its debts, short-term or long, *right then*. If you own any of it at the time, your investment is compromised if not gone.

In a strong economy, few give this risk any thought. They do not imagine that companies, governments and their agencies will ever cease paying interest due. Many people also erroneously believe that the debt issued by government-sponsored enterprises, such as U.S. mortgage insurers Fannie Mae and Freddie Mac, are government-guaranteed, but they're not. *You* take the risk when you buy their debt or their investment products.

Some money market funds realized early on that they could buy slightly riskier debt issues in order to squeeze out an extra 0.1 percent annual yield above that of their competitors, which they could then advertise to attract deposits. Others began to try to top *them* using the same tactics. Some funds have ended up owning a lot of weak debt. To the extent that a money-market fund's holdings are downgraded, the fund is that much riskier. Funds do not report downgrades to you or warn you if they think any of their holdings may be at risk. You hear about it only via the loss statement that you receive in the mail.

In a depression, many money market funds will shock their depositors when they report losses. Once the process of debt defaults begins, to whom — and at what price — will the funds sell their portfolios if they wish to replace their risky assets with safer ones? They are all on the same ship, and there are few lifeboats.

The Safest Cash Equivalents Inside the U.S.

The safest cash equivalents in a depression are the very best near-term debt instruments, issued by a strong enterprise or government. The strongest such issues today lie *outside* the United States. In the U.S., the primary option is short-term Treasury securities, which includes not only Treasury bills but also longer-term notes and bonds that are within months of maturity, which can be purchased on the secondary market. For the time being, and for the investor who must or prefers to keep all assets inside the United States, Treasury bills or money market funds that hold only short-term U.S. Treasury debt appear to be the best financial haven available next to bullion-type gold and silver coins. These investments might also be attractive for some investors outside the U.S., although there is always currency risk to take into account, because if the dollar falls against your home currency, you will lose money.

The beauty of safe near-term debt is that instead of getting killed by rising interest rates, you can benefit from them. In 1931, the Fed was forced to raise its discount rate in the face of deflation in order to prop up the value of a falling dollar. Other investments fell harder as a result, but holders of very short-term T-bills who kept purchasing new ones at expiration watched their returns increase. This is a good way to defend your portfolio against rising interest rates.

Treasury bills and "Treasury only" money market funds have the added advantage of incurring no state income tax obligation on the interest they pay, which saves you some money if you live in a state with an income tax. Most of these funds also allow you to write checks on the account, so you will be getting a fairly safe yield on what amounts to your checking account. Usually they limit check amounts to $100 or more each, so you will still need a bank checking account for smaller checks, but that shouldn't put much of your total wealth at risk.

You could choose to buy Treasury bills directly from a broker or the U.S. Treasury Department from instructions available at its websites, www.publicdebt.treas.gov and www.treasurydirect.gov. For the record, you no longer get actual Treasury bills for your money. You get a bookkeeping entry that *says* you own Treasury bills. The Treasury department makes it easy to roll over your position automatically upon expiration, but on the other hand, you get none of the amenities of a money-market fund. You do get a modicum of additional safety from more direct ownership. Like many money-market funds, Treasury-only funds are bonded by insurance companies against fraud or theft. However, in a depression environment, such a bond is only as good as its insurer (see Chapter 24). Also, if the fund's custodial bank fails, your T-bills could be under wraps until things are sorted out. So buying T-bills directly from the government has the same advantage as holding actual gold in your hand as opposed to stock shares or warehouse receipts: There is no middleman. If top domestic safety and uninterrupted liquidity are crucial to your investment plan, go ahead and buy T-bills directly. Otherwise, the funds should serve. Personally, I prefer to err on the side of being as safe as possible.

Despite what virtually everyone assumes, there are some risks in owning T-bills, directly or indirectly. For example, you could lose some of the value of your certificates or fund shares if there were a rush to sell debt assets in general or merely a panic over possible U.S. government insolvency, either of which could drive the prices of short-term Treasury debt down (and their interest rates up) until the market recovered its equilibrium or confidence. Aside from the above-mentioned risks associated with funds, the only way for holders of Treasury bills to lose all their money would be for the U.S. government to default on its debt.

A federal government default is not impossible. The U.S. Treasury's $3.4 trillion debt and extensive unfunded government liabilities will present significant financial burdens in a depression. The deepest depression in three centuries could force Treasury issues down to junk status, like so many South American IOUs. Despite this risk, the U.S. government still has immense taxing power, and its world-class reputation should attract a share of capital if there is a "flight to quality" during a worldwide monetary crisis. As many stocks and bonds collapse during the crash, those who thought they were pretty smart investing in historically overpriced stocks, Russian and Argentinean bonds, retail consumer debt, junk bonds and worse will come to realize, "We need to sell these losers for what we can get and buy something else with the money we have left." In such a situation, money is likely to flow into what investors perceive as stronger issues. These could well include Treasury bills, making their issuer, the U.S. Treasury, even more liquid. Of course, politics could scuttle this potential. Foreign governments could outlaw money exports, or the U.S. could become politically unstable, reducing its status as an investment haven. The truth is that no one can know exactly how Treasury securities will fare in a major depression. What I *can* say is that, apart from special situations in the corporate realm that I dare not attempt to anticipate, T-bills are probably the safest U.S.-based interest-bearing investment. The next section will present attractive alternatives to holding short-term U.S. Treasury securities.

Of the many hundreds of money market funds in the United States, surprisingly few hold exclusively short-term U.S. Treasury obligations. Among the largest fifteen of these funds, only five have all these features: no other required accounts, no

5 LARGEST TREASURY-ONLY MONEY MARKET FUNDS WITH NO TRANSACTION CHARGES OR LIMITS Source: Weiss Ratings, Inc.		
Fund Name	**Toll-Free No.**	**Web Address**
American Century Capital Presv Fund I	(800) 345-2021	www.americancentury.com
JPMorgan 100% US Treas MMF/Morgan	(800) 348-4782	www.jpmorganfunds.com
One Group US Treas Secs MMF/CI A	(800) 480-4111	www.onegroup.com
Schwab US Treasury Money Fund	(800) 435-4000	www.schwab.com
Vanguard Treasury MMF	(877) 662-7447	www.vanguard.com

Table 18-1

transaction limits and no separate charges for printing checks, bounced checks or wire transfers into or out of your account. Table 18-1 provides a list. All of these funds' costs are covered by their "expense ratios," i.e., the percentage of your account that they charge as a management fee. They do vary, so do some comparative shopping. Also, investigate the banks they use and choose the safest. If you would like to examine the full list of Treasury-only money-market funds, contact the following:

Weiss Ratings, Inc.
Website: www.weissratings.com
Email: wr@weissinc.com
Address: P.O. Box 109665, Palm Beach Gardens, FL
    33410
Phone: 800-289-9222 and 561-627-3300
Fax: 561-625-6685

While I am comfortable saying that T-bills are the safest asset to hold inside the United States this side of gold and silver, *At the Crest of the Tidal Wave* warned that *some* day, even Treasury bills would probably become risky. If the dollar ever re-enters its long-term bear market, and particularly if it goes into free-fall, then even soaring short-term Treasury yields might not be able to overcome investors' imperative to get out. Each uptick in yield would be a yet greater burden to the government in the form of debt service, a fact that might frighten T-bill investors as much as entice them. If the federal government defaults, it might resort to a desperate action such as declaring that Treasury bills are now long-term bonds, to be paid off in ten years instead of ten weeks. You don't want to be stuck with any such deal.

If you come to believe that T-bills will get into trouble, you should buy safe foreign short-term debt or gold and silver to protect your capital. For details, see the next section and Chapter 22. Always be vigilant; always be practical; always try to get out of a potentially risky investment *before* others perceive that risk. If you need help, Elliott Wave International continuously monitors risks and opportunities in these markets from the standpoint of price trends and investor psychology.

Finding the Safest Cash Equivalents Outside the U.S.

For the globally sophisticated investor, there are excellent alternatives to U.S.-based debt. Most people hesitate to look outside their own areas, but if you have substantial capital to protect, you should expand your geographical horizons. The first reason is for the sake of diversity (*targeted* diversity, not the willy-nilly type), but there is a better reason: The safest investment debt resides within the safest financial systems.

Even if a debt-issuing *entity* is financially secure, events that are barely its fault might compromise it. For example, a manufacturer or municipality might be fully sound, except that it unwarily entrusts all its reserves to a single bank, and the bank fails. Suddenly, the issuing entity is in financial trouble, and its debt is much riskier.

So ideally, you should begin by identifying a country whose financial system is among the soundest available. According to SafeWealth Group, a firm of wealth preservation experts, *Switzerland* is the standout in this respect in Europe, and *Singapore* is the standout in Asia, currently and for the immediately foreseeable future.

Swiss voters are financially conservative. Under the Swiss Constitution, citizen-led referendums and initiatives can, and often do, challenge or revoke government policies or legislation, keeping excesses in check. Swiss citizens also have the highest savings rate in Europe, which helps liquefy the local banking system. Singapore issues no short-term debt because the government, with its conservative spending policy, doesn't need short-term money. The country's bank reserves are strong because its citizens have a 25 percent savings rate mandated by law, which they routinely exceed. For comparison, the savings rate in the U.S. has fallen in the past 18 years from an average rate of 10 percent all the way down to zero. (Figures actually dropped to a 4 percent *negative* savings rate — i.e., spending exceeding income — but U.S. statisticians adjusted the definition of savings, so the lowest rate officially recognized to date is 0.2 percent of disposable income.) Moreover, each of these countries has a small total government debt relative to its financial base. Switzerland's national debt load is only about 170 billion Swiss francs, a fraction of the 3 trillion Sfr deposited in that country's banks, much of which would surely be freely available to refinance Swiss government debt given difficult times, when capital seeks conservative investments. Thus, while keeping in mind that politics can change, it appears at this time far less likely that a Swiss or Singaporean government entity will renege on its jurisdiction's obligations than perhaps any other government entities in the world.

The next step is to find the safest debt issues within one or both of the safest countries. In Switzerland, Swiss Money Market

Claims (the equivalent of T-bills), near-term Swiss Confederation bonds and carefully selected cantonal (a canton is a district) bonds are probably as close to safe debt as you can get. Singapore's safest offerings are long-term government bonds with nearby maturities.

To be even safer, you will want to get more specific. While most Swiss cantons' paper has a top safety rating, the standard rating services, as we will see in Chapter 25, do not take the possibility of severe system-wide financial pressures into account. It is advisable, then, to invest in a canton that has little debt and a history of balancing its budget even in tough times.

As you can probably tell by now, this is a field for specialists. I am not one of them. If you are a major institution or Arab oil magnate, you probably already get good advice. Otherwise, as far as I know, the SafeWealth Group is the best option. It has researched banks, insurance companies and debt issuers and isolated those that it believes have the highest level of safety on the planet. It has also identified wealth managers who focus primarily on protecting and preserving capital as opposed to aggressive growth with risk. Wherever you reside, if you would like to own a portfolio of the safest short-term foreign debt or even a fund of U.S. Treasury bills through a safe Swiss institution, this is a good place to start. Be aware that the available custodial institutions typically require minimum investments beginning at 100,000 Sfr or more. You may contact the firm as follows:

> SafeWealth Group Service Center
> Cari Lima, Senior Vice President
> Email: clientservices@safewealthgroup.ch
> Address: Grand-Rue 114, 2nd Level East,
>   CH-1820 Montreux, Switzerland
> Phone: (from U.S. 011) 41-21-966-7200
> Fax: (from U.S. 011) 41-21-966-7201

SafeWealth Group's services are often rendered with no direct cost to the client. Equally comforting, SafeWealth traditionally counsels people as if a global financial disaster lay immediately around the corner, so you don't have to explain concerns that most investment counselors view as little different from paranoia. As the old saying goes, I may be paranoid, but that doesn't mean there isn't someone following me. In the final analysis, it is better to be safe and wrong than exposed and wrong.

Protecting Against Hyperinflation

When a central bank prints banknotes rapidly to fund government spending, the result is hyperinflation. I expect deflation in the U.S., not inflation. Nevertheless, I conceded in Chapter 13 that monetary foresight cannot be 20/20. Also, you may live in a country that *is* in a position to hyperinflate.

If you face a currency-based hyperinflation, some aspects of your financial defense are substantially different from those that you will use to protect against deflation. For example, you do not want to hold *anything* denominated in the hyperinflating currency, and you do not want to sell local stocks short. You can protect yourself best with a portfolio of notes and bills denominated in stable foreign currencies, along with gold and silver (see Chapter 22).

Small investors in qualified countries outside Europe who are afraid of home currency hyperinflation have an option, too. The Prudent Safe Harbor Fund issues from the same fund family that offers the Prudent Bear Fund (see contact information in Chapter 20). This fund invests primarily in sovereign foreign notes and bonds of major European nations, but part of the fund (typically around 15 percent) is invested in gold stocks and gold bullion. The fund is also appropriate for Europeans who antici-pate deflation. The minimum is an affordable $2000. Keep in mind that European currencies can fall in value, too, and interest rates for European bonds can fluctuate as much as those in other areas. This fund is fine for some of your holdings, but you must be sure of your market analysis to use it for the bulk of your assets.

A Combination Strategy

Observe that one defense works for both a deflationary crash *and* a local hyperinflation: *holding notes and bills of strong issuers, denominated in a stable currency.* If you are worried about either deflation or hyperinflation in your country and want to protect against it, you should explore a mechanism through which you can hold a portfolio of the highest-grade near-term debt with the option of switching its denomination easily from one currency to another so that you can keep your money continuously lodged with the most conservative and stable governments. If you want to have a handle on the most likely future trends among the world's currencies, Elliott Wave International's services can help you. Of course, if a worldwide hyperinflation were to spare no currency at all, then precious metals would be your primary recourse. To prepare even for that remote possibility, you should also have a mechanism already in place to convert your holdings quickly to precious metals. If you can meet the minimums associated with their recommended institutions, SafeWealth Group can help you make all these arrangements under one roof. If you are a small investor, you can still achieve close to the desired result by choosing the most liquid banks, money market funds and precious metals available to you, using the lists and leads in this chapter and Chapters 19 and 22 as a guide.

Chapter 19:

How To Find a Safe Bank

Risks in Banking

Between 1929 and 1933, 9000 banks in the United States closed their doors. President Roosevelt shut down *all* banks for a short time after his inauguration. In December 2001, the government of Argentina froze virtually all bank deposits, barring customers from withdrawing the money they thought they had. Sometimes such restrictions happen naturally, when banks fail; sometimes they are imposed. Sometimes the restrictions are temporary; sometimes they remain for a long time.

Why do banks fail? For nearly 200 years, the courts have sanctioned an interpretation of the term "deposits" to mean *not* funds that you deliver for safekeeping but a *loan* to your bank. Your bank balance, then, is an IOU from the bank to you, even though there is no loan contract and no required interest payment. Thus, legally speaking, you have a claim on your money deposited in a bank, but practically speaking, you have a claim only on the loans that the bank makes with your money. If a large portion of those loans is tied up or becomes worthless, your money claim is compromised. A bank failure simply means that the bank has reneged on its promise to pay you back. The bottom line is that your money is only as safe as the bank's loans. In boom times, banks become imprudent and lend to almost anyone. In busts, they can't get much of that money back due to widespread defaults. If the bank's portfolio collapses in value, say, like those of the Savings & Loan institutions in the U.S. in the late 1980s and early 1990s, the bank is broke, and its depositors' savings are gone.

Because U.S. banks are no longer required to hold any of their deposits in reserve (see Chapter 10), many banks keep on hand just the bare minimum amount of cash needed for everyday transactions. Others keep a bit more. According to the latest Fed figures, the net loan-to-deposit ratio at U.S. commercial banks is 90 percent. This figure omits loans considered "securities" such as corporate, municipal and mortgage-backed bonds, which from my point of view are just as dangerous as everyday bank loans. The true loan-to-deposit ratio, then, is 125 percent and rising. Banks are not just lent to the hilt; they're past it. Some bank loans, at least in the current benign environment, could be liquidated quickly, but in a fearful market, liquidity even on these so-called "securities" will dry up. If just a few more depositors than normal were to withdraw money, banks would have to sell some of these assets, depressing prices and depleting the value of the securities remaining in their portfolios. If enough depositors were to attempt simultaneous withdrawals, banks would have to refuse. Banks with the lowest liquidity ratios will be particularly susceptible to runs in a depression. They may not be technically broke, but you still couldn't get your money, at least until the banks' loans were paid off.

You would think that banks would learn to behave differently with centuries of history to guide them, but for the most part, they don't. The pressure to show good earnings to stockholders and to offer competitive interest rates to depositors induces them to make risky loans. The Federal Reserve's monopoly powers have allowed U.S. banks to lend aggressively, so far without repercussion. For bankers to educate depositors about safety would be to disturb their main source of profits. The U.S.

government's Federal Deposit Insurance Corporation guarantees to refund depositors' losses up to $100,000, which *seems* to make safety a moot point. Actually, this guarantee just makes things far worse, for two reasons. First, it removes a major motivation for banks to be conservative with your money. Depositors feel safe, so who cares what's going on behind closed doors? Second, did you know that most of the FDIC's money comes from other banks? This funding scheme makes prudent banks pay to save the imprudent ones, imparting weak banks' frailty to the strong ones. When the FDIC rescues weak banks by charging healthier ones higher "premiums," overall bank deposits are depleted, causing the net loan-to-deposit ratio to rise. This result, in turn, means that in times of bank stress, *it will take a progressively smaller percentage of depositors to cause unmanageable bank runs.* If banks collapse in great enough quantity, the FDIC will be unable to rescue them all, and the more it charges surviving banks in "premiums," the more banks it will endanger. Thus, this form of insurance compromises the entire system. Ultimately, the federal government guarantees the FDIC's deposit insurance, which sounds like a sure thing. But if tax receipts fall, the government will be hard pressed to save a large number of banks with its own diminishing supply of capital. The FDIC calls its sticker "a symbol of confidence," and that's exactly what it is.

Some states in the U.S., in a fit of deadly "compassion," have made it illegal for a bank to seize the home of someone who has declared bankruptcy. In such situations, the bank and its depositors are on the hook indefinitely for a borrower's unthrift. Other states have made it illegal for a bank attempting to recover the value of a loan to seize any of a defaulting mortgage holder's assets other than the mortgaged property. In such situations, the bank assumes the price risk in the real estate market. These states' banks are vulnerable to severe losses in their mortgage portfolios and are at far greater risk of failure.

Many major national and international banks around the world have huge portfolios of "emerging market" debt, mortgage debt, consumer debt and weak corporate debt. I cannot understand how a bank trusted with the custody of your money could ever even *think* of buying bonds issued by Russia or Argentina or any other unstable or spendthrift government. As *At the Crest of the Tidal Wave* put it in 1995, "Today's emerging markets will soon be *sub*merging markets." That metamorphosis began two years later. The fact that banks and other investment companies can repeatedly ride such "investments" all the way down to *write-offs* is outrageous.

As most of us know, banks and mortgage companies lend money to consumers via credit cards, auto loans and mortgages. You may not know that they then package and re-sell those loans as investments to portfolio managers, insurance companies, pension funds and even trust departments at other banks. The issuing banks keep most of the interest paid by the consumers in exchange for guaranteeing a small interest payment (today less than 2.5 percent) on the package. These investments are called "securitized loans," and banks and mortgage companies have issued $6 trillion worth of them. This high sum implies that if you have a managed trust, invest in a debt fund or have insurance or a pension, you are almost surely dependent upon some of these deals.

When banks sell the packages, they get back as much money as they lent out in the first place, so guess what. They can go right out and roll the same percentage of their deposits out again and again as new consumer loans. Investors in the packages are, in a sense, new depositors.

If the issuing banks get in trouble some day and can't pay, the owners of the debt packages will then have dibs on the interest payments from the consumers. If those payments dry up, they have that great collateral to fall back on: vacant homes, used cars and truckloads of worn VCRs and other household junk. If a depression is on, what will that collateral be worth?

If such deals don't sound that solid to you, then why are so many institutions making these investments? Because they're buying them with OPM: Other People's Money…your money. And besides, it's "guaranteed" and backed by "collateral"!

This scheme, like so many others in existence today, works only as long as the debtors and the economy can keep up the pace of interest payments, some of which are as high as 17 percent. In a major economic downturn, this credit structure will implode. Banks that have followed this course will be stressed, and so will their customers.

Many banks today also have a shockingly large exposure to leveraged derivatives such as futures, options and even more exotic instruments. The underlying value of assets represented by such financial derivatives at quite a few big banks is greater than the total value of all their deposits. The estimated representative value of all derivatives in the world today is $90 trillion, over half of which is held by U.S. banks. Many banks use derivatives to hedge against investment exposure, but that strategy works only if the speculator on the other side of the trade can pay off if he's wrong.

Relying upon, or worse, speculating in, leveraged derivatives poses one of the greatest risks to banks that have succumbed to the lure. Leverage almost *always* causes massive losses eventually because of the psychological stress that owning them induces. You have already read of the billion-dollar debacles at Barings Bank, Long-Term [sic] Capital Management, Enron and other institutions that speculated in leveraged derivatives. It is traditional to discount the representative value of derivatives because traders will presumably get out of losing positions well before they wreak destruction. Well, maybe. It is at least as common a human reaction for speculators to double their bets when the market goes against a big position. At least, that's what bankers *might* do with *your* money.

Today's bank analysts assure us, as a headline from *The Atlanta Journal-Constitution* put it on December 29, 2001, that "Banks [Are] Well-Capitalized." Banks today are indeed generally considered well capitalized compared to their situation in the 1980s. Unfortunately, that condition is mostly thanks to the Great Asset Mania of the 1990s, which, as explained in Book One, is probably over. Much of the record amount of credit that banks have extended, such as that lent for productive enterprise or directly to strong governments, is relatively safe. Risky at this juncture are loans to weak governments, real estate developers, government-sponsored enterprises, stock market speculators, venture capitalists and consumers (via credit cards and consumer-debt "investment" packages). One expert advises, "The larger, more diversified banks at this point are the safer place to be." That assertion will surely be severely tested in the coming depression.

There are five major conditions in place at many banks that pose a danger: (1) low liquidity levels, (2) dangerous exposure to leveraged derivatives, (3) the optimistic safety ratings of banks' debt investments, (4) the inflated values of the property that borrowers have put up as collateral on loans and (5) the substantial size of the mortgages that their clients hold compared both to those property values and to the clients' potential inability to pay under adverse circumstances. All of these conditions compound the risk to the banking system of deflation and depression.

Financial companies are enjoying big advances in the current stock market rally. Depositors today trust their banks more than they trust government or business in general. For example, a recent poll asked web surfers which among a list of seven types of institutions they would most trust to operate a secure identity service. Banks got nearly 50 percent of the vote. General bank trustworthiness is yet another faith that will be shattered in a depression.

Well before a worldwide depression dominates our daily lives, you will need to deposit your capital into safe institutions. I suggest using two or more to spread the risk even further. They must be far better than the ones that today are too optimistically deemed "liquid" and "safe" by rating services and banking officials.

Safe Banking in the United States

If you must bank in the U.S., or if you prefer it, choose the best bank(s) available. I believe that even in a deflationary crash, many of the safest U.S. banks have a good shot at survival and even prosperity. The reason is that relatively safe banks, if they have the sense to inform the public of their safety advantage, are likely to become *even safer* during difficult times. Why? Because depositors in a developing financial crisis will move funds out of the weakest banks into the strongest ones, making the weak ones weaker and the strong ones stronger. One of the great ironies of banking is that the more liquid a bank, the less likely it is that depositors will conduct a run on it in the first place.

Weiss Ratings, Inc. provides one of the most reliable bank-rating services in America. (See Chapter 18 or the last section of this book for contact information.) CEO Martin Weiss has graciously consented to provide a practical guide for this book. Table 19-1 lists what his researchers consider the two strongest banks in each state in the union. Table 19-2 lists what they consider the 24 strongest *large* banks in the U.S. For our purposes, I see little point in listing the weakest banks, but if you want to know which ones they are, you can find them listed in the brand-new

THE TWO HIGHEST-RATED BANKS IN EACH STATE

Source: Weiss Ratings, Inc. (based on 03/31/03 data, updated for 2nd edition)

Name	City	State	Total Assets in millions	Weiss Safety Rating
Alaska				
FIRST NB ALASKA	ANCHORAGE	AK	1,967.3	A+
MOUNT MCKINLEY MSB	FAIRBANKS	AK	187.9	A
Alabama				
CITIZENS BANK OF WINFIELD	WINFIELD	AL	150.0	A
FIRST BK OF BOAZ	BOAZ	AL	106.6	A+
Arkansas				
FIRST ARKANSAS B&T	JACKSONVILLE	AR	259.5	A+
FIRST NB IZARD CTY	CALICO ROCK	AR	110.1	A+
Arizona				
COMMUNITY BK OF ARIZONA	WICKENBERG	AZ	412.5	A-
VALLEY COMMERCE BK	PHOENIX	AZ	142.2	A-
California				
FARMERS & MERCHANTS BK	LONG BEACH	CA	2,573.3	A+
SAVINGS BK OF MENDOCINO CTY	UKIAH	CA	617.1	A+
Colorado				
FARMERS ST BK	FORT MORGAN	CO	143.1	A+
MOUNTAIN STATES BK	DENVER	CO	273.9	A
Connecticut				
CITIZENS NB	PUTNAM	CT	221.2	A+
LIBERTY BK	MIDDLETOWN	CT	2,067.9	A+
District of Columbia				
NATIONAL CAPITAL BK OF WA	WASHINGTON	DC	185.4	A+
ADAMS NB	WASHINGTON	DC	208.9	A-
Delaware				
FIRST NB OF WYOMING	WYOMING	DE	189.1	A+
BALTIMORE TRUST CO	SHELBYVILLE	DE	334.6	A
Florida				
FIRST NB OF MT DORA	MT DORA	FL	118.6	A
FIRST GUARANTY B&TC	JACKSONVILLE	FL	276.3	A
Georgia				
FARMERS & MERCHANTS BK	COMER	GA	112.3	A+
BANK OF LA FAYETTE	LA FAYETTE	GA	158.1	A+
Hawaii				
CENTRAL PACIFIC BK	HONOLULU	HI	2,025.7	A-
BANK OF HAWAII	HONOLULU	HI	9,473.1	A-
Iowa				
IOWA SVG BK	DIKE	IA	27.2	A+
STATE BK OF WAVERLY	WAVERLY	IA	124.3	A+
Idaho				
BANK OF COMMERCE	IDAHO FALLS	ID	500.2	A+
FARMERS NB OF BUHL	BUHL	ID	276.1	A
Illinois				
GERMANTOWN T&SB	BREESE	IL	250.6	A+
STATE BK OF LINCOLN	LINCOLN	IL	164.0	A+
Indiana				
FIRST ST BK	BOURBON	IN	83.6	A+
STATE BK OF LIZTON	LIZTON	IN	187.5	A

Table 19-1

Kansas				
FIDELITY ST B&TC	DODGE CITY	KS	119.6	A+
FARMERS & DROVERS BK	COUNCIL GROVE	KS	101.0	A+
Kentucky				
KENTUCKY-FARMERS BK	ASHLAND	KY	132.6	A+
EAGLE BK	WILLIAMSTOWN	KY	140.8	A+
Louisana				
FIRST NB-DE RIDDER	DE RIDDER	LA	162.1	A+
EVANGELINE B&TC	VILLE PLATTE	LA	395.6	A+
Massachusetts				
FOXBOROUGH SVGS BK	FOXBORO	MA	121.5	A+
NEWTON SO CO-OP BK	NEWTON	MA	226.7	A+
Maryland				
MIDDLETOWN VALLEY BK	MIDDLETOWN	MD	134.6	A+
CALVIN B TAYLOR BKG CO	BERLIN	MD	360.2	A+
Maine				
FRANKLIN SVGS BK	FARMINGTON	ME	290.1	A
MECHANICS' SVGS BK	AUBURN	ME	193.1	A-
Michigan				
CHELSEA ST BK	CHELSEA	MI	176.8	A+
FARWELL ST SVG BK	FARWELL	MI	92.7	A+
Minnesota				
FIRST NB OF BEMIDJI	BEMIDJI	MN	337.8	A+
FIRST ST BK OF WYOMING	WYOMING	MN	103.5	A
Missouri				
FIRST NB	CAMDENTON	MO	234.7	A+
FIRST NB	CAMDENTON	MO	144.7	A+
Mississippi				
BANK OF NEW ALBANY	NEW ALBANY	MS	294.1	A+
FARMERS & MERCHANTS BK	BALDWYN	MS	135.5	A
Montana				
YELLOWSTONE BK	LAUREL	MT	258.8	A+
CITIZENS ST BK OF CHOTEAU	CHOTEAU	MT	48.7	A
North Carolina				
BANK OF GRANITE	GRANITE FALLS	NC	718.2	A
HIGH POINT B&TC	HIGH POINT	NC	613.4	A
North Dakota				
SARGENT COUNTY BK	FORMAN	ND	64.4	A
SCANDIA AMERICAN B&TC	STANLEY	ND	59.8	A
Nebraska				
MCCOOK NB	MCCOOK	NE	171.1	A
NEBRASKA ST B&TC	BROKEN BOW	NE	79.7	A
New Hampshire				
PISCATAQUA SVGS BK	PORTSMOUTH	NH	179.7	A
CLAREMONT SVGS BK	CLAREMONT	NH	260.3	A
New Jersey				
SUMITOMO TR & BKNG CO USA	HOBOKEN	NJ	325.9	A+
CUSTODIAL TRUST CO	PRINCETON	NJ	503.6	A+
New Mexico				
WESTERN BK	ARTESIA	NM	96.7	A+
FIRST NB-RUIDOSO	RUIDOSO	NM	50.2	A+
Nevada				
HOUSEHOLD BK NEVADA NA	LAS VEGAS	NV	4,277.2	A-
FIRST NB OF ELY	ELY	NV	46.6	A-

Table 19-1 (cont'd)

New York				
BANK OF MILLBROOK	MILLBROOK	NY	119.4	A+
MITSUBISHI TR & BKNG CORP	NEW YORK	NY	588.2	A+
Ohio				
FARMERS SVG BK	SPENCER	OH	198.6	A+
SAVINGS BK	CIRCLEVILLE	OH	195.0	A+
Oklahoma				
OKLAHOMA B&TC	CLINTON	OK	102.8	A+
FIRST NB&TC CHICKASHA OK	CHICKASHA	OK	225.0	A
Oregon				
PIONEER TR BK NA	SALEM	OR	212.0	A+
CLACKAMAS COUNTY BK	SANDY	OR	146.6	A
Pennsylvania				
NEFFS NB	NEFFS	PA	186.7	A+
SEWICKLEY SVGS BK	SEWICKLEY	PA	231.8	A+
Rhode Island				
CENTREVILLE SVGS BK	W WARWICK	RI	707.7	A+
TALBOTS CLASSIC NB	LINCOLN	RI	9.0	B-
South Carolina				
BANK OF YORK	YORK	SC	144.6	A+
ARTHUR ST BK	UNION	SC	215.3	A
South Dakota				
FIRST FIDELITY BK	BURKE	SD	212.9	A+
PIONEER B&TC	BELLE FOURCHE	SD	280.9	A
Tennessee				
CITIZENS BK	CARTHAGE	TN	428.4	A+
FIRST NB OF MCMINNVILLE	MCMINNVILLE	TN	307.3	A+
Texas				
FIRST ST BK	BURNET	TX	128.5	A+
FIRST NB OF ALBANY	ALBANY	TX	197.0	A+
Utah				
BRIGHTON BK	SALT LAKE CITY	UT	191.3	A
MORGAN STANLEY BK	W VALLEY CITY	UT	2,918.0	A+
Virginia				
BURKE & HERBERT B&TC	ALEXANDRIA	VA	1,114.5	A+
AMERICAN NB&TC	DANVILLE	VA	613.6	A+
Vermont				
PEOPLES TR CO OF ST ALBANS	ST ALBANS	VT	193.8	A-
UNION BK	MORRISVILLE	VT	231.7	A-
Washington				
FIRST INDEPENDENT BK	VANCOUVER	WA	658.0	A
HORIZON BK	BELLINGHAM	WA	820.9	A+
Wisconsin				
SHELL LAKE ST BK	SHELL LAKE	WI	108.6	A+
SECURITY NB OF DURAND	DURAND	WI	198.4	A+
West Virginia				
PEOPLES BK OF MULLENS	MULLENS	WV	118.6	A+
BANK OF CHARLES TOWN	CHARLES TOWN	WV	192.8	A
Wyoming				
FIRST ST BK OF NEWCASTLE	NEWCASTLE	WY	94.4	A+
CONVERSE COUNTY BK	DOUGLAS	WY	156.9	A

Table 19-1 (cont'd)

STRONGEST LARGE BANKS IN AMERICA			
Source: Weiss Ratings, Inc. (based on 3/31/03 data, updated for 2nd edition)			
Bank Name	**State**	**Weiss Safety Rating**	**Total Assets (in millions of $)**
Apple Bk for Svgs	NY	A-	5604
Bancorpsouth Bk	MS	B+	10,337
Bank of America Georgia NA	GA	B+	7,993
Bank of Hawaii	HI	A-	9,473
Citibank-Delaware	DE	B+	7,335
Citizens Business Bk	CA	B+	3,395
Columbus B&TC	GA	A-	4,091
Comerica Bk-Texas	TX	B+	4,563
Commerce Bk NA	MO	B+	11,335
Emigrant Svg Bk	NY	A	9,832
Fifth Third Bk	MI	B+	51,761
Fifth Third Bk	OH	B+	25,130
Fifth Third Bk IN	IN	A	7,974
Fulton Bk	PA	B+	3,897
Household Bk SB NA	NV	A-	4,277
Hudson City Svgs Bk	NJ	A	14,913
International Bk of Commerce	TX	B+	5,130
Mellon Bk NA	PA	B+	26,450
Mercantile Safe Deposit & TC	MD	A	4,514
New York Community Bk	NY	B+	12,002
Silicon Valley Bk	CA	A-	3,932
Texas St Bk	TX	B+	4,024
Trustmark NB	MS	B+	7,146
Weebanco Bk	WV	B+	3,349
Whitney NB of New Orleans	LA	B+	7,178

Table 19-2

Ultimate Safe Money Guide, by Martin Weiss (John Wiley & Sons, 2002). Weiss' book is a good complement to this one for many reasons. Aside from banks and insurance companies (see Chapter 24), his firm also rates mutual funds, brokerage firms, HMOs and corporations with common stock.

There are other independent and reliable bank rating sources. Among them, Veribanc, Inc. has been in the ratings business the longest. The service covers banks, S&Ls and credit unions. The company's classifications rank financial institutions not just on their present standing but also on their future outlook, which is what you should care about. Using a clear, simple rating system, it assesses capital strength, asset quality, management ability, earnings sufficiency, liquidity and sensitivity to market risk.

IDC Financial Publishing, Inc. also publishes highly specific and easy-to-interpret quarterly financial ratings that track the financial safety of U.S.-based banks, savings and loan institutions and credit unions. You will find their contact information below:

Veribanc, Inc.
Website: www.veribanc.com
Email: service@veribanc.com
Address: P.O. Box 1610, Woonsocket, RI 02895
Phone: 800-837-4226/800-442-2657
Fax: 781-246-5291

IDC Financial Publishing, Inc.
Website: www.idcfp.com
Email: info@idcfp.com
Address: P.O. Box 140, Hartland, WI 53029
Phone: 800-525-5457 and 262-367-7231
Fax: 262-367-6497

If, despite all your precautions, you come to suspect that any of your chosen banks face the risk of closure, move your money to a safer bank immediately. If you cannot identify a safer bank, then do not hesitate to withdraw all of your money in cash. If you are not first in line, you may forfeit the opportunity.

Safe Banking Worldwide

A free market in banking would provide every imaginable service, from 100% safekeeping for a fee to 100% lending with a large return. To preserve their reputations, bankers would have an incentive to be extremely careful with your money. Monopoly money and regulated banking have produced quite another result. Nevertheless, there still exist a few banks in the world that mainly provide a wealth preservation service as opposed to interest income and daily transactional conveniences. If you want the utmost safety for capital storage, if a bit less convenience, you must use these banks. The safest banking institutions in the world reside in countries that (1) do not have, and are unlikely to impose, exchange controls or wealth transfer restrictions and (2) have a low overall debt-to-deposits ratio. Not surprisingly, the top candidates are the same as those with the safest debt: Switzerland and Singapore.

Nevertheless, do not fall into the trap of choosing any Swiss bank just because it's Swiss. Today's largest Swiss banks, with their fat portfolios of derivatives, are at immense risk of failure if a depression occurs. Furthermore, they have branches worldwide and are thus vulnerable to the whims of numerous governments. The best course of action is to locate smaller, safer local Swiss banks. Austria's low debt per capita makes it a good backup alternative. If you want to find a safe bank, these jurisdictions are the place to begin.

Using stringent bank-rating requirements, SafeWealth Group has identified banks in these countries that earn its highest rating for survivability in a global depression. This "Class 1" rating requires an aggressively discounted liquidity ratio of at least 75 percent, an otherwise nearly unheard-of 35 percent net liquid equity ratio (i.e., the percentage of a bank's capital that is free and accessible at all times), a low derivatives/capital ratio, no derivatives held on a speculative basis, a low amount of deposits held at other banks and that the bank operate in a single nation so that the rules it must follow are clearly defined.

A 75 percent aggressively discounted liquidity ratio means that deposits are held in such liquid investments that even if the bank were suddenly faced with demands from depositors to withdraw 75 percent of the total money in the bank, given a few days or weeks, it could do so. There are even a very few banks in the world with liquidity ratios at or above 100 percent. In other words, they could pay off *all* their depositors, *in full*, on very short notice. Many banks couldn't pay off 10 percent of their depositors quickly, and the world's weakest banks would be hard-pressed to service *any* above-normal level of simultaneous withdrawals. And that is in *today's* benign financial environment, never mind a depression environment.

If you are serious about safety and can meet a recommended bank's account minimum, you should set up a relationship with a Class 1 bank. SafeWealth Group can help you cut through red tape to establish relationships with such banks and other institutions. You need to go through a representative because these private Swiss banks do not readily accept accounts from any individual, corporation or trust representative that walks through the door, a policy that reflects their general conservatism. They will accept a new account only if its ownership and purpose are completely above board and will not endanger the bank's reputation. If you meet these standards, SafeWealth Group can secure the proper introductions for you in most cases and guide you through the process. (See Chapter 18 or the final section of this book for contact information and typical minimums.) If you are a Swiss or Singaporean resident and have ready access to such institutions, by all means stay put as long as local politics remain stable.

Act While You Can

My subscribers have been reading about the strategies outlined here in Book Two since 1998. When it comes to safety, it is always best to act early. Due largely to aggressive governmental policing of illegal activities such as the drug trade, money laundering, tax evasion and terrorist financing, average honest people do not enjoy the free, ready access to financial institutions that they did a few years ago. Some banks are now obliged to meet with prospective clients in person to satisfy suitability rules. There can be little doubt that if a crisis climate comes to pass, you could face many more obstacles if not outright denial of service. If you are truly intent on preserving your wealth, you should resist the temptation to procrastinate under the presumption that you can rely on the status quo. Opportunities close down all the time. For example, the two safest banks in London no longer accept non-British clients. In the U.S., the bank deemed the safest in the nation two years ago no longer takes out-of-state accounts. A few of my prudent subscribers got in after I recommended it, but now the procrastinators have to look elsewhere. This is a lesson. Don't delay, or the institutions now available to protect your savings may close their doors to you. Another word of warning: Bank ratings can change. The smart approach is to keep in touch with the services that rate banks seriously to make sure your bank(s) continue to qualify for a high safety rating.

Once you move the bulk of your investment funds into the safest cash equivalents, and after you have chosen a safe bank or two for savings and transactions, then and only then should you consider speculating in the stock market with a small portion of your capital. That is the subject of the next chapter.

Chapter 20:

Should You Speculate in Stocks?

Perhaps the number one precaution to take at the start of a deflationary crash is to make sure that your investment capital is *not* invested "long" in stocks, stock mutual funds, stock index futures, stock options or any other equity-based investment or speculation. That advice alone should be worth the time you spent to read this book.

In 2000 and 2001, countless Internet stocks fell from $50 or $100 a share to near zero in a matter of months. In 2001, Enron went from $85 to pennies a share in less than a year. These are the early casualties of debt, leverage and incautious speculation. Countless investors, including the managers of insurance companies, pension funds and mutual funds, express great confidence that their "diverse holdings" will keep major portfolio risk at bay. Aside from piles of questionable debt, what are those diverse holdings? Stocks, stocks and more stocks. Despite current optimism that the bull market is back, there will be many more casualties to come when stock prices turn back down again.

Not only will many stocks fall 90 to 100 percent, but so will a substantial number of stock mutual funds, which cannot exit large equity positions without depressing prices and which have the added burden to you of one percent (or more) annual management fees. The good news is that we will finally find out who the few truly good fund managers are and which ones were heroes by virtue of being around for a bull market.

Don't presume that the Fed will rescue the stock market, either. In theory, the Fed could declare a support price for certain stocks, but which ones? And how much money would it commit to buying them? If the Fed were actually to buy equities or stock-index futures, the temporary result might be a brief rally, but the ultimate result would be a collapse in the value of the Fed's own assets when the market turned back down, making the Fed look foolish and compromising its primary goals, as cited in Chapter 13. It wouldn't want to keep repeating *that* experience. The bankers' pools of 1929 gave up on this strategy, and so will the Fed if it tries it.

Short Selling Stocks and Trading in Futures and Options

Short selling is a great idea at the onset of a deflationary depression, at least from a *timing* standpoint. Shares of vulnerable banks and other financial companies in particular are a great downside bet. The current stock-market rally, so far a pitifully weak response to record Fed-induced liquidity in 2001, is providing a great general short-selling opportunity, per all the evidence in Chapters 6 and 7. You should avoid shorting special situations such as defense and natural resource stocks, which can move counter-trend, or at least fall less precipitously, when international tensions rise. Buying "leaps," which are long-term puts, on stocks and stock indexes would be a fine speculation. If you do not already know by experience what the terms "short selling" and "leaps" mean, I recommend that you avoid engaging in these activities.

Unfortunately, there could well be *structural* risks in dealing with stocks and associated derivatives during a major retrenchment. Trading stocks, options and futures could be extremely problematic during a stock market panic. Trading systems tend to break down when volume surges and the system's operators become emotional. When the exchange floor became a hurricane of paper in 1929, it would sometimes take days to sort out who had bought and sold what and then determine whether investors and traders could afford to pay for their positions. You can experience the turmoil vicariously in any good history of the 1929 crash. To give you a flavor of what goes on, read this description, from one of my subscribers, of the tumult during a comparatively mild panic forty years ago:

> I worked for Merrill Lynch in New York in 1962 during the collapse. I well recall the failure of the teletype in our office and inexperienced clerks calling in the orders to the main office. I recall many of the screw-ups: buys called in as sells and vice versa. Some stocks had nicknames like Bessie (Bethlehem Steel), Peggy (Public Service Electric and Gas), and I recall the clerks calling in the orders by the stocks' nicknames and the person on the other end not knowing what the hell they were talking about. All the while, the market was collapsing.

Do you think investors and brokers will behave differently now that so much stock trading is done on-line? I don't. Do you think the experience will be "smoother" because modern computers are involved? I don't. In fact, today's system — much improved, to be sure — is nevertheless a recipe for an even bigger mess during a panic. Investors will be so nervous that they will screw up their orders. Huge volume will clog website servers, disrupting orders entered on-line. Orders may go in, but confirmations may not come out. A trader *might not know* if his sale or purchase went through. Is he in or out? Quote systems will falter at just the wrong time. Phone lines from you to the broker and from the broker to the floor will be jammed, and some will go down. Computer technicians will be working overtime while being distracted worrying about their own investments. Brokers will be operating on little sleep and at peak agitation, since most brokers are themselves bullish speculators. They will enter orders incorrectly. Firms will begin to enact and enforce tighter restrictions on trading and margin. Price gaps will trigger stops at prices beyond the ability of some account holders to pay. You, the wise short seller, could survive all these problems only to discover that your broker has gone bankrupt or has been shut down by the SEC or that its associated bank has had a computer breakdown or that its assets are depleted or frozen.

Unless you are prepared for such an environment, don't get suckered into this maelstrom thinking that the bear market will be business as usual, just in the other direction. If you want to try making a killing being short in the collapse, make sure that you are not overexposed. Make sure that if the system locks up for days or weeks, you will not be in a panic yourself. Make sure that in a worst-case scenario, the funds you place at risk are funds you could lose.

Inverse Index ("Short") Mutual Funds

A somewhat more conservative speculation would be to invest in inverse index funds, also called short funds or bear funds, which are bets on falling stock indexes. These funds go up in value as stock index futures fall in value, and vice versa. I recommended inverse index funds in *The Dick Davis Digest* for both 2000 and 2001, and they beat everything else both years. The stock market should have several more down years ahead, and bigger ones at that.

In the U.S., you will find inverse S&P index funds at Rydex and ProFunds. Rydex has Ursa, which is the largest inverse index fund available, and ProFunds has the Bear ProFund. Rydex also has Arktos, which moves inversely to the NASDAQ 100 Index.

For seasoned speculators who can time the market well, Rydex offers Tempest, which is *doubly* short the S&P index, and Venture Fund, which is doubly short the NASDAQ 100. Also, they may be traded twice a day, not just at the close. ProFunds has the UltraBear fund and the UltraShort OTC fund, which are doubly short the S&P and NASDAQ 100, respectively. I am serious about using such funds *only if you are already a seasoned speculator*. You must be extra careful any time you use leverage, because leverage heightens your emotions, making them an even worse enemy to success.

The companies that offer short funds also offer money-market funds and "long" index funds too, so with a brief phone call, you can easily move your money to take advantage of swings in either direction or "park" it for safety. Speaking of parking, Rydex's money-market fund owns only instruments issued, guaranteed or backed by the U.S. government or its agencies or instrumentalities, making it safer than the average money market fund.

For information on these two mutual fund companies, contact the following:

Ursa Fund, Arktos Fund, Tempest Fund, Venture Fund
Website: www.rydexfunds.com
Address: Rydex Series Funds, 9601 Blackwell Rd,
         Suite 500, Rockville, MD 20850
Phone: 800-820-0888 and 301-296-5406
Minimum: $25,000

Bear ProFund, UltraBear, UltraShort 100
Website: www.profunds.com
Address: ProFunds, 7501 Wisconsin Ave, Suite 1000,
         Bethesda, MD 20814
Phone: 888-776-1970 or 240-497-6400
Minimum: $15,000

Before you invest in bear index funds, you need to understand something important about how they work, which can be a good or bad thing, depending upon the market environment.

Holders of shares make money depending upon the *short-term percentage change* that the market undergoes each day or half day. In a persistently trending market, this situation is better than a short sale. Theoretically, the market can go down five percent per week indefinitely. If the market does fall a long way in a straight line, these funds could compound your return well beyond that of a normal short sale, which at most can gain 100 percent. Also, while the shares of these funds lose value in an up market, they do not lose all of their value, as a short sale can when a stock doubles.

On the other hand, this attribute in some circumstances can present a big problem. To understand it, follow this example: You invest $100,000 in a doubly leveraged short S&P 500 fund with the index at 1000, which is a $200,000 short S&P 500 exposure. The next day, the index rises 10%, so you have lost $20,000. The short fund automatically resets your exposure to twice your equity at the end of the day, so your new exposure is short $160,000. The next day, the index returns to 1000, but your equity rises only to $94,545 because the percentage decline from the higher level is only 9.09 percent, and you didn't have enough exposure on the way back to make up your initial loss. The index is unchanged, but you lost money. The same negative result occurs when the index initially goes your way and then returns to its starting point. Critics call this attribute "beta slippage." This problem is compounded when markets are in a trading range and further when leveraged funds reset twice a day. Since markets often fluctuate within sideways trends, this aspect of inverse index funds can be a negative attribute for long-term investors. To make these funds work in all environments, you have to be a successful market timer. Achieving that goal when you are restricted to trading in and out only once or twice a day *at a particular time* is difficult. If you can do it, then use these vehicles. If not, there is an alternative to the rescue.

Customized Dynamic Index Allocation

The brainchild of Stanford M.B.A. Robert R. Champion, Bermuda-based Invesdex, Ltd has developed an Internet-based instrument called MarketPlus, which is a liquid, fully asset-backed over-the-counter investment contract that has the look and feel of an online trading account. It offers a selection of major world equity and debt indexes, currencies, commodities, and a money-market index. You create your own return parameters by customizing your contract to the performance of one or more of these assets, long or short. You also get to choose the leverage you want, from zero (conservative) up to 3-to-1. To avoid beta slippage, your exposure is normally not reset unless and until you choose to do so. You can adjust allocations as often as every half-hour, far more often than index funds allow. This frequency is somewhat restricted compared to a futures account, but with MarketPlus, you cannot lose more than your investment because the system resets your exposure to your initial ratio if your loss exceeds certain limits. What's more, all gains — even when indexed to the money-market rate — are capital gains and are not taxed until funds are withdrawn from the instrument. To invest in MarketPlus, you must be a professional financial adviser, money manager or experienced "Qualified Investor," which means that you must have a net worth in excess of US$1 million and be able to invest at least US$100,000 in the contract. Currently available only to non-U.S. investors, MarketPlus is due to become available to U.S. investors in 2003. For information, contact the following:

Invesdex, Ltd
Website: www.invesdex.com
Email: info@invesdex.com
Address: P.O. Box HM 1788, Hamilton HM HX,
        Bermuda

Phone: 441-296-4400
Fax: 441-295-2377
President & CEO: Valere B. Costello
Minimum: $100,000

Managed Bear Funds

You may also wish to consider a portfolio of short or hedged stocks, managed by an expert. Actively managed bearish stock funds are designed to benefit from a declining stock market. There are very few around today because the stock mania of the 1990s drove most of them out of business. The public hasn't been interested; in fact, it has moved money out of bear funds since the 2000 top! A few courageous money managers have maintained this alternative.

One example in the U.S. is the Prudent Bear Fund, which maintains short positions in individual stocks and indexes and also buys put options. The fund is about 70 percent short. This short percentage typically does not vary greatly, says president David Tice. The fund maintains some long positions, which account for up to 15 percent of its assets. Longs include special situations such as shares of certain small-cap companies and natural resource stocks such as gold and silver mining companies. The fund is no-load. It is about $200 million in size. Tice is fully apprised of the long-term risk in the stock market and the financial world.

Another example is the Comstock Capital Value Fund, which is positioned to profit from a declining market with a combination of index puts and shorts of both individual stocks and stock futures. With the leverage of puts taken into account, the fund is the equivalent of over 100 percent short. The fund also has positions in long-term U.S. Treasury bonds and the Euro currency. The firm's other fund is the Comstock Strategy Fund, which is conservatively positioned to benefit from a bear market, using puts to approximate a 70% net short position. The funds' managers, Charles Minter and Martin Weiner, have been writing free web commentary which (amazingly) calls for a long-term bear market in a deflationary environment. You can read it free on their website.

Another bear fund is the Gabelli Mathers Fund. Manager Henry van der Eb takes a conservative approach, making it attractive if you are unconvinced of the bear's imminence or ultimate severity. The fund also offers tax-sheltered gains due to tax-loss carry-forwards, "earned" during the bull market.

For information on these funds, contact the following:

Prudent Bear Fund
Website: www.prudentbear.com
Email: info@prudentbear.com
Address: 8140 Walnut Hill Lane, Suite 300, Dallas, TX
           75231
Phone: 800-711-1848 and 214-696-5474
Minimum: $2000
Manager: David Tice

Comstock Capital Value Fund and Strategy Fund
Website: www.comstockfunds.com
Email: info@comstockfunds.com
Address: 24 S Main Street, Yardley PA 19067
Phone: 215-493-7076
Fax: 215-493-8083
Minimum: $1000
Managers: Charles Minter and Martin Weiner

Gabelli Mathers Fund
Website: www.gabelli.com/mathers.html
Email: info@gabelli.com

Address: One Corporate Center, Rye NY 10580
Phone: 800-422-3554
Minimum: $1000
Manager: Henry van der Eb

A Personal Portfolio Consultant

Well-heeled investors around the world have an interesting option. Asset Allocation Consultants, Ltd. can help you set up any type of portfolio management you want. Its proprietary analytical system maintains the track records of thousands of managers and among them profiles a number of ideal allocations. The firm assesses your situation and then recommends one or a small combination of managers that it deems best suited to manage your funds according to that assessment. The cost to you is often nothing, since the firm asks the managers it selects to reimburse you for the consulting fees that you incur out of the management fees normally charged to your account. Some refuse, but many agree.

For the safety-conscious, Asset Allocation Consultants has set up a popular *market-neutral* strategy. It splits your portfolio between two equity managers, one with a proven record of choosing longs, the other with a proven record of choosing shorts. The idea is that the manager investing in the direction of the market does extremely well, while the other manager's selection expertise mitigates his counter-trend position. Ideally, the market is thereby "neutralized," so you get good stock selection on both sides without naked exposure to market-trend risk.

If you have a market bias, you can increase the ratio of funds split between the short and long manager or tilt the group by adding an extra manager on the long or short side. As an aggressive bear-market strategy, the firm can also, for example, identify three appropriate managers on the bear side and split your money

among them. This way, you get more expertise working for you
while simultaneously reducing the risk of having one manager go
sour. Remember, this is not an index fund where you must lose
money if the market goes up or make only so much if it goes down.
The best "bear" managers do far better than the market when it's
trending down, and some of them have made money even in rising trends because they're good at picking the most vulnerable
stocks to short. The company has also identified single "market
neutral" managers who are adept at both the long and short side
of stock selection.

  Senior partner Ted Workman reports that clients utiliz-
ing the Market Neutral Strategy achieved a return of 54.2 percent
for the two years of 2000 and 2001 against an S&P performance
of *minus* 21.9 percent. His website also posts individual managers' largest drawdowns (i.e., the percentage slips in portfolio value
from each higher peak to the next trough), so you can assess
those as well. Naturally, as with all investments, there are no
guarantees, so make sure the chosen plan makes sense for you.
The only drawback is that the minimum investment for this program is pretty high, at $500,000. For information, contact the
following:

   Asset Allocation Consultants, Ltd.
   Website: www.assetallocating.com
   Email: enquiries@assetallocating.com
   Address: P.O. Box 613 Station "Q", Toronto, Ontario
     M4T 2N4, Canada
   Phone: 800-638-5760 and 416-762-2330
   Fax: 416-762-3793

Portfolio Managers Who Are Not Afraid To Be Bearish

You can also find portfolio managers who are not afraid to be bearish. There are surely many in the world. I personally know of only a few, and they may or may not be the best. In the U.S., an example is Lang Asset Management (www.langasset.com), which selects medium-to-large-cap stocks that look overvalued and shorts them. The manager doesn't use options or derivatives and attends each account individually. In Asia, Marc Faber Ltd. (www.gloomboomdoom.com), and in Europe, Zulauf Asset Management AG (Grafenauweg 4, CH-6301 Zug, Switzerland; phone: (US: 011) 41-41-724-5701, email: zam@zuam.ch), provide bearishly oriented management. Minimum funding requirements range between $100,000 and $3 million.

To find more leads, check out the Hedge Fund Association at http://www.thehfa.org and Planet Hedge Fund at http://planethedgefund.com/catlinks/indi.html. Hedge funds are only as good as their managers. Some fund managers use huge leverage and can "blow up," losing everything on a bad bet. The more spectacular of those make the newspapers; there are others that just go quietly. If you want to go this route, choose wisely and make sure that you satisfy yourself that the money manager you choose deals with safe banks. I have not investigated that aspect of any of these funds. By the way, Asset Allocation Consultants does monitor many of these managers and can help you decide which ones might be best for you.

Temporary Opportunity?

The opportunity to make money on the downside in a deflationary crash can hardly be overstated, because *you will be making more dollars as the value of dollars is soaring*. It's a double benefit. Will it always be there?

I recall only one time when authorities banned buying in a bull market. The Comex futures exchange banned orders "to open" in silver futures in January 1980 to save their own skins, since many exchange members were short. Most investors were long, so their only allowed course was to sell. By changing the rules, the exchange profited and investors got killed. (For more on that story, read *Silver Bonanza*, by James Blanchard and Franklin Sanders, published by Jefferson Financial, 2400 Jefferson Highway, Suite 600, Jefferson, LA 70121, phone 504-837-3033.)

In a bear market, bullish investors always come to believe that short sellers are "driving the market down," when in fact, the decline is almost entirely due to selling from within their own over-invested ranks. Sometimes authorities outlaw short selling. In doing so, they remove the one class of investors that *must* buy. Every short sale (except when stocks go to zero) must be *covered*, i.e., the stock or derivative contract must be purchased to close the trade. A ban on short selling creates a market with no latent buying power at all, making it even less liquid than it was. Then it can dribble down day after day, unhindered by the buying of nervous shorts. Like all other bans on free exchange, a ban on short selling hurts those whom it is designed to help.

The Japanese government is currently discussing a ban on short selling. If authorities in your country decide to disallow short selling, the bad news is that this option will be closed to you. The good news is that they usually take such actions near major bottoms, so it will probably be about the proper time to cover shorts and start composing your "buy" list anyway.

Chapter 21:

Should You Invest in Commodities?

Figures 21-1 through 21-9 show what happened to commodities in dollar terms from 1929 through 1938. Pay particular attention to what happened in 1929-1932, the three years of intense deflation in which the stock market crashed. As you can see, commodities crashed, too.

You can get rich being short commodity futures in a deflationary crash. This is a player's game, though, and I am not about to urge a typical investor to follow that course. If you are a seasoned commodity trader, avoid the long side and use rallies to sell short. Make sure that your broker keeps your liquid funds in T-bills or an equally safe medium.

There can be exceptions to the broad trend. A commodity can rise against the trend on a war, a war scare, a shortage or a disruption of transport. Oil is an example of a commodity with that type of risk. This commodity *should* have nowhere to go but down during a depression. From 1929 to 1933, for example, after oil had already fallen substantially over preceding years, it plummeted another 80 percent in price. The odds of a repeat performance, however, are lessened by the fact that 4/5 of the world's known oil reserves are in Asia. Aside from France, political entities in general have squandered their nations' forty-year opportunity to have responsible companies replace the cumbersome, costly and dangerous old models of energy production with

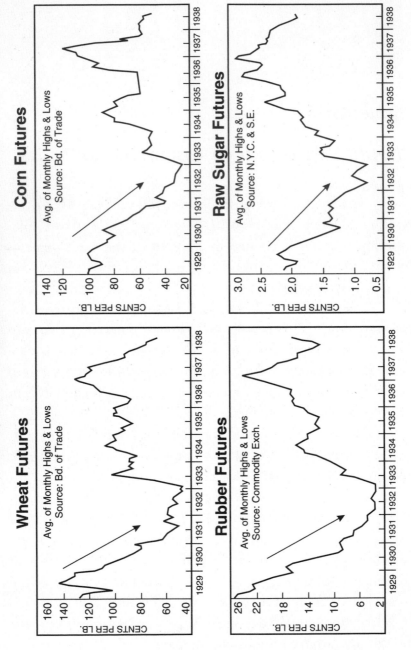

Prices of Commodities, 1929 — 1938

Wheat Futures
Avg. of Monthly Highs & Lows
Source: Bd. of Trade
CENTS PER LB.

Corn Futures
Avg. of Monthly Highs & Lows
Source: Bd. of Trade
CENTS PER LB.

Rubber Futures
Avg. of Monthly Highs & Lows
Source: Commodity Exch.
CENTS PER LB.

Raw Sugar Futures
Avg. of Monthly Highs & Lows
Source: N.Y.C. & S.E.
CENTS PER LB.

Figures 21-1 through 21-4

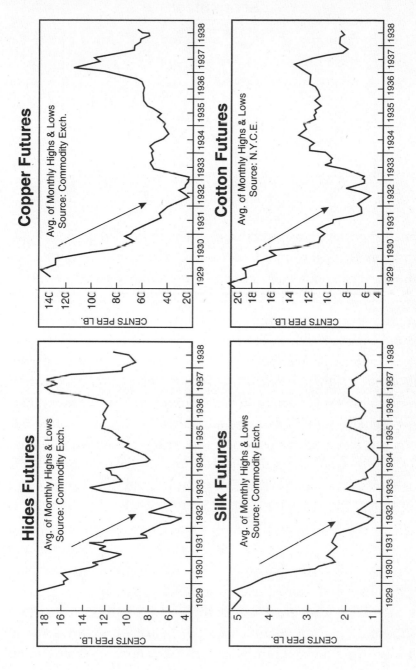

Figures 21-5 through 21-8

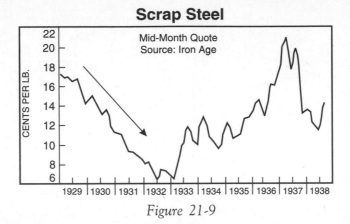

Figure 21-9

nuclear power plants, which (absent politics) can produce mul-
tiples more energy at far less cost, risk and pollution. Because of
these policies, many nations are deeply vulnerable to a cessation
of oil shipments from unstable nations. So oil may be a good
short, but it's a risky one. Be careful with any commodities that
could experience shortages.

Some people today who are concerned about economic
upset are touting commodities, mostly because they look for a
replay of the inflationary 1970s. Commodities have been jumping higher since October, and advocates are vehement. I do not
buy this argument, at least not as of today. As shown in Figure
21-10, the Commodity Research Bureau (CRB) commodity index has tracked the S&P, with a slight lag, since mid-1998. Gold
and silver have also joined in the latest stock rally. As I see it,
this correlation means that most assets lately are moving up and
down more or less together, probably as liquidity expands and
contracts. If so, then any deflation will crush hard-asset prices
right along with share prices, just as it always has.

Even if I came to expect the prices of hard assets to rise, I
still would not put commodities on the top of my list. I would
buy gold and silver, for three reasons: First, unless you own an oil
company or the like, you can't own physical commodities; you

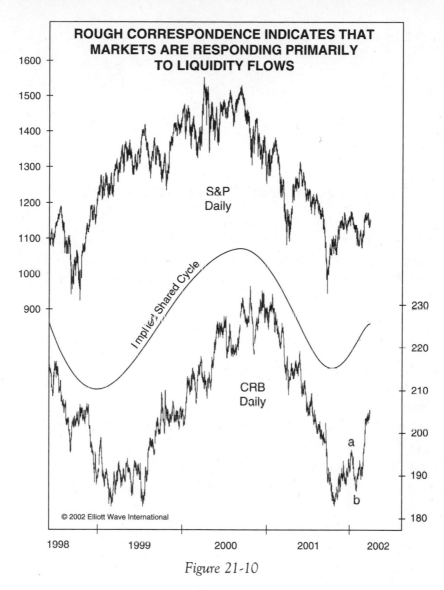

Figure 21-10

have to own them through a promise to deliver, called a futures contract. With respect to gold and silver, you can own the physical asset. Second, gold and silver are cheap, and third, they have monetary value. If there truly is a panic into real goods, I cannot imagine a scenario in which those two would be excluded.

Chapter 22:

Should You Invest in Precious Metals?

Precious metals are likely one day to become the most important asset class to own. From the mid-1970s to the mid-1980s, investors were dedicated to owning gold and silver for safety. Today, people are utterly disinterested in gold or silver, which sets the stage for an opportunity.

First, some brief background. Currencies today are fictions, but few realize it. Sometime during this century, people will question the validity of the fiat money system. The 1970s may prove to have been just a warm-up in a world battle for real money. Governments may exercise their powers to keep the fiat paper money system afloat, defending their currencies with various schemes and legal restrictions, but in the end, gold will win.

Why is gold such a desirable commodity? At the top of the list is its impeccable utility as a store of value. Relentless inflating has caused chronic value losses in currencies. The U.S. dollar has dropped in value by an estimated 94 percent (exact values depend upon the benchmark) since the Fed came into being. These collapses have destroyed the financial security of the working class, the middle class and retirees. If modern money had a tangible basis, then workers could have saved for their retirement in a true store of value, and retirees would have far more buying power in their golden years. It is already a pity to observe hard-working people unable to save a penny. It will be heart wrenching to see innocent people suffer during the ultimate resolution of central banks' credit-expansion policies. Gold also contributes to long-run productive stability. By setting up central banks with monopoly powers dedicated to paper money, governments traded that stability for an international casino in which money manipulators thrive at the expense of producers and savers.

It is dangerous to entrust any service crucial to survival to a statutory monopoly or government regulation. When the Russian government handled food production and distribution, central planners reported over seven straight decades of "bad weather," food shortages and starvation. Similarly, with the Bank of England, the Fed and their worldwide counterparts in charge, central planners report decades of "rising prices," monetary debasement and the impoverishment of savers. Periodic credit inflation would occur in a free market as well, but its effects would be limited because real money cannot be inflated, and prudent people and institutions could choose to opt out of a credit binge in favor of real money. A free people would choose the best money, and I have no doubt that it would be gold.

Is the Precious Metals' Bear Market Over?

Despite the verity of gold as the best form of money, there is a right time for everything. Advisors who have insisted upon inflation's inevitability have kept their followers in gold and silver for 21 years as they plummeted 70 percent and 93 percent respectively in *dollar* terms, while the dollar was losing purchasing power at the local store. This is no mean feat insomuch as no other commodity has accomplished it. These losses, even forgetting the massive opportunity costs, have been staggering.

Right now, I think it likely that gold and silver will fall into their final dollar price lows at the bottom of the deflation because that is what happened to silver in the last great deflation.

Figure 22-1

Figure 22-1 shows that although silver had undergone most of its bear market by the time of the 1929 high in the stock market, it still followed commodities and paper assets down during the deflation to a final low in December 1932. There is rarely sufficient reason to bet heavily on cycles behaving differently from an established pattern, and this cycle's history implies that the precious metals' bear market is not quite over yet. If this deflation acts like the last one, then at the coming bottom, we will have a great buying opportunity for gold and silver — maybe the greatest ever.

Most gold bugs today assert that gold and silver are a "deflation hedge," a "war hedge," and a "depression hedge," claims that the record does not convincingly support. The price history of 1931 is instructive in showing that there was a year-long mid-depression rally in the price of silver, which ended on a spike, indicating brief panic buying. Investors of that time were likewise convinced that silver would provide counter-trend solace during monetary difficulty. They were remembering silver's positive performance during the preceding difficult times of 1914-1919, which were inflationary. Similarly, today's precious metals enthusiasts have the inflationary 1970s in mind. However, the actual troubles in the 1930s were, and in this case are expected to be, deflationary.

The fact that people "rushed into gold" in the early 1930s has been a mainstay of the gold advocates' argument. They rarely tell the whole story. I suspect that people bought gold then because the U.S. government had fixed the price, at $20.67 per ounce. While everything else collapsed, gold was soaring in relative value, and its value gains were guaranteed. Who wouldn't buy it? If the government had fixed the price of any other substance, people would have invested in that instead. Like silver in the 1930s, gold today is free to trade at market price, which means that it can go down during a dollar deflation. I cannot guarantee that it will; I can only state that there is no good case to be made that history indicates otherwise.

Buy Gold and Silver Anyway

You might be surprised to find that I advocate holding a healthy amount of gold and silver anyway. There are several reasons for this stance:

First, it *could* be different this time, for some reason I cannot foresee. In a world of fiat currencies, prudence demands hedging against a rush to tangible money.

Second, these metals should perform well on a *relative* basis compared to most other investments. Unlike so many commodities, they will not fall 90 percent from today's prices, much less to zero, like so many stocks and bonds. These metals are downright inexpensive compared to their top values in 1980. Silver today costs only about 8 percent of its peak dollar value. Relative to home prices and stock prices, the metals have never been cheaper. So even if the precious metals continue to decline, they will fall much less in percentage terms than most other assets because they have already fallen so far.

Third, the question of whether there will be further bear market in the metals is important primarily to speculators and quibblers. Gold and silver have declined in dollar value for over two decades, which is between 90 percent and 100 percent of the total time I had expected them to fall. It may not be prudent to try to finesse the final months.

Fourth, the metals should soar once the period of deflation is over. Notice in Figure 22-1 that silver rebounded ferociously after it bottomed in 1932, tripling in just two years, rewarding those who continued to hold it. If deflation again keeps precious metals prices down, the rebound after the bottom should be no less robust. Given the likely political inflationary forces, it could well be much stronger. So by all means, you want to own precious metals prior to the onset of the post-depression recovery.

Fifth and foremost, if you buy gold and silver now, *you'll have it*. If investors worldwide begin to panic into hard assets, locking up supplies, if governments ban gold sales, if gold and silver prices go through the roof, you won't be stuck entirely in paper currency. You will already own something that everyone else wants.

Be aware that the present legalities of gold and silver ownership could change. This political risk isn't fantasy, even in the Land of the Free. In 1933, President Roosevelt outlawed gold ownership for U.S. citizens and imposed a ten-year prison sentence on anyone who refused to surrender his gold to a Federal Reserve Bank within 25 days. (The following year, the government began a long campaign of fixing the price of newly mined silver, though each level was temporary and closely reflected market forces.) The ban on gold stayed in place for over four decades, until President Ford lifted it on the first day of 1975.

Should you buy gold and silver now? The answer depends on how much you are willing to pay for the added breadth in your portfolio and for their current availability. If you are willing to see the dollar value of the precious metals drop another 30 percent or more before they rise substantially, then I would say, that's the price you're willing to pay for insurance against later unavailability and for greater portfolio stability under an unexpected inflation scenario. If you want to arrange for capital safety in every way that you can manage, then diversification into real money is a necessary part of that effort.

How To Buy Gold and Silver

I do not advocate buying gold and silver in paper form by way of futures contracts, gold-backed bonds from the Russian government or ownership certificates connected to commingled accounts at storage facilities. After all, which is better — owning actual gold or some entity's promise to pay it? For maximum safety, you should own gold and silver in physical form, outright.

One-kilo bars are widely traded globally, but "standard bars" of 400 fine ounces are the primary form of gold and silver used by central banks and recognized by the U.S. Comex, the London Bullion Market Association and the Tokyo Commodity Exchange (TOCOM). So that is the most liquid medium for storing substantial wealth in gold.

Coins are a good medium for smaller portfolios. Even larger ones should include their share of coins because some day tangible money could once again become a medium of exchange, at least temporarily. To that end, be sure to avoid rare coins that have a "collectibility" premium. Many dealers recommend paying up for rare coins because in 1933 some collectible gold coins were exempt from U.S. government confiscation. The "cutoff" point for rarity was never codified, though, and there is no guarantee that any such law, much less exactly the same law, will go into effect in your jurisdiction. Any future confiscation in your country may include gold coins with a small collectibility premium because investment strategies built around them are well known. By all means, though, if the argument makes sense to you, pay the premium and sleep better for it.

The best-known and most liquid "bullion" style gold coins are American Eagles, South African Krugerrands, Canadian Maple Leafs and Australian Nuggets. As for silver, Americans should own a bag or two of circulated U.S. silver coins. Most coin dealers can get you these items. After you have a core position, accumulate the metals at a pace with which you are comfortable, preferably on price declines. Every time myopic central banks and panicked debtors push the price of gold and silver down, buy some more.

It is probably not a good idea to invest in gold *stocks* at this juncture. As shown in Chapter 17 of *At the Crest*, during common-stock bear markets, stocks of gold mining companies have more often gone down than up. The exception is in relatively rare five to ten-year periods of accelerating inflation. That is not the risk we face today. Few people know that from the top day in the Dow in 1929 to the bottom day in 1932, gold mining shares rose only slightly *even though the U.S. government propped up the companies' product by fixing its price.* Mining shares did not soar in value until the stock market as a whole turned up. Today the government does not fix the price of gold, so in the deflation we currently face, gold mines will enjoy no false advantage over any other companies. Their stocks will probably rally when the overall stock market rallies (as they are doing now), but they have no built-in support as they did in the 1930s, so they are likely to disappoint those who invest in them. (Of course, if the government's policy on gold changes, then so might the outlook for mining share prices.) Also be aware that there are risks attending the independence of mining companies. Owning gold shares means betting that no government will nationalize the mines whose shares you own. Owning gold shares is fine at the top of a Kondratieff economic cycle when inflation is raging, such as occurred in the 1970s, but not in its final years when deflation is raging and political tensions are their most severe. For a detailed case against gold stocks for the current bear market, please see Chapter 17 of *At the Crest of the Tidal Wave*.

In 1933, Roosevelt's Executive Order stated, "Your possession of these proscribed metals and/or your maintenance of a safe-deposit box to store them is known to the Government from bank and insurance records. Therefore, be advised that your vault box must remain sealed, and may only be opened in the presence of an agent of The Internal Revenue Service." Most banks were only too happy to comply because gold prohibition promised their salvation, or so they believed. If your government decides to confiscate gold, your country's banks will be recruited in the operation. If it happens sometime in the coming crash, the reason will probably be "fighting terrorism." By the way, this potential is a good reason to refrain from keeping any important personal papers in bank safe deposit boxes in any jurisdiction where such an action is possible. Otherwise, you may have to wait a while for permission to access the contents.

If you would like to buy gold and silver, your options are much more limited than they were twenty years ago, when everyone seemed to be in the business. Here are some suggestions. If you want to buy at least $100,000 worth of gold and/or silver bars and store them in one or more of the safest depositories in the world, contact SafeStore, Ltd., via the SafeWealth Group.

While SafeWealth's approach is second to none, those who prefer using a U.S.-based consulting firm that advertises similar services may wish to investigate Asset Strategies International. ASI likewise helps clients diversify globally through precious metals storage as well as bank accounts, insurance and portfolio management. Their recommended institutions' minimums are as low as $25,000, which may be helpful to you. Their focus is much more on service than on ultimate capital protection, so if you decide to work with this firm, be sure to insist upon safety. You can find ASI through the following means:

Asset Strategies International, Inc.
Website: www.assetstrategies.com
Email: assetsi@assetstrategies.com
Address: 1700 Rockville Pike, #400, Rockville MD 20852
Phone: 800-831-0007 and 301-881-8600
Fax: 301-881-8600
Principals: Michael Checkan and Glen Kirsch

If you want to buy bullion-style gold coins or circulated silver coins inside the U.S. and store them domestically, check out the dealers listed below. (Fidelitrade also offers an exchange-approved depository.) Be sure to cross-check prices before buying.

Fidelitrade
Website: www.fidelitrade.com
Email: info@fidelitrade.com
Address: 3601 North Market Street, Wilmington, DE
        19802
Phone: 800-223-1080 and 302-762-6200
Fax: 302-762-2902
CEO: Mike Clark

Hancock & Harwell
Website: www.raregold.com
Email: info@raregold.com

Address: Suite 310, 3155 Roswell Rd., Atlanta, GA 30305
Phone: 888-877-1782 and 404-261-6566
CEO: Robert L. Harwell

Investment Rarities, Inc.
Website: www.gloomdoom.com
Email: jcook@investmentrarities.com
Address: 7850 Metro Parkway, Suite 213, Minneapolis,
    MN 55425-1521
Phone: 800-328-1860 and 612-853-0700
CEO: James R. Cook

Miles Franklin Ltd.
Website: www.milesfranklin.com
Email: milesf@ix.netcom.com
Address: 3601 Park Center Building, Suite 120, St. Louis
    Park, MN 55416
Phone: 800-822-8080 and 952-929-7006
Fax: 952-925-0143
CEO: David M. Schectman

Straight Talk Assets, Inc.
Website: www.coinmoney.com
Email: straighttalk@mindspring.com
Address: P.O. Box 1301, Gainesville, GA 30503
Phone: 800-944-9249 and 770-536-8045
CEO: Glenn R. Fried

Well-heeled investors should round out their holdings
with platinum. Platinum is a precious metal, and in recent decades, its coinage has established it as an emerging monetary metal
as well. Platinum has several advantages over gold and silver,
not the least of which is that it packs more value per ounce. If
you can afford to diversify to this extent, ask your metals dealer
about platinum bars and coins.

Chapter 23:

What To Do With Your Pension Plan

Make sure you fully understand all aspects of your government's individual retirement plans. In the U.S., this includes such structures as IRAs, 401Ks and Keoghs. If you anticipate severe system-wide financial and political stresses, you may decide to liquidate any such plans and pay whatever penalty is required. Why? Because there are strings attached to the perk of having your money sheltered from taxes. You may do only what the government allows you to do with the money. It restricts certain investments and can change the list at any time. It charges a penalty for early withdrawal and can change the amount of the penalty at any time.

What is the worst that could happen? In Argentina, the government continued to spend more than it took in until it went broke trying to pay the interest on its debt. In December 2001, it seized $2.3 billion dollars worth of deposits *in private pension funds* to pay its bills.

In the 1930s, the world heard a lot of populist rhetoric about why "rich" people should be plundered for the public good. It is easy to imagine such talk in the next crisis, directed at requiring wealthy people to forfeit their retirement savings for the good of the nation.

With the retirement setup in the U.S., the government need not be as direct as Argentina's. It need merely assert, after a stock market fall decimates many people's savings, that stocks are too risky to hold for retirement purposes. Under the guise of protecting you, it could ban stocks and perhaps other investments in tax-exempt pension plans and restrict assets to one category: "safe" long-term U.S. Treasury bonds. Then it could raise the penalty of early withdrawal to 100 percent. Bingo. The government will have seized the entire $2 trillion — or what's left of it given a crash — that today is held in government-sponsored, tax-deferred 401K private pension plans. I'm not saying it will happen, but it could, and wouldn't you rather have your money safely under your own discretion?

By the way, if you are normally in a high tax bracket and find yourself in a year with zero income or significant business losses, you can cash out part or all of your plan with either less tax (since you will be in a lower tax bracket) or no tax, if your earned-income losses cancel out the income from the plan. If you are under the age of 59½, you will normally have to pay a penalty, which is currently 10 percent of the value of the distribution. If you use the funds to pay for college tuition, though, you can even avoid the penalty. When you cash out your plan, you can still keep the money in the same investments if you wish, but then they will be in your own name, not in the name of a plan. Be sure to consult a tax advisor before proceeding.

Perhaps you have no such opportunity for a tax saving and do not want to pay the penalty attached to premature withdrawal. If your balance is high enough, you may wish to consider converting your retirement plan investments into an annuity at a safe insurance company (see Chapter 24). It is highly likely (though not assured) that such investments would be left alone even in a national financial emergency.

If you have money in a captive corporate or government employee retirement plan with limited options, move it out of stock and bond funds. Park it in the safest money market fund available within the plan. Investigate the rules that pertain to cashing out and decide your next course of action.

If you or your family owns its own small company and is the sole beneficiary of its pension or profit sharing plan, you should lodge its assets in a safe bank or money market fund. As an alternative, depending upon your age and requirements, you may consider converting it into an annuity, issued by a safe insurance company. Such insurance companies are few and far between, but the next chapter shows you where to find them.

Chapter 24:

What To Do With Your Insurance and Annuities

If you believe that your fortunes are not dependent upon junk bonds, you might be in for a surprise. If you have life insurance, especially if you have a "guaranteed rate of return" insurance policy, your policy may depend upon the performance of junk bonds. Many large insurance companies failed in the comparatively mild recession of the early 1990s because they backed their policies with junk bonds. The economic contraction that insurance companies now face is *three degrees larger* than that one (Grand Supercycle as opposed to Primary). Your insurance nest egg, to put it bluntly, may be at risk.

Some insurance companies guarantee a minimum return on "equity-indexed annuities" while letting you participate in the market's gains but not its losses. An article in a major financial magazine calls these plans "a bear-proof way to ride the market" that "removes downside risk," but the way it's done involves zero-coupon bonds, index options and other exotic vehicles. This scheme will surely blow up, and if it does, the guarantee will stress the insurance companies that sell these policies.

Even traditionally safe insurance companies are massively exposed to losses during a major deflation because they invest in standard vehicles such as stocks, bonds, real estate and "securitized" consumer loan packages. Some venerable insurance companies in Europe have become compromised not from their own investments but because banks that today are awash in leveraged derivatives purchased them some time in the past ten years.

A deflationary vise will put double pressure on the solvency of insurance companies. As the values of most investments fall, the value of insurance companies' portfolios will fall. Conversely, as the economy weakens, more and more people will decide to cash out their policies. Insurance companies become hard-pressed to honor the value of whole-life policies when there is a net outflow of cash at the same time that their property and stock investments are declining in value.

When insurance companies implode, they file for bankruptcy, and you can be left out in the cold. I know, because my insurance broker placed our insurance with, of all the companies in the world, Confederation Life. In 1994, it collapsed, along with Baldwin United and First Executive Corporation, which were huge institutions. See what happened when I didn't do the necessary research? If you think that you can rely on your broker to recommend a safe insurance company, think again. Brokers shop mainly for price, and when they do look into safety, they rely on rating services that don't do a good job (see Chapter 25). As it turned out, I was lucky. Government and industry leaders in both the U.S. and Canada worked for three years to distribute the policies to other companies. When my policy moved, it carried *another* full year's cash-out restriction, and all the while, I was still required to pay the premiums. The only reason that the deal finally made it through was that the North American financial boom continued throughout the 1990s, and other insurance companies felt safe taking on the additional obligations.

When a bust is in force, few insurance companies are willing or able to take over a stressed company's policy obligations, which have little collateral behind them. If your insurance company fails, your investment of a lifetime will be gone. It's happened to many people and will happen to many more.

Whole-life policies are almost always a terrible idea under a fiat money system. During inflationary times, their real value grows far more slowly than it appears, if at all, because the purchasing power of the monetary unit declines. During deflationary times, the policy your family is counting on to protect against death or old age can disappear if the company fails.

One option is to cash out such policies and buy term insurance instead. With term insurance, you can keep an eye on the fortunes of various companies and switch from one to another. Talk to your insurance broker about the courses of action open to you.

On the other hand, an interesting "deflation bonus" can also come available if you're careful. If you have whole-life insurance or an annuity with a *sound company*, you can actually come out way ahead because *the values and payouts are denominated in currency*. During deflation, the value of cash rises, so in terms of purchasing power, each dollar of value in your policy will be able to purchase more goods and services than it previously did. All you need to do is find a sound company.

Where To Buy Your Insurance Policies

At minimum, you should move your whole-life insurance policy or annuity to a sound insurer as soon as possible. If you delay one day too long in moving your policy, and the company's assets are frozen, you will have no recourse.

As far as I can tell, Weiss Ratings, Inc. produces the most reliable ratings of U.S. insurance companies. Their system is also simple and straightforward. Unlike the maze of gradations such as "Bbb+" and so on that other services use, the Weiss system simply reads like a report card, from A+ down to F, adding only a set of

"E" grades prior to F. Weiss considers any company rated B- or above to have "good" financial safety but recommends that you do business with companies rated B+ or better. In normal times, that assessment is probably all you need. However, if you believe that there is a reasonable risk of that rare and devastating event, a deflationary crash and depression, why not demand the absolute best? Table 24-1 lists all U.S. insurance companies that Weiss rates A+. The two companies on this list that are also on Weiss' list of the 25 largest insurance companies rated B+ or higher are marked with an asterisk.

Of course, as prudent as these judgments may be, these ratings do not fully take into account other considerations that will be crucial in a depression. For example, what bank(s) does your insurer use to hold its assets and make transactions? If an insurer's main bank implodes, its situation could become chaotic.

THE SAFEST U.S. INSURERS			
Source: Weiss Ratings, Inc. (based on 03/31/03 data, updated for 2nd edition)			
Company Name	Domicile State	Weiss Safety Rating	Total Assets (in millions of $)
LIFE & HEALTH INSURERS			
American Family Life Ins Co	WI	A+	2,834.4
Country Life Ins Co	IL	A+	4,294.5
State Farm Life & Accident Asr Co	IL	A+	1,126.1
State Farm Life Ins Co*	IL	A+	32,601.6
Teachers Ins & Annuity Asn Of Am *	NY	A+	144,727.7
PROPERTY & CASUALTY INSURERS			
Government Employees Ins	MD	A+	9,271.47
Interins Exch of the Automobile Club	CA	A+	3,592.58
Tennessee Farmers Asr	TN	A+	544.69
Tennessee Farmers Mutual Ins	TN	A+	1,369.45
United Services Automobile Asn	TX	A+	12,952.01
USAA Casualty Ins	TX	A+	4,146.74

*These are among the largest 25 insurers rated B+ or higher.

Table 24-1

This one factor could override even an insurer's A+ credit rating. Ratings can change for all sorts of reasons. For maximum confidence, keep abreast of Weiss' ratings as they pertain to the companies you choose. (See contact information in the last section of this book.)

As if there were not already enough to worry about, the currency denomination of your policy may also prove crucial. If the currency in which you expect to be paid collapses in value, so will your plans for retirement.

Again, SafeWealth Group specializes in minimizing all these risks by identifying the safest insurance companies in the world as well as those among them that use safe banks as custodians of their funds. Better yet, it can identify the ones that also allow you to designate the currency denomination(s) of your choice within their policies. Such provisions for ultimate safety are particularly important for annuity arrangements, estate planning and capital-preservation programs that utilize insurance contracts.

The main point is to make sure that you assess the vulnerability of your insurance policies and annuities now. If you are satisfied, fine. If not, take appropriate action before your insurance company, its bank, or you, become too stressed to adapt.

Chapter 25:

Reliable Sources for Financial Warnings

Safety Ratings for Financial Institutions

The most widely utilized rating services are almost always woefully late in warning you of problems within financial institutions. They often seem to get news about a company around the time that everyone else does, which means that the price of the associated stock or bond has already changed to reflect that news. In severe cases, a company can collapse before the standard rating services know what hit it. When all you can see is dust, they just skip the downgrading process and shift the company's rating from "investment grade" to "default" status.

Examples abound. The debt of the largest real estate developer in the world, Olympia & York of Canada, had an AA rating in 1991. A year later, it was bankrupt. Rating services missed the historic debacles at Barings Bank, Sumitomo Bank and Enron. Enron's bonds enjoyed an "investment grade" rating four days before the company went bankrupt. In my view, Enron's bonds in particular were transparently junk well before their collapse. Why? Because the firm employed an army of traders in derivatives, which is an absolute guarantee of ultimate failure even when it's *not* a company's main business.

Sometimes there are structural reasons for the overvaluation of debt issues. For example, investors buy the debt offerings of Fannie Mae, Freddie Mac and the FHLB because they think that the U.S. government guarantees them. It doesn't. All that these companies have is the right to borrow money from the U.S. Treasury, $2.5 billion in the case of Fannie and Freddie and $4 billion in the case of the FHLB. That credit line represents less than ¼ of 1 percent of each company's outstanding mortgage loans, so it is a drop in the bucket. Worse, because of that advantage, the bonds that these companies issue are exempt from SEC registration and disclosure requirements because they are simply *presumed* to be safe. Managers of these companies are going to be utterly shocked when a depression devastates their portfolios and their earnings. Investors in these companies' stocks and bonds will be just as surprised when the stock prices and bond ratings collapse. Most rating services will not see it coming.

A few companies take a stringent approach to rating institutional safety. I listed three good U.S. bank-rating firms in Chapter 19. Weiss Ratings, Inc. has quite reliable, detailed ratings on a broader range of U.S. institutions. For example, while most analysts never saw the Enron disaster coming, Weiss placed Enron on its "Corporate Earnings Blacklist" in April 2001 and cited the company as being "highly suspect of manipulating its earnings reports." Two quarters later, the scandal broke, and countless employees and investors — people who hadn't the foggiest notion about taking the precautions I'm suggesting to you in this book — lost everything.

SafeWealth Group uses an even more stringent "survivability indicator" for financial institutions globally, taking not just the present balance sheet and corporate structure into account but also the institution's projected viability in a financial crisis or depression. SafeWealth is not in the ratings publishing business, but in response to inquiries, it will introduce qualified individuals, companies and trusts to its highest-rated institutions.

Investment Advice from Brokers

Throughout my career, I have advised people not to trust a brokerage firm's "fundamental" (as opposed to technical) analysts to warn you about anything. Brokerage firm analysts are notoriously poor at market timing. Besides being beholden to their corporate clients, which gives them an extreme bullish bias, most of these analysts use the wrong tools. Even when they are independent thinkers, they are usually not students of market psychology and thus have no idea how to figure out when a stock is probably topping. In fact, brokerage firm analysts are typically cheerleaders for a stock just as it is topping out and during most of its fall. Over 20 years ago, when I worked as a Technical Market Specialist at Merrill Lynch, I watched as an analyst kept a "buy" rating on a maker of CB radios while its stock dropped from 19 to 1. Nothing has changed. According to reports, 11 out of 16 analysts covering Enron had a "buy" (some even emphasized "strong buy") on the stock four weeks before the company declared bankruptcy and well after the decline in the stock price had wiped out its investors. As most people have subsequently learned, brokerage firm analysts almost never use the word "sell." If they really think a company's stock is dangerous, they label it a "hold." The problem with trying to follow this guideline, though, is that they usually label a stock that way after its bear market has run most or all of its course. To avoid being hurt by these strategists, you need independent market analysis.

Useful Newsletters in a Bear Market

Most newsletters these days are wet behind the ears. Their focus is touting stocks to buy. That was fine for the bull market, but it probably isn't now. At all times ideally, but particularly in a global bear market, you need input from seasoned analysts who cover the financial world with healthy skepticism and are as good at warning you about what investments to avoid as they are at suggesting what actions to take. Besides my own company's publications (see final section of this book), here are a few that I like:

The Gloom, Boom & Doom Report
Website: www.gloomboomdoom.com
Email: info@gloomboomdoom.com
Address: 3308 The Center, 99 Queens Rd. Central, Hong
      Kong
Phone: (U.S. dial 011) 852-2-801-5410
Fax: 852-2-845-9192
Editor: Marc Faber

Grant's Interest Rate Observer
Website: www.grantspub.com
Email: webmaster@grantspub.com
Address: 2 Wall Street, New York, NY 10005
Phone: 212-809-7994
Fax: 212-809-8426
Editor: James Grant

The International Speculator
Website: www.internationalspeculator.com
Email: info@internationalspeculator.com
Address: P.O. Box 84911, Phoenix AZ 85071
Phone: 800-528-0559 and 602-252-4477
Fax: 602-943-2363
Editor: Doug Casey

Safe Money Report
Website: www.safemoneyreport.com
Email: wr@weissinc.com
Address: Weiss Research, P.O. Box 31689, Palm Beach
      Gardens, FL 33420

Phone: 800 236 0407 and 561-627-3300
Fax: 561-625-6685
Editor: Martin D. Weiss

SafeWealth Report
Email: clientservices@safewealthadvisory.com
Address: SafeWealth Services SA – Service Center,
        Grand-Rue 114, 2nd Level East,
        CH-1820 Montreux, Switzerland.
Phone: (in U.S., dial 011) 41-21-966-7200
Fax: (in U.S., dial 011) 41-21-966-7201
Production Manager: Jane V. Scott

All that most of these services can do is offer you ideas. In the
end, you will have to make up your own mind with the evidence
that they present.

Chapter 26:

How To Ensure Your Physical Safety

In essence, bull and bear markets are social mood trends. Social mood trends have consequences.

A positive social mood has positive social consequences. The great bull market of the past quarter-century created a wonderful world. Major antagonists in the areas of politics, religion and race kissed and made up. The Cold War ended. Communism collapsed. Markets became global and sophisticated. The world embraced, to one degree or another, capitalism and freedom. The Information Age was born. Even country music got raucous and happy. In the 1990s, people felt secure, and today wealth abounds.

Generally speaking, that environment has been safe, profitable and fun. However, social mood trends are a two-way street. When the positive trend ends, a negative one takes over for a while. Those trends have social consequences, too: destructive ones, which affect finance, the economy, politics and all kinds of social relationships.

This book focuses mostly on finance. If you get out of investments that will lose most of their value in a crash and keep your money safe, you will be quite wealthy in terms of your purchasing power. Unfortunately, that's not all there is to a major bear market. Depressions are a mess. You may have money, but certain goods might be scarce or rationed. You might be financially smart yet get caught in a war zone.

It may not be much fun to contemplate the social effects of downtrends, but it is important. It's true that if you become financially devastated, you can't take advantage of great investment opportunities. But if you encounter physical risk, you may not even be around to try.

In order to profit from and enjoy an uptrend, you and your family must be fully protected during the preceding downtrend. Then, at the bottom, you can rise above the general despair and take full advantage both financially and emotionally of the next expansive increase in positive social mood.

Elliott waves portend many social changes, and you can anticipate them to some degree by understanding what I call socionomics. There is not room to explain the idea in this book. For a taste of how useful socionomics can be, review these comments on one result of social mood change that the forecasted bear market was expected to exhibit:

"Foreigners will commit terrorist acts on U.S. soil...."
— *At the Crest of the Tidal Wave* (1995)
Chapter 21, p.435

"The impulse to build shows up in the construction of record-breaking skyscraper buildings at social-mood peaks. At troughs, few buildings are built, and many of those already in place may be burned or bombed out of existence."
— *The Wave Principle of Human Social Behavior and the New Science of Socionomics* (1999)
Chapter 14, pp.229-230

"The Middle East should be a complete disaster. You've got at least three major religions in that area that all dislike each other, and the truce of the bull market has already been tenuous, so that area is going to blow up."
— *The Elliott Wave Theorist*, August 2001 issue

The 9/11/01 attack on the World Trade Center and the ensuing war in Afghanistan have borne out these observations, and we are as of yet only two mild years into the bear market.

By the way, some commentators write as if the terrorist attack caused the recession, but the stock market topped out a year and a half earlier, and the economy began contracting half a year earlier. Attacks such as this *result* from negative social-mood trends, which is why a socionomist can generally anticipate the tenor of behavior that manifests in such acts. Such manifestations are always a matter of frequency and degree. There is always some social unrest, even in the late stages of a bull market, but conflict always escalates in a bear market. For more on this theme, please see Chapters 14-16 of *The Wave Principle of Human Social Behavior and the New Science of Socionomics* (by far my most important book). For a fuller discussion of what to expect socially in the bear market, please read Chapter 21 of *At the Crest of the Tidal Wave*.

Polarization and Conflict

The main social influence of a bear market is to cause society to polarize in countless ways. That polarity shows up in every imaginable context — social, religious, political, racial, corporate, by class and otherwise. In a bear market, people in whatever way are impelled to identify themselves as belonging to a smaller social unit than they did before and to belong more passionately. It is probably a product of the anger that accompanies bear markets, because each social unit seems invariably to find reasons to be angry with and to attack its opposing unit. In the 1930s bear market, communists and fascists challenged political institutions. In the 1970s bear market, students challenged police, and blacks challenged whites. In both cases, labor challenged management and third parties challenged the status quo.

In bear markets, rallies, marches and protests become common events. Separatism becomes a force as territories polarize. Populism becomes a force as classes polarize. Third parties, fourth parties, and more, find constituents. Bear markets engender labor strikes, racial conflict, religious persecution, political unrest, trade protectionism, coups and wars. In the area of personal behavior, part of the population gets more conservative, and part gets more hedonistic, and each side describes the other as something that needs reform. One reason that conflicts gain such scope in depressions is that much of the middle class gets wiped out by the financial debacle, increasing the number of people with little or nothing to lose and anger to spare.

The Erroneous Timing of Previous Concerns

In the late 1970s and early 1980s, survival was a big topic. There were million-seller books about where to buy electric generators, how to choose bulletproof vests, storing dried foods and so on. This occupation of course coincided with an approaching major bottom in a 16-year bear market (in inflation-adjusted terms). By then, you shouldn't have been wasting your time with it; you should have been buying stocks and bonds. The ideal time to address safety concerns is at the beginning of a downtrend, not at the end.

In 1999, near the all-time high in stocks, many people were again concerned for their physical safety, but this time, it was for the wrong reason. They feared that the "Y2K" computer glitch would shut down the civilized world. In the heat of the international obsession over this issue and in answer to many emails to the Message Board on our website, I answered that the free market would take care of that problem. Until the social mood trend turned down, as evidenced by a major downturn in the stock averages, there was little to fear on that scale.

Anticipated events such as those rarely cause global disruption. Major trends of increasing pessimism, anger and fear do cause global disruption, and that's what a bear market is. After January 1, 2000, all the worriers over Y2K evaporated. Complacency reigned again, just when financial risk was at its greatest. That's also when physical safety should have become a real concern. The eruption of terrorist activity in recent months is a product of a bear market, so you see my point.

Some Thoughts on Preparedness

Exactly what to do about your physical safety is a difficult problem. Living in a populous area or near a military installation or an important infrastructure site is somewhat dangerous in times of social unrest. If you are physically tied to a job in such a spot, decisions about relocating are even more difficult than otherwise.

I know people who have farmland in the country, a retreat in the mountains or a self-sufficient home. Others buy guns or learn self-defense. These are fine ideas if you can fit them into the requirements and desires of your life. But for such preparations to be useful, you have to find yourself in a position where you need them. Usually in a major bear market, you are less likely to encounter a mob, a criminal or a terrorist than to face state-sponsored controls within your own country or military attack from without, and there may be little that a retreat or karate can do for you in those situations.

Nevertheless, if you determine that you need this type of preparation, now is a good time to dig out that old list of "Y2K" items and buy from it whatever you would like to have — such as an electric generator, a few months' worth of emergency dried foods, a video surveillance system, defensive weapons, etc. — some at half the prices that they were selling for in late 1999. Being prepared for terrorism is hardly an unreasonable idea.

Here are some web locations to help you with aspects of physical preparedness. Some of them link to other sites, so once you get in the loop, you will find many more resources.

Disaster Preparedness
>   http://www.oism.org/nwss/s73p908.htm
>   http://www.fema.gov

Basic Survival
>   http://www.survival-center.com/index.htm
>   http://www.ki4u.com/nuclearsurvival/list.htm

Home Security, Disaster Information
>   www.joelskousen.com

Dried Foods
>   www.alpineaire.com
>   www.fcs.uga.edu/pubs/current/FDNS-E-34-CS.html

Water Testing
>   www.calcon.net/~prt

Air Testing
>   www.envirotester.com

Self Defense
>   www.kravmagainc.com

Some disaster-related literature can be more upsetting than helpful. Always stop and think: Is this course of action necessary? Is there a more sensible alternative? There is little point in taking much time, effort and cost to prepare for disastrous events that are highly unlikely or which can be judiciously avoided.

Chapter 27:

Preparing for a Change in Politics

The Elected Leader's Fortunes

Figure 27-1 uses U.S. electoral history to show that when the stock market is rising, reflecting a positive social-mood trend, voters tend to maintain the incumbent leader. When stocks collapse, the leader is thrown out in a landslide or by other means; though the instances are rare, there are no exceptions to this rule. Voters do not appear to care which party is in power at such times; they just throw whomever they perceive to be in charge, and his party, out of power.

National leaders always make things worse for themselves by (1) claiming credit when the economy does well, thereby implying that it's their fault when it doesn't, and (2) vowing to enact economy-boosting measures when the economy weakens, thereby supporting the fiction that they can control it, which puts their opponents in a position to claim that those policies failed.

A leader doesn't control his country's economy, but the economy mightily controls his image. When the economy contracts, that image suffers, and the voters throw him out. This is true of elected rulers all over the earth. For an instructive case in point, study the fortunes of U.S. president Richard Nixon, who won a second term in a landslide in late 1972 at a major top and was hounded from office less than two years later as the Dow

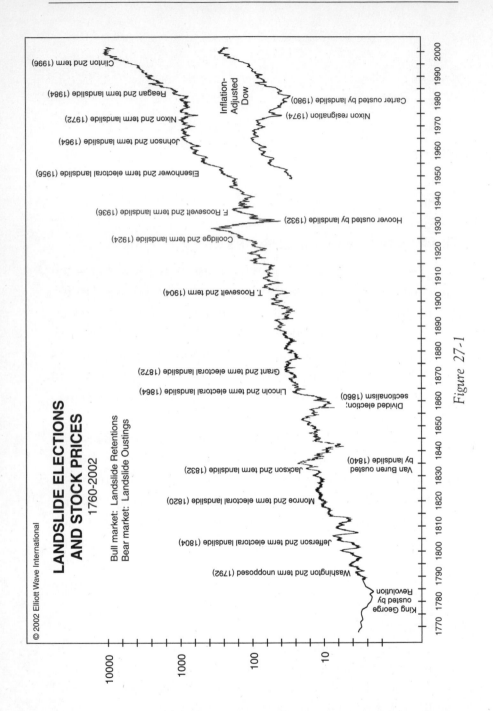

LANDSLIDE ELECTIONS AND STOCK PRICES
1760-2002

Bull market: Landslide Retentions
Bear market: Landslide Oustings

© 2002 Elliott Wave International

King George ousted by Revolution

Washington 2nd term unopposed (1792)

Jefferson 2nd term electoral landslide (1804)

Monroe 2nd term electoral landslide (1820)

Jackson 2nd term landslide (1832)

Van Buren ousted by landslide (1840)

Divided election: sectionalism (1860)

Lincoln 2nd term electoral landslide (1864)

Grant 2nd term electoral landslide (1872)

T. Roosevelt 2nd term (1904)

Coolidge 2nd term landslide (1924)

F. Roosevelt 2nd term landslide (1936)

Hoover ousted by landslide (1932)

Eisenhower 2nd term electoral landslide (1956)

Johnson 2nd term landslide (1964)

Nixon 2nd term landslide (1972)

Reagan 2nd term landslide (1984)

Clinton 2nd term (1996)

Inflation-Adjusted Dow

Nixon resignation (1974)

Carter ousted by landslide (1980)

Figure 27-1

suffered its largest decline since 1937-1938. Or consider George Bush, who enjoyed record presidential approval ratings in 1991 yet lost the election just a year later amidst the deepest slide in S&P companies' earnings since the 1940s. In Argentina, which recently has suffered financial ruin after a deflationary crash, the president saw his public approval drop from 70 percent to 4.5 percent in just two years. The country then ran through four successive presidents in a matter of weeks. Those voters wanted *all* the bums thrown out.

If there is a deflationary crash, the incumbent leader of your nation, no matter how popular he is early in his term, will not win re-election if stock prices are much lower on election day. The financial and economic decline during his term and the defeat that follows will not be primarily his fault, though the majority will insist that they are. If the decline is a drawn-out affair, more than one successive leader could suffer defeat at its hands.

The Public, Not the President, Controls the Trend

People who hear me say in speeches that the markets and the economy affect the election of the leader more so than vice versa invariably gasp in incredulity. In the U.S., Republicans say, "How can you say that Ronald Reagan's conservative policies cannot be credited for the economic improvement of the 1980s, which led to 8 out of 10 years of expansion?" To which I reply, "Then do you also credit Franklin Roosevelt's liberal policies for the economic improvement of the 1930s, which led to 11 out of 12 years of economic expansion?" (You can switch these lines when a Democrat asks you the question.) Or more poignantly, "Do you credit Adolf Hitler for the dramatic economic upturn in Germany after he assumed power in 1933?"

What is really happening is that these leaders got into power because the people, despairing over their depression, demanded the ouster of the incumbents. The trend turned, and the new leader got the credit. Sometimes, voters at market bottoms do elect leaders with better economic policies. Usually, they don't.

Conversely, leaders in power during financial collapses are rarely directly at fault. Usually years of mismanagement by others set the stage. The leaders in power at the time, though, always appear inept, because they take actions designed to "help the economy," which fail, or they decline to take actions and are blamed for fiddling while Rome burns. Regardless of what they do or don't do, the public blames them and their party and kicks them out.

Political Stresses in Major Bear Markets

As we discussed in Chapter 26, bear markets create social *polarization*; in the political realm, that means *radical politics*. That much I can guarantee in the upcoming depression. Who wins the battles or the war is not scripted beforehand, except that the incumbents perceived to be in power lose.

In recent years, voter turnout has been low, races have been lackluster and close, and politics have been middle-of-the-road, with little difference between the major parties. Get ready for dramatic political changes.

In the U.S. stock collapse of 1835-1842, a brand-new political party (the Whigs) won the presidential election in 1840 and another (the Democrat Republicans), which had held power for forty years, soon afterward dissolved. In the election of 1860, following the stock bottom and deep recession of 1859, politics were so polarized that many states did not list all the presidential candidates on their ballots. A new party (Republican) won its first election. The following year, the Civil War broke out. The election of 1932, near the bottom of the Great Depression, was less tense but still a watershed, which led to the transformation of the United States into a semi-socialist state.

Given the projected size of this bear market, look for nations and states to split and shrink. Look for regional governments to challenge national ones. There is no way to know *exactly* where such splits will erupt, but they will erupt somewhere.

International politics will become increasingly dangerous. The number of annual nuclear explosions, whether for testing or attack, waxes and wanes inversely with the stock market. (For a graph, see Chapter 16 in *The Wave Principle of Human Social Behavior.*) Look for an increased number of nuclear explosions during the bear market.

Debt and fiat money create political risks. Overseas investors and central banks own 45 percent of the U.S. Treasury's bonds in the marketplace. The largest investors are Japan and China. Ultimately, the turmoil of a record-breaking debt liquidation could force the Treasury or the Fed to renege on some of its obligations, which could have extreme political consequences and turn global sentiment viciously against the U.S. On the other hand, an irony arises in the area of currency. The Fed's September 2001 bulletin reports that an estimated 90 percent of the new $100 bills ordered by the Federal Reserve Bank of New York are used to "satisfy foreign demand." According to a 1994 *New York Times* article, "In Russia, Romania, Tajikstan, China, Vietnam and other countries [the U.S. dollar] has become 'the official unofficial tender.'" Since 70 percent of dollar currency is overseas, a major dollar-based credit deflation would transfer 70 percent of the surviving dollars' expanding purchasing power to non-U.S. holders of dollar bills. Americans hold a larger percentage of IOUs, while others hold a larger percentage of the real thing, that is, to the extent that it *is* real. What political decisions such a situation may cause are anyone's guess, and so are the consequences.

What To Do If You Have Political Aspirations

If there is a major stock market crash, you want to run for office near the bottom. You will be revered by the public and historians if you win. George Washington, Abraham Lincoln,

Franklin Roosevelt and Ronald Reagan were all elected at or
near the bottom of severe downtrends, and all have an exalted
place in American history.

Third parties do well in tough times; so do outsiders and
radicals; incumbents do poorly. So if you are a non-incumbent
political animal, you can plan now to take advantage of the situation. If you want to be a politician, plan to run for office on any
party ticket but that of the primary leader in your country who
rode the trend down.

Why Politics Matter in the Context of This Book

At some point during a financial crisis, money flows
typically become a political issue. You should keep a sharp eye
on political trends in your home country. In severe economic
times, governments have been known to ban foreign investment,
demand capital repatriation, outlaw money transfers abroad, close
banks, freeze bank accounts, restrict or seize private pensions,
raise taxes, fix prices and impose currency exchange values. They
have been known to use force to change the course of who gets
hurt and who is spared, which means that the prudent are
punished and the thriftless are rewarded, reversing the result from
what it would be according to who *deserves* to be spared or get
hurt. In extreme cases, such as when authoritarians assume power,
they simply appropriate or take *de facto* control of your property.

You cannot anticipate every possible law, regulation or
political event that will be implemented to thwart your attempt
at safety, liquidity and solvency. This is why you must plan ahead
and pay attention. As you do, *think about these issues* so that when
political forces troll for victims, you are legally outside the scope
of the dragnet.

Chapter 28:

How To Identify a Safe Haven

As I said in Chapter 26, the real risk of social unrest will probably involve not so much roving itinerant bands looting your home – a classic fear that is rarely realized — as much as *international conflict* and *domestic repression*. In a bear market, both international and domestic tensions increase, and the resulting social actions can be devastating.

Far more people in the past century had their lives wrecked or terminated by domestic implosions than by war. Whether you lived in Russia in the 1920s, Germany in the 1930s, Europe in the 1940s, China in the late 1940s, Cuba in 1959 or Cambodia in the 1970s, the smart thing to do early was to get out of Dodge. However, if you ever make such a decision, you will have to be lucky as well as smart. The people in Europe who decided in 1937 to move away before things got worse were the prudent ones. But one or two of them might have said, "Let's go somewhere far away and safe. Let's go out to the Pacific and live on one of those sleepy islands in the Philippines." In other words, you might guess wrong.

One good guide to the world's developing crisis spots is Richard Maybury's *Early Warning Report*. If you are an Asian, African or Middle Eastern resident, his analysis is especially pertinent. Maybury has also published some excellent primers on

inflation and justice. You may contact him through the following means:

> *Early Warning Report*
> Website: www.richardmaybury.com
> Email: pmc701@aol.com
> Address: P.O. Box 84908, Phoenix, AZ 85701
> Phone: 800-509-5400 and 602-252-4477
> Fax: 602-943-2363
> Editor: Richard Maybury

If you live in a country with unstable politics, you should
think about where you might go if things get oppressive. Like
everything in a developing crisis, it is imperative to be prepared
well before you have to make a final decision.

Some readers, admittedly only a few, may find merit in
the idea of spending some time outside of their home countries
while a depression unfolds. After researching the international
scene for free and stable Western-style English-speaking countries, I find five top candidates: the United States, Canada,
Australia, New Zealand and Ireland.

The world's #1 choice for refuge is the United States.
Indeed, the philosophical foundation of the United States and
its (sometimes dormant) embodiment by many of its citizens
bodes well for a low likelihood of severe domestic repression.
Nothing is impossible, of course, and some people argue that the
history of civilizations suggests that, on a multi-century basis at
least, the peak of U.S. world power is at hand and repression will
follow. Potentially more dangerous is the international threat.
The U.S.'s penchant for involving itself in other countries' dis-
putes has made it a prime target for terrorists and certain
governments. Any sustained or coordinated effort by America's
enemies could make domestic life highly unstable. Alternatively,
if authoritarians assume power at the federal level near the bot-

tom of a depression (which happened throughout Europe and Asia in the 1930s and 1940s), difficulties could arise from domestic sources.

Simply *preparing* to move might not prove to be enough. Before you actually take that crucial action, your country of choice might shut its borders. Your country of *origin* might shut its borders. If terrorists infect a city in your nation with a biological warfare agent, you may be banned from entering any other nation. If you ever reach the point that you are sure you want a foreign refuge, you should move right then. If you choose a safe haven, and if the threats pass, you can always return to your home country.

At minimum, make sure that your passport is current, since demand for passports may increase later and delay processing. Another great idea is to obtain a "green card" or permanent resident visa in the country to which you would probably move if you came to such a decision. Usually they are issued for a period of five years or so, at which time you must renew them from inside that country. Permanent resident visas generally cost about $US 4000 in legal fees to obtain, although most attractive countries have do-it-yourself forms available on the Internet. Like everything else, though, getting an extended visa takes time. You have to fill out forms and meet fairly stringent requirements. Even if you are quick and efficient, your legal representative or your host government might not be. Silly roadblocks can crop up that require another piece of paper, and so on. The point is, to get what you want, act early. Before actually packing up to move, you should consult an attorney in your chosen country so that you understand its laws.

A great way to get to know other countries from your armchair is by way of the *Eyewitness Travel Guides*, by Dorling Kindersley Publishing. They are not only packed with information, like most travel guides, but they are also loaded with breathtaking and informative photos. Their current cost is $24.95 each. For specific information about these countries' visitation and extended visitation policies, investigate the following websites:

United States: www.bcis.gov
Canada: www.cic.gc.ca/english
Australia: www.immi.gov.au
New Zealand: www.immigration.govt.nz
Ireland: www.justice.ie

Some of these sites are easier to use than others; you may have to poke around to find what you want. Sometimes web addresses change. If any of these sites move, or if you wish to investigate countries other than those listed above, just perform an Internet search on key words. Most immigration offices have their own websites.

I thought about filling up a couple of chapters with the pros and cons of these and other nations, but in the end, what really matters is what matters to *you*. Some of these countries have a better set of laws, others better weather, others a better culture, others better infrastructure, others more convenience. I am unfamiliar with non-English speaking countries that other people have been recommending, such as Argentina, Chile and Costa Rica, partly for the reason that I am unconvinced that they would be stellar havens of peace in a global depression. There are also many beautiful small island countries around the world, which rarely seem to be the focus of international conflict. You will have to sift through the data, the books and the brochures and decide for yourself. Of course, the best way to approach such a question is to visit selected locations personally. They make great vacation spots, so you will hardly regret it. Who says contemplating a depression can't have its pleasures?

Chapter 29:

Calling in Loans and Paying off Debt

People and institutions that best weather the system-wide debt liquidation of a deflationary crash and depression are those that take on *no debt* and extend *no risky credit*. This is the ideal situation for most people most of the time, anyway.

Handling Credit

In this book, we have already covered many topics that pertain to the problem of risky credit. Make sure that you do not lend your money to a weak debt issuer, whether corporate, governmental or any other entity. If you have already done so, trade it for something better.

There is also the question of personal credit extension. Have you lent money to friends, relatives or co-workers? The odds of collecting any of these debts are usually slim to none, but if you can prod your personal debtors into paying you back before they get further strapped for cash, it will not only help you but it will also give you some additional wherewithal to help those very same people if they become destitute later.

Handling Debt

If at all possible, remain or become debt-free. Being debt-free means that you are freer, period. You don't have to sweat credit card payments. You don't have to sweat home or auto repossession or loss of your business. You don't have to work 6 percent more, or 10 percent more, or 18 percent more just to stay even.

If you can afford it, the best mortgage is none at all. If you own your home outright and lose your job, you will still have a residence. When banks are throwing others out of their homes, you will still have a place to live. If you can't pay the rent on your business space, you can move your business into your house. And so on. I would rather own a crackerbox outright than have a mansion with mortgage payments I can barely make.

Consider the bank's situation in times of financial stress. Suppose you have paid off enough of your mortgage so that you own 50 percent of your home, which reflects the average equity held by homeowners nationwide. Suddenly, you find that you can't make further payments because of money problems in a depression. At that point, even if house prices had fallen by a whopping 50 percent, your bank would see it as no drop at all. It can place your property (actually *its* property) on the market. If the house sells for only 50 percent of its peak value, the bank gets 100 percent of its outstanding loan back. You can see why banks are pressured to sell properties in such situations. Of course, you end up homeless after slaving to pay off half the mortgage on the house over many years. That's what happens to many homeowners in a depression.

I suppose it might be possible to be creative in an otherwise impossible situation. Some people might decide to borrow as much of the home's value as possible, put the proceeds in a safe money-market fund and use those funds to meet the mortgage, thus assuring no missed payments for the duration. The problem with this idea is that many people are their own worst enemies, and they lack the discipline to protect the needed cash. They can find themselves both broke and homeless either way.

One way out of a debt load is personal bankruptcy. I don't recommend it because it isn't honest. People lent you their hard-earned money; you should pay it back. If you truly are a victim of unforeseen circumstances and must declare bankruptcy, apologize to your creditors and tell them that you hope the experience taught them a lesson about under-collateralized lending.

Chapter 30:

What You Should Do If You Run a Business

Avoid long-term employment contracts with employees. Try to locate in a state with "at-will" employment laws. Red tape and legal impediments to firing could bankrupt your company in a financial crunch, thus putting everyone in your company out of work.

If you run a business that normally carries a large business inventory (such as an auto or boat dealership), try to reduce it. If your business requires certain manufactured specialty items that may be hard to obtain in a depression, stock up.

If you are an employer, start making plans for what you will do if the company's cash flow declines and you have to cut expenditures. Would it be best to fire certain people? Would it be better to adjust all salaries downward an equal percentage so that you can keep everyone employed?

A cynic might recommend that if you are an employer, you should try to pay in stock or options, but if you share the expectations presented in this book, that course of action would be dishonest. Besides, an employee who gets gypped is hardly going to serve your company well. Don't forget, depressions don't last forever; when the next upturn comes, you will want a loyal staff to help you prosper in it, and they will want a healthy company to help them prosper, too. To encourage that result, pay what and how you need to for the talent you require.

Most important, make sure you get *paid*. If you sell retail, don't be responsible for large amounts of credit. If you are a supplier to other businesses, give a discount for cash up front. Try to cut back on the number of firms that habitually pay you 60, 90 or 120 days in arrears of your providing products or services to them. The higher your "accounts receivable," the more you are expending effort and money in exchange for debt. If the businesses whom you supply go under, you won't collect on monies owed. Worse, you may even lose the last few payments they did make to you. Did you know that bankruptcy law allows lawyers to *recall* all payments that a defunct firm made within 90 days before it filed for bankruptcy? Who do you think pays for the legal costs of handling a bankrupt business? You do, the hapless supplier. But if you operate for cash up front, at least you won't have to send back the latest payments *and* forfeit the rest of what you are owed. A moment's thought will reveal how dangerous this law will be in a depression, as payout call-backs will stress or perhaps even crush businesses on the margin that needed those previous payments to survive. By the way, if you have arrangements in which you supply goods for others to sell, be sure to file a UCC Financing Statement in the office of the Clerk of Court in the county where your seller resides. This statement gives constructive notice of a secured party's interest in its own property and keeps the bankruptcy vultures from trying to claim that your consigned property is a debt of the bankrupt company.

If you manage a bank, insurance company, money management firm or other financial institution, try to work out of your speculative derivative positions, particularly bullish ones. Reduce stock market risk as much as possible. If you *must* be heavily invested in stocks — for example if you manage a stock mutual fund — hedge your positions with options. Tidy up your mortgage portfolio. Get rid of all second-tier debt paper. If you have invested in municipal bonds, consumer debt, real estate debt, junk bonds or anything other than top-grade paper, sell it at today's lofty prices. Get on a solid footing with investments that are high quality, liquid and commonly understood.

Finally, plan how you will take advantage of the next major bottom in the economy. Positioning your company properly at that time could ensure success for decades to come.

Chapter 31:

What You Should Do with Respect to Your Employment

Over the past decade, more and more companies have been compensating employees with stock options instead of money. In 2001, over half of America's large public companies were paying over half of their employees in stock options. As a market analyst, I am fascinated with the value of these figures as a reflection of society-wide stock-market optimism. As someone trying to help you, I see them as a trap that you should avoid.

If you have no special reason to believe that the company you work for will prosper so much in a contracting economy that its stock will rise in a bear market, then cash out any stock or stock options that your company has issued to you (or that you bought on your own).

If your remuneration is tied to the same company's fortunes in the form of stock or stock options, try to convert it to a liquid income stream. Make sure you get paid actual money for your labor.

If you have a choice of employment, try to think about which job will best weather the coming financial and economic storm. Then go get it.

If you are entrepreneurial, start thinking of ways to serve people in a depression so that you will prosper in it. For example,

I am writing this book. Think about what people will need when times get hard. Some people automatically think that providing services for strapped people is the right choice when they think "depression." Certainly, opportunities are there. At the same time, that's not where much of the money is. Many people will *not* have their assets tied up in the stock market or other risky investments, and if deflation occurs, their real purchasing power will soar. At the bottom of the Great Depression, 70 percent of the population had jobs, and they were quite well off. You can prosper by providing services to the solvent and the wealthy. Offering services to creditors may also yield steady employment. For example, because so much of today's debt is consumer debt, the repo business will probably thrive. There will also be a boom in bankruptcy services in a depression; maybe you can keep out of debt by helping others manage theirs.

If you have charitable impulses, this is the time to exercise them. Government services will shrink in a depression, and many people will be suffering. If you are *really* creative, find a way to help destitute people and make money doing so.

Unfortunately, I don't have all the answers for your situation. You know your skills and tastes better than I do. Now is the time to take account of them.

Chapter 32:

Should You Rely on Government To Protect You?

In one sense, the answer is yes. You always have to live somewhere. If you are fortunate enough to live in a safe, free country, you can probably tell that those benefits are greatly a product of its philosophy of government. To that extent, you should rely on the best government you can find. Other than that, government can be a disappointing guardian.

Compounding the Problems

Government is rarely prepared for national financial calamities or economic depressions, and when it is, they are unlikely to occur. This is not a result of personal failures so much as an aspect of collective human nature. People are often prepared for the past but rarely for the future.

Generally speaking, the intelligent way for an individual to approach the vagaries of his or her financial future is to have *savings* or buy *insurance*. Governments almost invariably do the opposite. They spend and borrow throughout the good times and find themselves strapped in bad times, when tax receipts fall. Like their counterparts around the world, the Social Security, Medicare, Medicaid and "welfare" systems in the U.S. have been dispersing billions of dollars throughout decades of mostly good times. Even today, political forces are trying to raise the government's payouts, for example to include coverage of mental as well as physical illness, which seems to be another express ticket to insolvency.

When the bust occurs, governments won't have the money required to service truly needy people in unfortunate circumstances. They are likely then to make things worse by extending "unemployment benefits," which sucks money away from employers and makes them lay off more workers, by raising the cap on retirement benefit taxes, which takes money away from employees and makes them unable to save and spend, and by increasing taxes generally, which impoverishes productive people so that they cannot spend and invest. It's sad, but the pattern is almost always the same.

Dependencies To Avoid

Don't rely on government programs for your old age. Retirement programs such as Social Security in the U.S. are wealth-transfer schemes, not funded insurance, so they rely upon the government's tax receipts. Likewise, Medicaid is a federally subsidized state-funded health insurance program, and as such, it relies upon transfers of states' tax receipts. When people's earnings collapse in a depression, so do the government's tax receipts, forcing the value of wealth transfers downward. Every conceivable method of shoring up these programs can lead only to worse problems. A "crisis" in government wealth-transfer programs is inevitable.

Don't rely on projected government budget surpluses. A couple of years ago, the U.S. government declared a budget surplus, projected it years into the future and predicted healthy trends for its wealth-transfer programs. Was that a proper conclusion? Well, in 1835, after over two decades of economic boom, U.S.

government debt became essentially fully paid off for the first (and only) time. Conventional economists would cite such an achievement as a bullish "fundamental" condition. (Any time an analyst claims to be using "fundamentals" for macroeconomic or financial forecasting, run, don't walk, to the nearest exit.) In actuality, that degree of government solvency occurred the very year of the onset of a 7-year bear market that produced two back-to-back depressions. Government surpluses generated by something other than a permanent policy of thrift are the product of exceptionally high tax receipts during boom times and therefore signal major tops. They're not bullish; they're bearish and ironically portend huge deficits directly around the corner.

Don't rely on any government's bank-deposit "insurance." The money available through the FDIC, for example, is enough to cover only a small fraction of U.S. bank deposits. As Japan's troubles increase, its government has proposed lowering the value of insured deposits; that could happen in any country. The whole idea of having other banks and taxpayers guarantee bank deposits is theft in the first place and thus morally wrong and thus ultimately practically wrong. Government sponsored deposit insurance has lulled depositors into a false sense of security. After the 1930s, when thousands of banks failed, depositors became properly wary of profligate banks. Today they don't know or care what their bank officers are doing with their money because they think that the government insures their deposits. Deposit insurance will probably save accounts in the first few distressed banks, but if there is a system-wide money and credit implosion, this insurance won't protect you.

Don't rely incautiously on government's obligations to you if you are a retired government worker. In Argentina in recent weeks, the government suspended state pension payments to 1.4 million retired state employees. It had no money to pay because times got tough, and it had never saved when times were good. The same thing could happen to many governments around the world, whether national, state or local, which pay billions of dollars annually in pensions. All of them are dependent either upon wealth transfer or upon managed funds that may or may not be properly invested.

Don't rely on all governments to pay their debts. In the 1930s, Fulton County, Georgia, where I grew up, was formed from two bankrupt counties that defaulted on their bonds. By 1938, state and local municipalities had defaulted on approximately 30 percent of the total value of their outstanding debt. Much of it was eventually resolved; some wasn't. U.S. investors today own billions of dollars worth of municipal bonds, thinking they are getting a great deal because that bond income is tax-exempt. This tax break may be a bonus in good times, but like so many seemingly great deals, this one will ultimately trap investors into a risky position. Governments that have borrowed to the hilt were running deficits even in the booming 1990s, so the risk of default in a depression is huge. If the issuers of your tax-exempt bonds default, you will have the ultimate tax haven: being broke. Quite a few munis are "insured," which salesmen will tell you means the same as "guaranteed." Such guarantees work fine until defaults drag down the insurers. That is to say, when you really need the supposed guarantees, they can fail. Given the huge extent of today's municipal indebtedness, such failures are inevitable.

Don't rely on your central bank, either. Ultimately, it is not in control of your country's stock market, bond market or interest rates. It mostly reacts to market forces. People think that the Fed "lowered interest rates" in 2001. For the most part, the *market* lowered interest rates. Declining interest rates are not a "first cause" designed to induce borrowing; rather, a dearth of borrowing is a "first cause" that makes interest rates decline. Interest rates on perceived safe debt always fall when an economy begins to deflate. So the record-breaking decline in short-term U.S. interest rates last year was not any kind of "medicine." It was not primarily *administered* but an *effect*. Japan's prime interest rate fell to nearly zero over the past decade because of its ongoing deflation. That drop in the cost of borrowing didn't change the economy. Why? Because the economy was in charge of the drop. The most that a central bank can do is distort normal market trends and make credit a bit tighter or looser than it would otherwise be. Unfortunately, every such distortion has a counterbalancing market-induced correction later. The Fed's record-breaking monetary looseness during 2001 has revived the economy and propped up asset markets for a few months, but it probably won't last much longer than that. Ultimately, it will simply serve to make the contraction worse.

Don't rely on government to bail out the banking system. When Barings Bank failed, the Bank of England declined to save Barings' depositors. The World Bank and the IMF did not bail out the banks that collapsed in Southeast Asia in 1997. The Japanese Ministry of Finance has not been bailing out troubled Japanese banks. No one is bailing out Argentina's banks today. The French government bailed out Credit Lyonnais in a series of bailouts from 1994 through 1998 that drained more than $20 billion from France's tax intake. This was not much of an exception, though, because the bank is state-owned. Financial institutions and the U.S. government, through the FSLIC and then the Resolution Trust Corporation, bailed out the Savings & Loan industry a dozen years ago to the tune of $481 billion. These were unfortunate actions. Yes, unfortunate, because they lulled French and American bank depositors, who might otherwise have become wary, into thinking that they are protected against anything. How many more bailouts can France afford? Or the U.S.? If many big banks get in trouble, prudence will dictate that even the richest governments stand aside. If instead they leap unwisely into bailout schemes, they will risk damaging the integrity of their own debt, triggering a fall in its price. Either way, again, deflation will put the brakes on their actions.

Don't expect government services to remain at their current levels. The ocean of money required to run the union-bloated, administration-stultified public school systems will be unavailable in a depression. School districts will have to adopt cost-cutting measures, and most of them will result in even worse service. Encourage low-cost free-market solutions, which will benefit both children and teachers. The tax receipts that pay for roads, police and jails, fire departments, trash pickup, emergency (911) monitoring, water systems and so on will fall to such low levels that services will be restricted. Look for ways to get better services elsewhere wherever it is legal and possible.

Don't rely on government "watchdogs." They rarely foresee disasters. U.S. regulators did not anticipate the Savings & Loan industry collapse. Subsequent investigation revealed several years of immense corruption. Enron created some 850 suspicious partnerships and employed an army of "inventive" accountants. Still, the SEC and the FASB were clueless about anything being amiss. A $68 billion company collapsed, impoverishing countless employees and creditors. Now the watchdogs in Congress are holding "hearings." Do you think this will help the employees and investors who bet the farm on Enron? Well, when the Insull utility trust similarly collapsed in 1931-1932, no investor was reimbursed a nickel; no manager ever went to jail. With 20/20 hindsight, Congress passed a few new laws.

Be smart. Don't let your financial future end up depending upon proceedings covered by C-Span.

Chapter 33:

A Short List of Imperative "Do's" and Crucial "Don'ts"

Recall the old Chinese character that entwines *crisis* and *opportunity* in the same glyph. Position yourself to take advantage of what's coming.

Don't:

- Generally speaking, don't own stocks.

- Don't own any but the most pristine bonds.

- Generally speaking, don't invest in real estate.

- Generally speaking, don't buy commodities.

- Don't invest in collectibles.

- Don't trust standard rating services.

- Don't presume that government agencies will protect your finances.

- Don't buy goods you don't need just because they are a bargain. They will probably get cheaper.

Do:

• Fight the inertia that will keep you from taking action to prepare for the downturn. Start taking steps now.

• Involve your significant others in your decisions. Put your home or business partners in tune with your thinking before it's too late.

• Talk to heavily invested parents or in-laws who may be planning to pass on their investments to you. See if you can get them to become safe and liquid.

• Think globally, not just domestically.

• Open accounts at two or three of the safest banks in the world.

• Invest in short-term money market instruments issued by the soundest governments.

• Own some physical gold, silver and platinum.

• Have some cash on hand.

• Make sure that you have insurance policies only with the safest firms and make sure that they deal only with safe banks.

• If you are so inclined, speculate conservatively in anticipation of a declining stock market.

• Sell any collectibles that you own for investment purposes.

• If it is right for your circumstances, sell your business.

• Make a list of things you want to buy at much lower prices when they go on "liquidation sale."

• If you want to have kids, hurry up. Statistics show that fewer people feel like doing so during a bear market.

• Give friends a copy of this book.

• Keep up with our *Bear Market Strategies* page, a continually updated report on-line at http://www. elliottwave.com/conquerthecrash.

• *Contact the services mentioned in this book!* I am a market analyst and forecaster, not a banker, insurer, money manager, institution rater or depression strategist. These services can help guide you through the maze. Some of them can help you design your whole strategy in a matter of days.

• Plan how to take advantage of the next major *uptrend*. For example, go back to school during the decline and come out with extra skills just as the economy begins to recover. Apprentice in a job for low pay and learn enough to start your own business at the bottom so you can ride the next big upwave of prosperity. Investigate troubled businesses to buy at the bottom at deep discounts.

• Smile! because you will not be jumping out of the window; you'll be preparing for the incredible opportunities listed in the next chapter.

Chapter 34:

What To Do at the Bottom *of a Deflationary* Crash and Depression

At the bottom of a crash and depression, reverse most of Chapter 33's investment "do's" and "don'ts." When the Elliott-wave pattern in the major stock market averages indicates that the collapse is over, take a good portion of your safely stored cash and do the following:

• Cover shorts, and buy stocks of surviving companies at fire sale prices.

• Buy depressed bonds from issuers that have survived.

• Buy more gold, silver and platinum.

• Buy prime pieces of investment property from distressed banks.

• Buy your favorite uninhabited home or mansion at pennies on the dollar.

• Buy the under-rented office building or the abandoned business facility you need for the cost of back taxes.

• Buy your favorite art and collectibles at bargain prices.

• Buy your own business back, start a business, or buy a distressed business cheap.

• Keep an eye on commodities. Generally, one would wait about two decades, when inflation begins to accelerate as the Kondratieff liquidity cycle approaches its peak, to buy them aggressively. Because a financial crisis could ignite hyperinflationary political forces at the bottom of the deflation, you might decide to buy some commodities then as a safety hedge. If the futures market survives the crash, the Rogers Raw Materials Fund should provide an excellent vehicle. It invests in an international basket of 35 commodities, continually adjusting it to maintain constant percentage weightings for each commodity. These maneuvers are a mechanical method of buying relative weakness and selling relative strength, which helps the fund's profitability. You can learn more about the fund at its website, www. rogersrawmaterials.com or by calling 800-775-9352 or 866-304-0450.

• Choose your location well and remain watchful of world affairs, because wars often break out during or shortly after depressions. (For more specifics, see Chapter 16 of *The Wave Principle of Human Social Behavior*.)

• Sit back and watch the investment markets in which you have invested turn up strongly and surprise the world.

You've survived! Now prosper!

SERVICES THAT CAN HELP YOU SURVIVE AND PROSPER IN A DEFLATIONARY DEPRESSION

A Word on Suitability

Most of the services listed in this book are suitable for all investors. Some are suited only for those of a certain level of expertise, wealth and/or income. In pursuing your chain of inquiries, you may occasionally discover some financial services that are unavailable to certain investors who fail to meet legal and financial criteria required by their nations' Accredited, Qualified and/or Professional Investor rules. These rules are intended for public protection and may prohibit your access to services not deemed suitable for you. Entities that need to comply with such rules should be able to explain which rules, if any, pertain to you. Most good service providers will try to ascertain whether their services are suitable for you and tell you honestly if they are not. As you explore and judge various courses of action, please forgive any entities that refuse to fulfill your desires because they are following legal requirements or their own stricter criteria for your protection.

I have endeavored to provide enough avenues of inquiry in this book so that readers at all strata of wealth — small to large — will find useful methods of protecting their wealth in times of deflation and depression. If you discover any that I haven't mentioned, please let me know so that I may investigate them for possible listing at our continually updated site for readers of this book at www.elliottwave.com/conquerthecrash.

We have positive information and impressions about the service providers listed in this book and believe them to have integrity. Nevertheless, we cannot endorse or guarantee other people's products or services. Therefore, it is imperative that each reader do his own proper investigation regarding suitability. I have experience with many of these service providers or know their CEOs personally. You will probably get even better service if you mention that you read about them in this book.

Consultant for Locating Top Money Managers

Asset Allocation Consultants, Ltd.
Website: www.assetallocating.com
Email: enquiries@assetallocating.com
Address: P.O. Box 613 Station "Q", Toronto, Ontario
     M4T 2N4, Canada
Phone: 800-638-5760 and 416-762-2330
Fax: 416-762-3793
CEO: Mark Edward "Ted" Workman
Minimum: $500,000

Consultants on the World's Safest Banks, Insurance Companies and Precious Metals Storage Facilities

Introductions to international wealth preservation managers, private banks, general inquiries, etc.:

SafeWealth Group — Service Center
Email: clientservices@safewealthgroup.ch
Sr. Vice President: Cari Lima
Address: Grand-Rue 114, 2nd Level East,
     CH-1820 Montreux, Switzerland
Phone: (U.S. dial 011) 41-21-966-7200
Fax: (U.S. dial 011) 41-21-966-7201
Qualified institutions' typical minimums:
     Insurance companies: 100,000 Sfr
     Precious metals storage: $100,000
     Banks: $300,000

Insurance company introductions:

SafeWealth Services SA
Email: icollis@safewealthservices.ch
President: Imogen Collis

Precious metals acquisition and storage:

> SafeStore Ltd. — Service Center
> Email: m.amos@safestoreservices.com
> President: Michael Amos

Wealth preservation private consulting:

> SafeWealth Consultants, Ltd.
> Email: clientservices@safewealthconsultants.com
> Sr. Vice President: Cari Lima

Consultants on International Diversification

> Asset Strategies International, Inc.
> Website: www.assetstrategies.com
> Email: assetsi@assetstrategies.com
> Address: 1700 Rockville Pike, #400, Rockville MD 20852
> Phone: 800-831-0007 and 301-881-8600
> Fax: 301-881-1936
> Principals: Michael Checkan and Glen Kirsch

Customized Dynamic Index Allocation

> Invesdex, Ltd
> Website: www.invesdex.com
> Email: info@invesdex.com
> Address: P.O. Box HM 1788, Hamilton HM HX,
>   Bermuda
> Phone: 441-296-4400
> Fax: 441-295-2377
> President & CEO: Valere B. Costello
> Minimum: $100,000

Inverse Index ("Short") Mutual Funds

> Bear ProFund, UltraBear, UltraShort 100
> Website: www.profunds.com

Address: ProFunds, 7501 Wisconsin Ave, Ste 1000,
Bethesda, MD 20814
Phone: 888-776-1970 or 240-497-6400
Minimum: $15,000

Ursa Fund, Arktos Fund, Tempest Fund, Venture Fund
Website: www.rydexfunds.com
Address: Rydex Series Funds, 9601 Blackwell Rd, Ste 500,
Rockville, MD 20850
Phone: 800-820-0888 and 301-296-5406
Minimum: $25,000

Managed Bear Funds

Comstock Capital Value Fund and Strategy Fund
Website: www.comstockfunds.com
Email: info@comstockfunds.com
Address: 24 S Main Street, Yardley PA 19067
Phone: 215-493-7076
Fax: 215-493-8083
Minimum: $1000
Managers: Charles Minter and Martin Weiner

Gabelli Mathers Fund
Website: www.gabelli.com/mathers.html
Email: info@gabelli.com
Address: One Corporate Center, Rye NY 10580
Phone: 800-422-3554
Minimum: $1000
Manager: Henry van der Eb

Prudent Bear Fund
Website: www.prudentbear.com
Email: info@prudentbear.com
Address: 8140 Walnut Hill Lane, Ste. 300, Dallas, TX
75231

Phone: 800-711-1848
Minimum: $2000
Manager: David Tice

Newsletters for Staying Globally Informed

Early Warning Report
Website: www.richardmaybury.com
Email: pmc701@aol.com
Address: P.O. Box 84908, Phoenix, AZ 85701
Phone: 800-509-5400 and 602-252-4477
Fax: 602-943-2363
Editor: Richard Maybury

The Gloom, Boom & Doom Report
Website: www.gloomboomdoom.com
Email: info@gloomboomdoom.com
Address: 3308 The Center, 99 Queens Rd. Central,
    Hong Kong
Phone: (U.S. dial 011) 852-2-801-5410
Fax: 852-2-845-9192
Editor: Marc Faber

Grant's Interest Rate Observer
Website: www.grantspub.com
Email: webmaster@grantspub.com
Address: 2 Wall Street, New York, NY 10005
Phone: 212-809-7994
Fax: 212-809-8426
Editor: James Grant

The International Speculator
Website: www.internationalspeculator.com
Email: info@internationalspeculator.com
Address: P.O. Box 84911, Phoenix, AZ 85071

Phone: 800-528-0559/602-252-4477
Fax: 602-943-2363
Editor: Doug Casey

The Long Wave Analyst
Email: ian_gordon@canaccord.com or
        rick_langer@canaccord.com (U.S.)
Address: Canaccord Capital, Suite 1200, 595 Burrard St.,
        Vancouver, BC, V7X 1J1 Canada
Phone: 604-643-0280 or 800-667-5771
Fax: 604-643-0152
Editor: Ian Gordon

Rosen Numismatic Advisory
Numismatic Counseling, Inc.,
Email: mauricerosen@aol.com
Address: P.O. Box 38, Plainview, NY 11803
Phone: 516-433-5800
Fax: 516-433-5801
CEO: Maurice Rosen

Safe Money Report
Website: www.safemoneyreport.com
Email: wr@weissinc.com
Address: Weiss Research, P.O. Box 31689, Palm Beach
        Gardens, FL 33420
Phone: 800-236-0407 and 561-627-3300
Fax: 561-625-6685
Editor: Martin D. Weiss

SafeWealth Report
Email: clientservices@safewealthadvisory.com
Address: SafeWealth Services SA – Service Center
        Grand-Rue 114, 2nd Level East,
        CH-1820 Montreux, Switzerland

Phone: (in U.S., dial 011) 41-21-966-7200
Fax: (in U.S., dial 011) 41-21-966-7201
Production Manager: Jane V. Scott

Physical Safety

This is a diverse field. See Chapters 26 and 28 for leads.

Portfolio Managers Who Are Not Afraid To Be Bearish

This is a large, specialized field. See Chapter 20 for leads.

Safety Ratings for U.S. Banks and Insurance Companies

IDC Financial Publishing, Inc.
Website: www.idcfp.com
Email: info@idcfp.com
Address: P.O. Box 140, Hartland, WI 53029
Phone: 800-525-5457 and 262-367-7231
Fax: 262-367-6497

Veribanc, Inc.
Website: www.veribanc.com
Email: service@veribanc.com
Address: P.O. Box 1610, Woonsocket, RI 02895
Phone: 800-837-4226 and 781-245-8370
Fax: 781-246-5291

Weiss Ratings, Inc.
Website: www.weissratings.com
Email: wr@weissinc.com
Address: P.O. Box 31689, Palm Beach Gardens,
          FL 33420
Phone: 800-289-9222 and 561-627-3300
Fax: 561-625-6685

U.S. Gold, Silver and Coin Dealers

American Federal Rare Coin & Bullion
Website: americanfederal.com
Email: info@americanfederal.com
Address: 14602 North Cave Creek Rd., Ste. C, Phoenix,
AZ 85022
Phone: 1-800-221-7694 or 602-992-6857
Fax: 602-493-8158
CEO: Nick Grovich

Fidelitrade
Website: www.fidelitrade.com
Email: info@fidelitrade.com
Address: 3601 North Market Street, Wilmington, DE
19802
Phone: 800-223-1080 and 302-762-6200
Fax: 302-762-2902
CEO: Mike Clark

Hancock & Harwell
Website: www.raregold.com
Email: info@raregold.com
Address: Suite 310, 3155 Roswell Rd, Atlanta, GA 30305
Phone: 888-877-1782 and 404-261-6566
Fax: 404-237-6500
CEO: Robert L. Harwell

Investment Rarities, Inc.
Website: www.investmentrarities.com
Email: jcook@investmentrarities.com
Address: 7850 Metro Parkway, Ste 213, Minneapolis, MN
55425-1521
Phone: 800-328-1860 and 612-853-0700
CEO: James R. Cook

Miles Franklin Ltd.
Website: www.milesfranklin.com
Email address: milesf@ix.netcom.com
Address: 3601 Park Center Building, Suite 120, St. Louis
        Park, MN 55416
Phone: 800-822-8080 and 952-929-7006
Fax: 952-925-0143
CEO: David M. Schectman

Straight Talk Assets, Inc.
Website: www.coinmoney.com
Email: straighttalk@mindspring.com
Address: P.O. Box 1301, Gainesville, GA 30503
Phone: 800-944-9249 and 770-536-8045
CEO: Glenn R. Fried

Watching the Fed

Federal Reserve Board
Website: www.federalreserve.gov
Phone: 202-452-3819

Ludwig von Mises Institute
Website: www.mises.org
Email: contact@mises.org
Address: 518 West Magnolia Avenue, Auburn, AL 36832
Phone: 334-321-2100
Fax: 334-321-2119
Book catalog: www.mises.org/product.asp?

The Money Market Observer
Wrightson Associates
Website: www.wrightson.com
Email: sales@wrightson.com
Address: Harborside Financial Center, Plaza V
        Jersey City NJ 07311

Phone: 212-815-6540
Fax: 212-341-9253
Editor: Lou Crandall

TrimTabs.com Investment Research
Website: www.trimtabs.com
Email: info@trimtabs.com
Address: 520 Mendocino Avenue, Suite 350,
Santa Rosa, CA 95401
Phone: 707-874-9546
Fax: 707-525-1011
Director: Michael Alexander
Editor: Charles Biderman

Wave Analysis, Economic Forecasting and Investment Recommendations

Elliott Wave International, Inc.
Website: www.elliottwave.com
Email: customerservice@elliottwave.com
Address: P.O. Box 1618, Gainesville, GA 30503
Phone: 800-336-1618 and 770-536-0309
Fax: 770-536-2514
Paid services: Books, financial periodicals, intensive
market coverage, flash alerts; European, Asian and
North American market coverage
Free services: Market Watch, Market Report, Club EWI,
Big Bear Cafe
Only for readers of this book: Continual free updates on
services that can protect you and your finances:
www.elliottwave.com/conquerthecrash
CEO: Robert R. Prechter, Jr.

Special Arrangements

Asset Allocation Consultants, Ltd. (www.assetallocating. com) gives away a free copy of *At the Crest of the Tidal Wave* with each consulting application. The firm buys the books from my publisher, so it's fine with me.

Lang Asset Management, Inc. (404-256-4100) offers *At the Crest of the Tidal Wave* for 50 percent off to anyone submitting an inquiry.

If you identify yourself as an EWI customer or a purchaser of this book, you can get SafeWealth Group's 39-page report, *Asset Survival in a Depression* (or a later title, depending upon timeliness) plus a full year of *The SafeWealth Report* for $299, well below the normal price of $450. To order, call Elliott Wave International at 800-336-1618 or 770-536-0309 or visit www.elliottwave.com/ specialoffer/swr.

Along with free updates to the preceding list of services, readers of this book can get special package prices on *The Elliott Wave Theorist*, *The Elliott Wave Financial Forecast* and our main book titles, including *Elliott Wave Principle*, *At the Crest of the Tidal Wave* and *The Wave Principle of Human Social Behavior* at www.elliottwave.com/conquerthecrash.

New for the second edition: In April 2002, world-famous author Tony Robbins read both *Conquer the Crash* and *The Wave Principle of Human Social Behavior* and absorbed the ideas in record time. On May 13, he interviewed me at my home about the markets, the economy and socionomics for his Powertalk series. This fun, intense three-hour discussion covers a wide scope and includes various nuances about coming events. If you would like to participate in that living-room experience, you can obtain the 3-CD audio set for a very reasonable $19.95 at the following web address: http://www.anthonyrobbins.com/prechter. Or order from Anthony Robbins Companies, 9888 Carroll Centre Rd., Ste 100, San Diego, CA 92126. Phone: 800-800-9639 or 858-535-6290.

New for the second edition: Readers of this book can purchase SafeWealth Group's three multi-page reports assessing the stock market crises and developing depressions in the **U.K.**, **Germany** and **Canada**. You may get each report for $49. Call Elliott Wave International at 800-336-1618 or 770-536-0309 or visit www.elliottwave.com/specialoffers/swg.

SUPPLEMENT FOR *2004*

A Year After Publication, Prechter's Batting Close to 1.000

"Well, it's been a year since the book came out. The S&P YTD is flat, even with its recent war rally, and it's down 20%+ for the past 52 weeks. We have a war on our hands, the public is hotly divided politically, and protestors are in the streets (I'm writing this from San Francisco's financial district). The Federal Reserve is just about out of options (despite Alan's claims to the contrary). Every day, it seems, *The Wall Street Journal* and *The New York Times* carry economic and business news that confirm many of his forecasts. So, if Prechter's not quite batting 1.000, he's still knocking an awful lot of pitches out of the park."

Supplement for 2004

In the year following the completion of *Conquer the Crash*, stock markets around the world fell precipitously. In the past six months, the stock market rebound has convinced most observers that a new bull market is underway and that an economic boom is resuming. Therefore, now seems like a good time to review the case presented in *Conquer the Crash* to see if it remains valid. In preparation for the coming year, this analysis was conducted in the late summer and early fall of 2003. All charts in this Supplement are completed with data available as of the first week of October, 2003.

UPDATE ON THE ECONOMY

On July 17, 2003, the National Bureau of Economic Research announced its decision that the economic recession that began in March 2001 ended in November 2001. That's fine, if one desires to fit definitions of recession into rigid quantitative nooks, but it's not the important story. To understand what is going on, please review "Hierarchy in Finance and Economics" on page 20, Figure 3-9 on page 30 and "Implications for the Economy" on pages 82-83 of this book. The points to glean from these discussions are: (1) economic trends are a result of social mood trends, and (2) *Elliott wave hierarchy governs the vigor of economic expansions and contractions.* All the evidence in Chapter 1 speaks to these points, and now we have more.

Figures A-1 through A-4 show how the first year and a half of the latest officially recognized recovery has fared relative to prior recoveries. The post-recession expansions from the 1940s through the 1980s (i.e., within wave III, IV and early in wave V; see Figure 1-2 for orientation) were very strong (see top line in each graph below). That attending wave ⑤ after 1991 was weaker (middle line), and the latest one, which is just a temporary respite within a Grand Supercycle bear market, is the weakest (lower

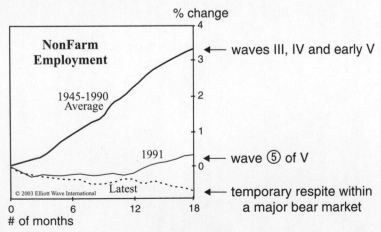

Figure A-1

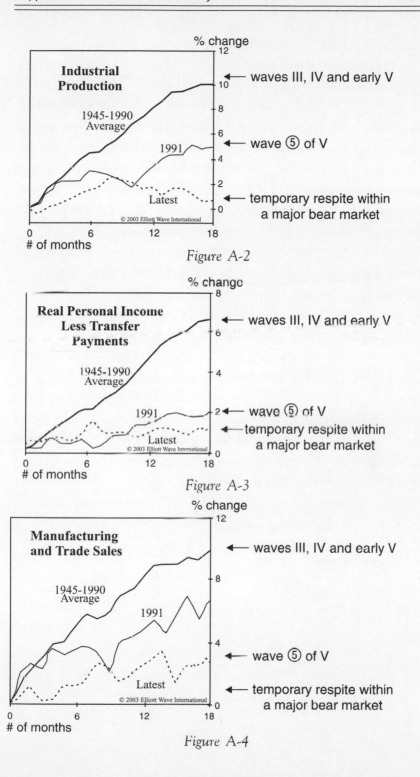

Figure A-2

Figure A-3

Figure A-4

line). *These are precisely the relationships of economic relative strength that Elliott waves imply and produce,* and they continue to unfold right before our eyes.

Even some of these weak statistics are probably overstated. Nearly half of recent GDP gains are due to defense spending related to the Iraq War. That is not production but its opposite: the destruction of resources. There is also the matter of so-called "hedonic" indexing, by which the government adjusts GDP upward when the quality of a product class (such as the speed of computer chips) improves. This practice makes GDP appear dramatically higher than it is. For example, since 1997, the government used hedonic indexing to add $130 billion to GDP in phony computer sales alone. One wonders if there has really been much of a recovery at all. Statistics such as job losses (see Figure A-1) cannot be adjusted and are probably truer gauges of the economy.

Apparently the wave progression in this bear market is along the lines of 1835-1842 in the U.S. and post-1990 in Japan, in which (per page 83) "the economy contracted over a longer period in two or more steps, with recoveries in between." Figures A-1 through A-4 are fully in line with our forecast, so the economic analysis of Chapters 1 and 8 remains on target. Although the NBER and most economists declare the contraction of 2001 "one of the shortest recessions on record," it's not a recession. It's part of a deflationary depression that is just getting started.

UPDATE ON THE STOCK MARKET

It has been 18 months since the first quarter of 2002, when *Conquer the Crash* applied market analysis to the question of the future course of the stock market. From peaks in the spring of that year, U.S. stock market averages, including those that made all-time highs in April 2002, fell an average 30 percent into early October 2002. Since then, the averages have rallied (so far) for a full year, and the Dow, which had fallen to 7200, is back to 9600. The rest of the world's major stock markets continued on to new lows in March 2003 but have rebounded since. The overwhelming consensus is that stocks have embarked upon a new bull market. Did the original analysis way overestimate the extent of the anticipated decline? In other words, *is the bear market already over?* The way to answer that question is to update all the key indicators presented in Chapters 4, 6 and 7.

Valuation Analysis

From their all-time highs in 2000, U.S. stocks fell on average *fifty percent*, as measured by the S&P Composite and Wilshire 5000 indexes. That is a long way down. Surely with a decline that big, stocks returned to a level at which they provide "good values," right?

Wrong. By every measure, stocks are still more expensive than they were at every major market top of the 20th century, including 1929. That's *top*, not bottom. With respect to past bottoms, stocks are still outrageously overpriced.

Dividend Yield

Figure A-5 updates Figure 6-1. The decline of 2002 and subsequent rebound have put the DJIA's annual dividend yield at 2.1 percent, still less than it was at the top minute in 1929. Most investors still don't care about yield. They remain convinced that

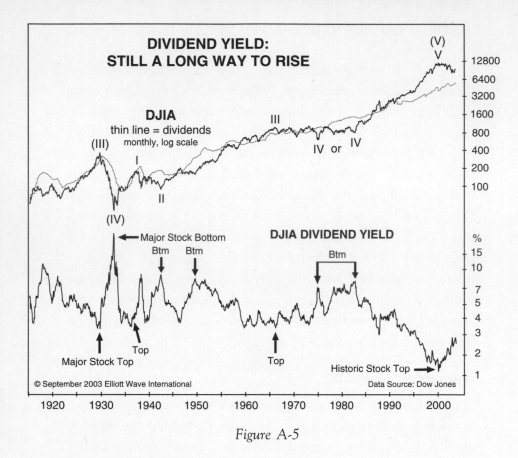

Figure A-5

their profits will come from capital gains in the new bull market, so who needs dividends?

In the late 1990s, it was popular to argue that low dividends were excusable because companies were presumably plowing profits back into the company to create growth. Today, it is popular to argue that low dividends still don't matter because interest rates in the money market have fallen so far that even low dividends are fairly attractive on a *relative* basis. But the interest rate cycle exquisitely fools investors. In 1980-81, interest rates were 16 percent, and few wanted to trade their high-yielding Treasury bills for stocks. That was a great time to buy stocks. Now that rates are down to one percent on federal funds, few want to trade their stocks for low-yielding Treasury bills. It is, naturally, a good time to sell stocks.

If history is a guide, the increasing fear behind a bear market will eventually make investors demand higher dividend income. The yield on the Dow should at least triple from today's level and will probably reach percentages in double digits before the bear market is over. In fact, as outrageous as it sounds, given that this bear market is one degree larger than that of 1929-1932, the annual dividend yield should at some point exceed that of the 1932 low, which was 17 percent.

Price-Earnings Ratio

The P/E ratio on the overall S&P index has receded, from 50 to 30. Has this adjustment provided bargains? The *highest* readings of the 20th century, at market *tops*, occurred in the upper 20s. At bottoms, it was around 7. The P/E ratio today is not bullish. Figure A-6 updates Figure 6-4. As you can see, the P/E ratio still has a long way down to go.

Many people say that the historically high P/E ratio looks reasonable when "E" is adjusted to account for *expected* earnings rather than having it express *actual* recent earnings. Of course it does! P/E ratios become extreme precisely because people think that "E" is going to rise or fall a lot, so they price stocks accordingly. At those wonderful buying opportunities of 1942, 1949 and 1982, actual P/E ratios hit new lows because analysts and investors expected a big economic contraction, which would have made earnings fall substantially. At those times, the low P/E looked reasonable because investors were sure that E would fall, meaning that their *expected* P/E was double or triple what the actual P/E was. But they were wrong. The very fact that so many analysts projected E much lower was an indication that they were extremely pessimistic, which is a sign of a bottom, not a top. We hear the same argument today, in reverse. Analysts and investors currently project E much higher because they expect (despite nearly two

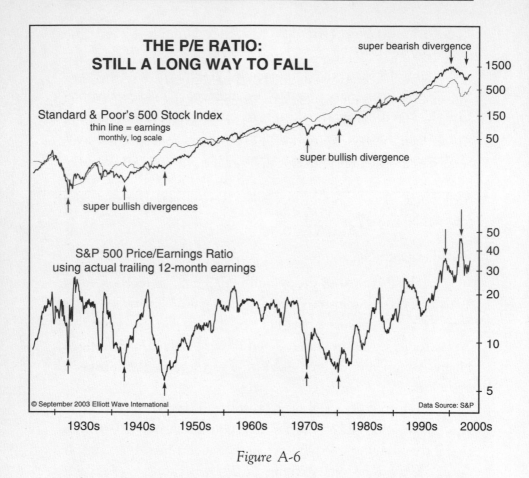

Figure A-6

years of extreme sluggishness for a supposed recovery) a big economic expansion, which would make earnings rise substantially. So, in their minds, the *expected* P/E is half of what the actual P/E currently is, making it "not really so bad." But the very fact that so many analysts project E much higher is an indication that they are extremely optimistic, which is the sign of a top, not a bottom. When stocks fall again, E is going to *contract*, not expand.

The implications of the rare trend-continuation signal described for the P/E ratio in Chapter 6 have nowhere near played out. If history is a guide, P/E — real P/E — will be in single digits before the bear market is over. Again, given the degree of the decline, the P/E ratio should fall below 6 sometime in coming decades.

Book Value and Bond Yield/Stock Yield

Figure A-7 updates Figure 6-3. This graph needs little elaboration. The price/book value and bond yield/stock yield ratios have indeed been on their way back to lower levels since their all-time highs in March 2000. Their retrenchment has brought them from the outskirts of the solar system near Pluto to approximately Jupiter. The crew members on this flight still have many packages of

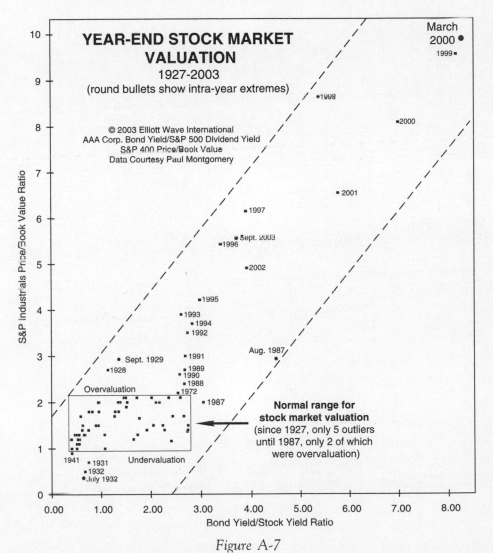

Figure A-7

dried soup and jars of Tang to tide them through the long remain-
der of their journey. As stated in Chapter 6, "if investors follow
their usual pattern, the decline will not end until there is at least
one bullet below and/or to the left of the box." That means a drop
to 1/3 of current levels, horizontally, vertically or both. In fact,
wave degree portends a record undervaluation, probably on both
measures, before the bear market is over.

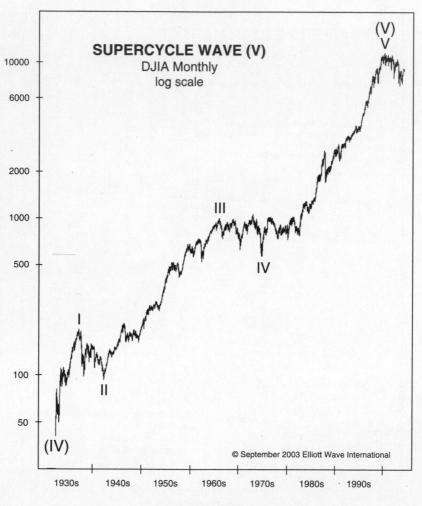

Figure A-8

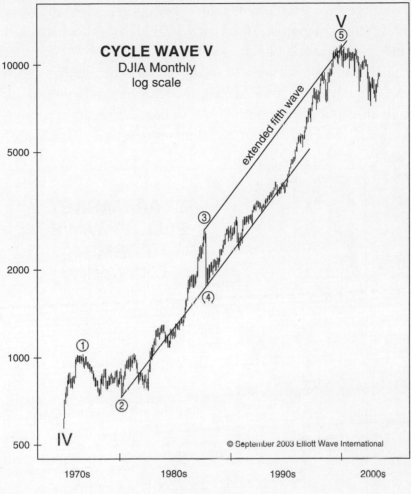

CYCLE WAVE V
DJIA Monthly
log scale

extended fifth wave

© September 2003 Elliott Wave International

Figure A-9

Elliott Wave Analysis

Was the bear market from early 2000 to late 2002 merely a high-level consolidation that will lead to new highs? Most people think so. Figures A-8 and A-9 update Figures 4-2 and 4-3.

Take a look at Figure 4-6 again and recall 9/11/2001, when the market was closed and the world was in panic, yet the Elliott wave form nevertheless portended an upside reversal. The projection called for the largest bear-market rally since the peak, which

in Elliott wave terms meant a three-step advance that would par-
tially retrace the decline from early 2001. That's what happened,
and then the market fell to new lows.

Examine the updated weekly graph of the DJIA in Figure
A-10 from mid-2001 to the present. You can see the big A-B-C
rally that took place following EWT's bullish forecast of September 2001. Now look at the formation from the top in March 2002,

Figure A-10

the time when *Conquer the Crash* was finished, to now. The Dow once again fell in *five* waves, and from the October low through today, the market has advanced in *three* waves. Study the right-hand side of Figure 3-1, and you will see that this is the form of a counter-trend movement, which in turn indicates that the larger trend remains down. Though the rally could travel a bit further, it has retraced 70 percent of the preceding decline, which is quite substantial for this stage in the wave structure. If this labeling is correct, the market is right back where it was in the "You Are Here" schematic in Figure 4-7 but at one smaller degree and further along the major downtrend.

Why does the market keep rallying on its way down? That's the nature of a fractal form; markets don't move in a straight line. Figure A-11 shows the DJIA from April 1930 to July 1932. When we step back from the graph after it is concluded, we see just one big, swift drop. In fact, there were many rallies, and each of them convinced many investors that the downtrend had ended. As historian John Brooks described the collapse,

> "[It] came with a kind of surrealistic slowness...so gradually that, on the one hand, it was possible to live through a good part of it without realizing that it was happening, and, on the other hand, it was possible to believe one had experienced and survived it when in fact it had no more than just begun."[18]

But as Yogi Berra might have said, "It wasn't over 'til it was over." The percentage gains of the Dow's rallies of the past three years are in the same ballpark as those in 1930-1932. The current bear market is of one larger degree than that of 1929-1932, so they are taking longer, but the fractal dynamics are the same.

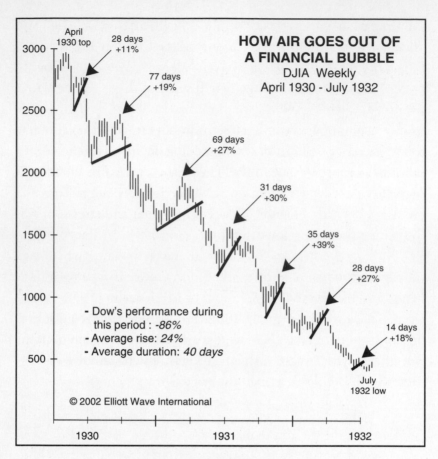

Figure A-11

Historically Optimistic Psychology — Again

Aside from the old canards about stocks being "underval-
ued" and always going up "long term," today we hear of a four-year
cycle bottom, a favorable presidential election cycle, that stocks
never fall more than three years in a row, and that they never fall
more than 50 percent in a bear market. All of these arguments
translate into the same old message: "Buy more and hold." It is
amazing, yet it can be no other way: Optimism today is as extreme
as it was in the first quarter of 2000, the first quarter of 2001 and

the first quarter of 2002. (See Chapter 7 for a recap of those times.) Here in early October 2003, investors and professionals of all types remain near the apex of the Slope of Hope.

Psychology of Economists

You might think that the bear market, the recession and the weak economic recovery would have impacted the aggregate opinion of economists by now. They haven't. In *The Wall Street Journal*'s mid-year 2003 survey of 54 economists, *not a single one* predicts that the economy will contract over the course of the next 6 to 12 months! The consensus is virtually identical to those that the WSJ has recorded at half-year intervals since the start of 2001, right before what the National Bureau of Economic Research later identified as the start of the last contraction. Economists polled project an average growth rate of 3.5% through the second quarter of next year. The Journal points out that this figure is no coincidence, as 3.5% is the average GDP growth rate since 1930. "Economists call it the long-run growth trend, and they believe that is what economic growth will revert to," reports *The Wall Street Journal*. As explained in *The Wave Principle of Human Social Behavior*, this is the same style of lagged linear projection in which conventional economists always engage. The economic growth rate from 1933 to 2001 (lagged one year from the stock market) generated by the Supercycle degree uptrend is one thing, and the growth rate (actually contraction rate!) from there forward will prove to be another. The market will not be near a bottom until the majority of economists becomes pessimistic.

Psychology of Money Managers

Money managers are also as bullish as ever. Figure A-12 updates Figure 7-3. As you can see, stock mutual funds today hold just 4.5 percent of their total holdings in cash. This is very near the level it was in the first quarter of 2000, at the all-time high in

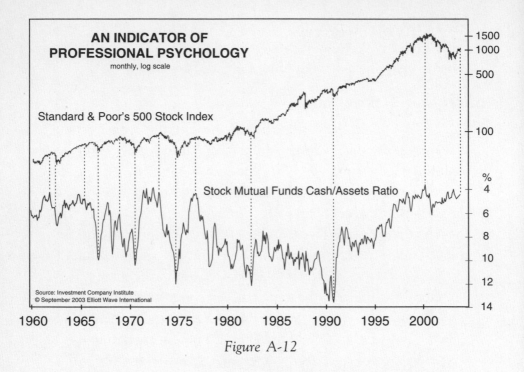

Figure A-12

the stock market. Money managers are convinced that October 2002 marked the start of a great new bull market, and they are invested up to their eyeballs to take advantage of the gains that are sure to come. The problem is that when cash levels are this low, there is little fuel left for buying. The optimism that such levels reflect is indicative of another rally *top*, not a bear market bottom.

Psychology of Brokerage Firm Analysts and Other Wall Street Strategists

The bear market has hardly fazed brokerage firm analysts. Figure A-13 updates Figure 7-1. As you can see, brokers still recommend that you keep 66 percent of your entire investment portfolio in stocks. This ratio will surely fall to new lows for its history before the bear market is over.

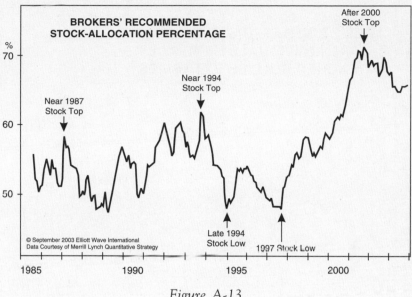

Figure A-13

Ned Davis Research surveys Wall Street strategists of all types. In recent months, strategists in the aggregate have been more bullish than at any time in the 17-year history of the data. (See the top graph in Figure A-14.) This fact is bearish, because it reflects a strong consensus of optimism, which is a characteristic of major market tops.

Psychology of Advisors

According to data from Investors Intelligence, independent newsletter writers are expressing their most bullish attitudes in at least 16 years. Consider: In the history of advisor polling, every major stock market bottom has followed 30 to 40 straight weeks during which there were more bears than bulls. For the past 50 straight weeks — nearly a year — there have been *more bulls than bears*. (See the middle graph in Figure A-14.) For 22 straight weeks, there have been more than *twice* as many bulls as

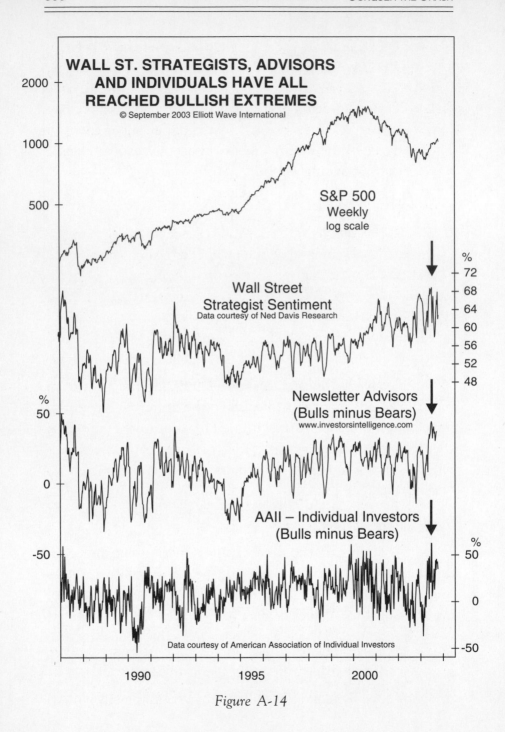

Figure A-14

bears, and for four out of the past five weeks, there have been an amazing *three times* as many bulls as bears! This is both a longer period of time and a greater disparity than existed at the all-time high in 2000. Considered relative to the stock market's moderate performance in the current rally, these readings are unprecedented. The potential for the stock market to disappoint expectations is therefore correspondingly large.

Psychology of the Public

The latest polls by the American Association of Individual Investors (AAII) shows that the public has again become convinced that the old bull market is back. In recent weeks, the bulls-minus-bears percentage among individual investors reached its highest level in the 16-year history of the survey, surpassing readings at previous market tops, including 1987 and 2000. (See the bottom graph in Figure A-14.) The public is typically skeptical that a new bull market has started when one actually has, but it is common for the majority to believe in a new bull market near the top of a bear-market rally.

The Media

Are the media pessimistic, as they have been at every major stock-market bottom in history? Read the evidence for yourself in the collage on the following pages.

The Smart Guys

Figure 7-7 showed that in 2001-2002, market professionals called "commercials" — the smart players — were short a record number of S&P futures contracts, and small traders — the naïve players — were long a record number. This is a classic situation early in a bear market. Given the dramatic drop in stock prices in 2002, it is clear which group made money (again) and which one

Brave Investors See Optimism Rewarded

—*USA TODAY*, July 1, 2003

Dow 20,000

Futurist Peter Schwartz takes a long view in predicting the coming "Long Boom."
— Forbes.com, July 21, 2003

Rising Hopes Worldwide Lift Markets; Growing faith that business activity will pick up fuels rally

—*Los Angeles Times*, July 8, 2003

Ready for liftoff?
The strongest three-month stretch since 1999 has the economy, and investors, straining skyward.
—*Christian Science Monitor*, July 7, 2003

A Real Recovery Is Coming Into View

Economists we surveyed were nearly unanimous. Count on a bounce.
—*BusinessWeek*, June 30, 2003

O.K., it's not 1999—buttech analysts are more bullish than they've been in years.
—*BusinessWeek*, June 30, 2003

'Economy 'aligned for a takeoff,' says Treasury chief
—*USA TODAY*, July 10, 2003

The 2003-2009 Bull Market Is Underway
—*The Bull & Bear Financial Report, June–July 2003*

The Market Looks Headed For Its First Winning Year Since 1999

—*Business Week*
June 30, 2003

MINISTERS ANTICIPATE GLOBAL UPTURN
—*Business Times, July 7, 2003*

BARRON'S
THE DOW JONES BUSINESS AND FINANCIAL WEEKLY   www.barrons.com   JUNE 16, 2003 $3.50

BULL RUN!

This rally is for real. Even if a summer lull sets in, stocks are likely to be 10% higher by year end. Credit rock-bottom interest rates, rising corporate profits and favorable tax policies.

Bulls back on Wall St.
—*San Francisco Chronicle*, July 1, 2003

The underlying fundamentals of this economy... offer the promise not only of a strong rebound, but also of a new era of economic growth ovation.
— *USA TODAY*,
July 15, 2003

Market's Sound Footing Inspires Confidence
—*The Washington Post, July 6, 2003*

Small Investors, Once Burned, Lead New Bull
—*The New York Times, June 22, 2003*

Top 10 Reasons to Be Bullish Again
—*NY Post, June 22, 2003*

By broad yardstick, stocks are a good buy
—*Chicago Sun Times*, July 7, 2003

10 Signs this Rally may be for Real —
Many analysts say latest rise is different
—*USA TODAY*, June 5, 2003

Stock Investors See Green In New Bull Market

—*Knight Ridder Tribune*, June 12, 2003

Optimism for Markets, Growth
—The Washington Post
August 24, 2003

Say Bye-Bye to the Bear.
—Louis Rukeyser's Wall Street
September 2003

Stock Market Is On Track for Year of Growth, Experts Predict
—Knight Ridder Tribune
September 2, 2003

WHY TECH WILL BLOOM AGAIN
—Business Week
August 25, 2003

Invest NOW

It's time to catch the next wave—the smart, safe way.
—Reader's Digest August 2003

Recovery On Track
The prevailing mood among economists has turned the most optimistic it has been in some time.
—USA Today
August 21, 2003

GET BACK IN
—Money, August 2003

Economic Strategist Sees Stocks Climbing Higher
—Knight Ridder Tribune, September 17, 2003

FINALLY, AN ECONOMY FIRING ON ALL CYLINDERS LOOK FOR A DOUBLE-DIGIT TURNAROUND
—Business Week, September 15, 2003

Global Economics Look Up
— The Wall Street Journal
August 12, 2003

The Bush Boom
"Virtually every sector of the economy is booming today, especially high-tech. Weak job growth is an anomaly and cannot last."
—The Wall Street Journal, September 15, 2003

IPO Market Picks Up Steam
—Knight Ridder Tribune Business News
August 26, 2003

Gaining Steam: This bull market is for real
—On Wall Street, September 1, 2003

September 2003

"We've just had one of the most impressive rallies of the past 50 years. Such strength almost never occurs on the eve of a major relapse." —Barron's
August 6, 2003

Consumers Predict Brighter Future
—Knight Ridder Tribune
August 27, 2003

Growth Bulls on Rampage
—Businessline
August 4, 2003

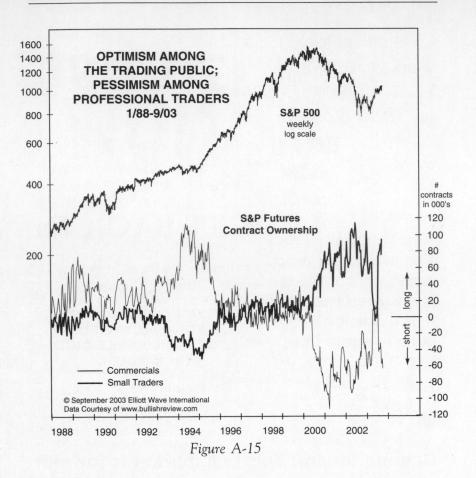

Figure A-15

lost. As you can see in Figure A-15, the recent rally has reinstated
a significant split between these two groups, as the commercials
are again betting on the downside, the public on the upside.

Another interesting statistic at this juncture is the report
that corporate insiders are dumping stock at a ratio of 36-to-1,
which is nearly *double* the rate that has occurred at major tops in
recent decades. These people are the closest to their own companies and can see how they're doing up close, and *they don't want to
hold their own shares at today's prices*. Economists want stocks, money
managers want stocks, Wall Street strategists want stocks, advisors want stocks, the public wants stocks, brokers want you to buy
stocks, and the media love stocks. But the commercials and insid-

ers are selling their heads off. Who do you think is likely to be making the right decision? That's the side that readers of *Conquer the Crash* are on.

I have avoided showing any indicators from the "momentum" class other than the advance/decline line of Figure 5-1. Generally speaking, they are more complex to interpret and less reliable than extreme readings in sentiment indicators, and this book is not intended as a comprehensive treatise on market analysis. The Volatility Index, however, has just matched low levels registered in March 2002, when *Conquer the Crash* was finished, and September 2000, when the S&P tested its all-time high. (See Figure A-16.) Low volatility indicates market complacency, which is exactly what the sentiment indicators currently reveal.

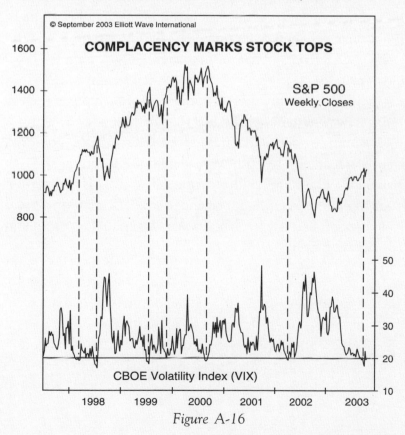

Figure A-16

Summary

Ongoing Elliott-wave analysis continues to indicate that the bear market is *not* over. The positions of the valuation and psychological indicators show that in fact, it is a *long way* from being over. For those who are positioned on the short side, the greatest opportunities are surely yet to come.

It is highly significant that several of the psychological indicators reveal more bullishness now than in April 2002, when the S&P 600 Small-Cap index made its all-time high (see Figure 4-8 for the picture through March), more than in 1Q 2000, when the Dow and S&P topped, the NASDAQ index breached 5000 in a blizzard of ticker tape, and the Internet stock mania was at its zenith, and more than in April 1998, when the advance-decline line topped out and the average stock made its all-time high. Similar degrees of bullish sentiment are reported from around the world. The extremity of optimism today recalls major intra-bear-market peaks such as those of April 1930, December 1968 and January 1973. Stock investors are once again caught up in the Big Dream. The persistent optimism of the past five years constitutes overwhelming evidence that it is indeed early within a prolonged global bear market. This string of readings reflects the antithesis of a bear-market bottom; it reflects a *top*. Given that it is occurring within a bear-market rally, it portends a *crash*. Every warning and recommendation made in *Conquer the Crash* remains proper and as pertinent as ever.

UPDATE ON OTHER MARKETS

Although real estate values in some areas (such as north Georgia, where I live) topped along with the stock market in 2000, the historically rapid decline in interest rates of 2001-2003 prolonged the housing boom in many areas. The fall in mortgage rates has prompted many people to purchase new homes and existing homeowners to borrow more on the value of their property. Normally, real estate prices peak about two years after stocks at a major top, but at this major top, it has taken more than three years. Housing is about the only sector holding up aggregate economic figures, and the borrowing binge that has supported it appears exhausted. As house prices and homebuilding turn down, the overall economy will accelerate downward. Like the stock market, real estate still has all the earmarks of a major *top*, not a bottom.

Treasury bonds have continued to follow the cycle shown in Figure 12-2 to a "T," as their rates have fallen to 4.2%. Figure A-17 shows an update. I nevertheless caution that continued

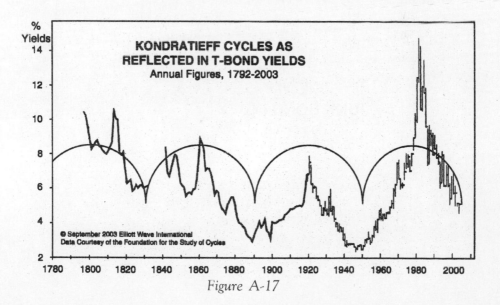

Figure A-17

stability in this sector is hardly assured, as Figure A-14 does not
include any bear markets of Grand Supercycle degree such as is
underway now. That's why my recommendation for capital
preservation is for safe *short-term* cash equivalents.

The widespread confidence that an economic expansion
is underway has also prompted another bounce in junk bonds.
This is wave (4) in the ongoing Elliott wave featured in Figure
15-4, as shown in Figure A-18. For anyone who got talked into
buying these issues any time in the past 15 years, this is another
belated opportunity to get out.

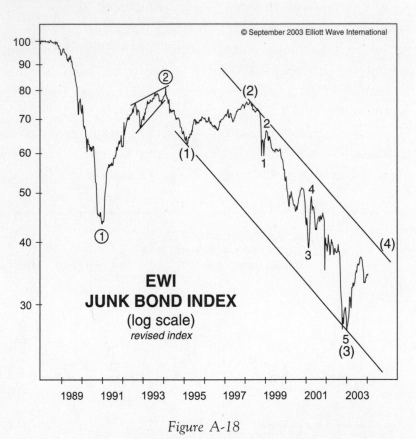

Figure A-18

Commodities continued their rally from 2001, following the curve shown in Figure 21-10 and updated in Figure A-19. The rally has probably ended. That curve is poised to turn down again, for both commodities and the stock market. At this juncture, then, all major markets — stocks, real estate, commodities and many bonds — are on the brink of responding jointly to deflationary forces. The "collapse" portion of the monetary cycle appears to lie directly ahead.

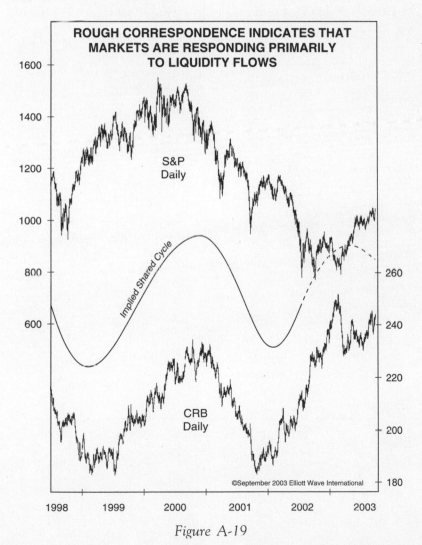

Figure A-19

Gold and silver are likewise holding near their highs for the past four years. Yet the wave pattern from the 1999 low appears corrective. Moreover, the substantial optimism toward gold and silver as well as a record disparity between the long speculators and the short commercials in gold futures argue in favor of the case that the precious metals have another phase of price weakness ahead. Therefore, the commentary on gold and silver in Chapter 22 remains applicable. If you are interested in the details of wave structure and price outlook, please request recent issues of *The Elliott Wave Theorist*.

UPDATE ON THE OUTLOOK FOR DEFLATION

Way back in November 1979, inflation was raging and precious metals were two months from their peaks in an explosive ten-year rise. That's when *The Elliott Wave Theorist* forecasted a dramatic shift in the monetary trend. It also outlined a scenario for the approaching second half of the monetary cycle that began in the 1940s. Here is the commentary from that time:

> The evidence I have available argues persuasively that at the very least we are reaching an interim peak in the inflationary spiral. Elliott counts suggest important tops in silver, gold, the commodity market indexes and short term interest rates.
>
> The incredible conjunction of "fives" in different markets all seem to point to the same conclusion: *The world is about to begin a phase of general disinflation.* **As I see it, a pattern of several disinflationary years leading to a deflationary trend later on would be a perfect scenario for the Elliott outlook for stocks. A gradual disinflation would create an optimistic mood in the country and lead to the conclusion that we may have finally licked the inflation problem. This sentiment would support a bull market in stocks for several years until the snowballing forces of deflation began to take over. At that point, a major deflationary crash would be impossible to avert, and the Grand Supercycle correction would be underway.**
>
> — *The Elliott Wave Theorist*, Special Report,
> "Commodities, Interest Rates and Inflation: A Major Top?"
> November 18, 1979

While the process took longer than originally expected, its trajectory was never in doubt. As the end of wave V in the Dow approached, Elliott Wave International publicly sounded the alarm for the final phase of the scenario:

"The true threat today is not inflation but deflation."

— *At the Crest of the Tidal Wave*, 1995, p.259

"The groundwork for a deflationary spiral is in place. In the not so distant future, we will be hearing about these less glamorous aspects of the deflationary cycle."

— *The Elliott Wave Financial Forecast*, February 2000

"The deflationary potential is historically large. [W]e risk overwhelming deflation in every corner of the globe."

— *Conquer the Crash*, March 2002

As investors of the time will recall, the general conviction in 1979-1980 was that inflation would endlessly accelerate. Wave analysis indicated an approaching *disinflation*. When stocks turned down in 2000, wave analysis signaled *deflation*. Figure A-20 shows

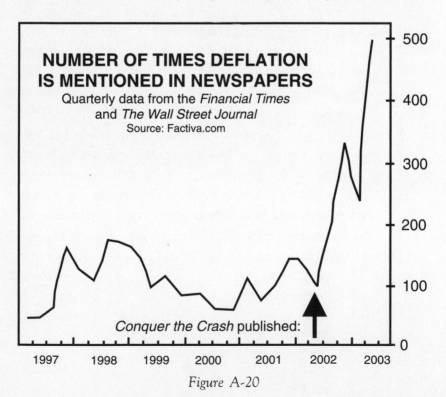

Figure A-20

that a general unconcern over prospects for deflation extended right up to the publication of *Conquer the Crash*.

What a difference a year makes. The term that was hardly given the respect of a hearing has since broken into the general consciousness, as the rarely used word *deflation* has become fashionable in financial discussion. It is fashionable, however, not to predict its occurrence but primarily to *dismiss* the idea that it has any serious likelihood of occurring. The president of the Federal Reserve Bank of Dallas said in May that there is "maybe one chance out of four"[1] that deflation will occur. This comment may sound simply like another dismissal of the risk, but careful perusal of news articles shows that the odds offered by those willing to express them are down from "1 in 10,000" back in the mid-1990s (when the global rate of inflation peaked) to "at most 1 in 50" from 2001 (see quotes in Chapter 13) to "1 in 4" now. This progression is highly instructive as to how conventional economists' opinions lag trends. The latest statement of odds came after a report that the Producer Price index for April fell 1.9 percent, which "was far larger than economists predicted."[2] Here are some more quotes, mostly from the past four months:

> "Not one economist [of 67 surveyed] said it was 'very likely' the economy would slip into deflation, and only 6% said it was 'somewhat likely.' About 95% said deflation was "not very likely" to happen."[3]

> "Fed policy-makers have mounted a virtuoso performance over the past six weeks to influence financial markets without even cutting rates. That should allay any worries that the Fed is in danger of running out of ammunition to stimulate the economy with interest rates already so low."[4]

> "The whole deflation story has been over-hyped...the economy does not lack for monetary fuel. Once money starts circulating through the economy at a more normal pace, the central bank won't be worrying about deflation."[5]

"The United States has too many good things going for it to make a forecast of deflation credible." "I don't believe that the United States is at the brink of significant and sustained deflation."[6]

"It is most unlikely that any future deflation will be as long or severe as it was in the Depression…. The Fed can conduct heterodox monetary policy, expanding the money supply by buying such things as long-term bonds. And ultimately, such a policy will stop the deflation."[7]

"In remarks broadcast to bankers in Berlin, Greenspan characterized the probability of crippling deflation as 'low'…. [He] said policymakers were…willing to 'lean over backwards' to contain deflationary forces."[8]

"There is little reason to believe that a monetary contraction is imminent. Few who are discussing this appear to have much understanding of what they are talking about. A renewal of price inflation, not deflation, should be our greatest concern."[9]

"Inflation is a Bigger Danger Than Deflation."[10]

"The best way to beat deflation is to aggressively increase liquidity by pumping up high-powered money. The Federal Open Market Committee did this in 1998 and 1999 [and] it can do so again."[11]

"Who's Afraid of Big Bad Deflation?" "Stocks Do Best Near Zero Inflation."[12]

"The idea that we are looking at a general deflation is wrong. There is simply no indication in the data of deflation."[13]

"[The] president of the Federal Reserve Bank of San Francisco…said, 'The chances of really experiencing declining prices is quite small.' He also said that the Fed has done research on whether deflation is a possibility, and its simulations have shown the probability is 'quite low' in 2003 and 2004."[14]

"Myth #5: We Are Staring Deflation in the Face. Inflation, as ever, is the sleeping dragon.... Deflation is still a fairy tale bogeyman at this stage — a Troll with which to frighten the children into silence and compliance."[15]

"Deflation Fears Are Irrational."[16]

Deflation Scare is Losing Air
Advisers, investors no longer concerned
Deflation Scare Is a Thing of the Past

Fears of deflation have been deflated.

Investors — virtually in a matter of weeks — have forgotten about the threat of deflation, and financial advisers are crossing it off their list of worries.

"It appears that the deflation-is-dead camp has won," says Keith B. Hembre, director of economic research for U.S. Bancorp Asset Management Inc. in Minneapolis. "It's a crowd psychology kind of thing."

A survey by the National Association for Business Economics in Washington backs the deflation-is-dead thinking. *None of the respondents to the May survey, all of whom were responsible for making macroeconomic predictions, predicted a decline in the consumer price index during the next two years.* [emphasis added]

"I would venture to say that, if anything, the position [against deflation] would have solidified" since May, says Tim O'Neill, president of the association and chief economist of the Toronto-based BMO Financial Group (formerly Bank of Montreal). Yet Mr. Hembre and other economists urge caution.

It's not going to happen here, says Nancy Kimelman, chief economist of SEI Investments in Oaks, Pa. "I have full faith in the American financial system to stop deflation in its tracks, and I think we're doing it."

Hers is a view widely held by financial advisers and others who are investing with abandon for the first time in years.

Brian Kohute, chief financial officer of the HJ Financial Group in Plymouth Meeting, Pa., says he is one of those people.

"We thought the risk of deflation was very heavy in the first half of the year," says the adviser, who oversees the $110 million his firm manages. "That's really changed" in the past few weeks.[17]

So, as they say, the more things change, the more they stay the same. Perhaps all these people will turn out right, but I think that the beliefs expressed above are simply an expression of the underlying social ebullience that is manifest in the stock market rally and economists' optimistic consensus. The progression of increasing attention paid to the deflation question, coupled with the continual denials that deflation will happen, appear to be part of a social psychological progression toward a credit crisis.

Even in this environment of extreme liquidity, prices have been falling for goods and services that are not considered "investments" (such as homes, stocks and precious metals) and not provided by government. Sure, medical care expenses and particularly insurance costs are soaring (50 percent in just the past three years), as are public school costs. What else can be expected from programs regulated or operated by government? (When government regulated the phone company, a long-distance call across the U.S. cost 75 cents a minute, ten times what it has proved to be worth in a competitive environment.) At the same time, in the relatively free market, prices are beginning to give way. Wages are slipping even as people are faced with higher house prices.

Something has to give, and *that something will be prices*. Global inflation, as measured by prices, has already declined from more than 30 percent per year in 1990-94 (*At the Crest* sounded a warning of the coming trend in 1995) to about 3 percent. Monetary trends are not a matter of *weeks*; they are a matter of decades, and this one isn't over. When the Dow turns down again and breaks 7000, it will signal the onset of a more intense phase of the deflationary progression.

On June 25, 2003, the Fed lowered the federal funds rate for the 13th time in a row, to one percent. This is the lowest level for interest rates since the early 1950s, immediately following the end of the last Kondratieff cycle (see Chapter 12). Chapter 13 asked, "What will [the Fed] do if the economy resumes its contraction, lower interest rates to zero? *Then what?*" It could be that the Fed has even less than one percentage point of room left to maneuver. The U.S. has a thriving money-market fund industry, which costs at least ½ percent of assets per year to administer. As it stands now, investors are getting extremely low returns from money-market funds. If the Fed were to let its funds rate drop to zero, investors' return after fees could go negative, which would make holding cash more attractive than holding debt, a situation the Fed surely wants to avoid. The monetary system appears to have reached the point at which those pesky reactionary forces discussed in Chapter 13 will come into play if the Fed tries any more "deflation-fighting," no matter what the mechanism.

Is the Fed really *fighting* deflation by aggressively lowering its interest rates? Everyone thinks so, but the result of deflation — its primary outward symptom — is lower prices. And what has the Fed been doing? It has spent over a year *lowering the price of renting money*. Within that period, in fact, the Fed has lowered prices more than anyone! It has participated in the initial phase of the deflationary process as if it were a merchant on the street discounting its wares to a disinterested public. It did so in response to slack demand for its product — credit — just as the auto manufacturers and others are doing with their products. Deflationary psychology brings about lower prices, and the Fed is lowering its prices.

The true power is not at the Fed but in the trend of social mood. Currently, the total credit supply is still rising, but commercial and industrial loans have fallen since 2001. In other words, lenders are exhibiting deflationary psychology in being unwilling to finance productive enterprise. Yet, ironically, they are quite willing to finance consumption via home, auto and credit-card loans. This dichotomy is untenable, as production is what ultimately pays for consumption. The speeding vehicle of debt-financed consumption is about to hit the brick wall of credit-starved (non)production. A new low in the stock market will announce the collision.

The Next Phase

As recounted above, people are finally talking about deflation (if only to dismiss it). The next word that should begin to slide into the lexicon is *depression*. I would like to feature quotes from authorities on the low likelihood of depression, but we find literally no professional economists, academics or Wall Street strategists even discussing the possibility. It is too remote even to mention! The term "depression" is where the word "deflation" was a few years ago, i.e., outside the general consciousness. Although no one is using that term now, soon it will be everywhere. The first phase will be widespread insistence that it can't happen, which will be the next clue that it is. The two "d" words in the subtitle to this book were anticipatory, published at a time when the likelihoods of their happening were (and still are) considered — as one economist said at the time about deflation — as remote as "being eaten by piranhas." Keep your toes on the riverbank.

UPDATE ON STRATEGY

The preceding market assessments show that the hard-to-find information in this book remains not only uniquely valuable but crucial to your financial survival. Think about it: If a 50 percent drop in the S&P 500 and the Wilshire 5000 indexes cannot bring value to the market or turn people bearish — two key requirements for a major bottom — how much more decline will it ultimately take? Chapter 8 already answers this question, and the state of the indicators today says that that assessment remains valid. Therefore, so does the advice.

I wish to emphasize even more strongly the admonition in Chapter 18 that "*some* day, even Treasury bills would probably become risky, [at which time] you should buy safe foreign short-term debt...." U.S. government obligations have become popular now, since Treasury bonds have soared in price as yields have fallen, at least until recent weeks. A depression could challenge the current consensus. T-bills are still likely better stores of value than stocks, real estate and corporate and municipal bonds. But if you have substantial wealth to protect, then for ultimate safety, you should by all means investigate ways to store your capital in the short-term obligations of government entities in Switzerland and Singapore, whose currencies appear sounder on a long-term basis than the U.S. dollar. Politics can change that assessment, so keep abreast of currency trends if you decide to go this route. Speculators who read this book early and followed the advice in Chapter 20 are positioned to make more money on the short side during the next wave down. The current time is not as ideal to sell short as 2000 was, but such an action taken now should still provide rewards.

Tables 18-1, 19-1, 19-2 and 24-1, which cover bank and insurance company safety ratings, have been updated according to the latest available data. Remember, to remain up to date on any new strategy ideas that we come across, visit elliottwave.com/conquerthecrash.

Being a safety advocate now is fine for the time being, but I do look forward to writing my next *bullish* book. If my timing is right, it will be just as out of favor as the super-bullish Elliott-wave predictions from 1978 and 1982 that the DJIA would quintuple. That's all right with me. I would rather be right than popular. I do hope, though, that you are one of the few who will be coming along for the ride when that great opportunity arrives.

A SECOND ONGOING ROUND-TRIP FORECAST

Outlining an entire monetary cycle (as recounted at the beginning of the "Deflation" section of this Supplement) is not the only round trip that Elliott-wave authors have predicted. 1978's *Elliott Wave Principle* forecast both a great bull market in stocks and a great bear market to follow. It is instructive to travel back in time to see how different things were then and how dramatically the social mood of the time contrasts with today's relentless optimism. Figure A-21 shows a picture of the DJIA as of 1978, when *Business Week* was reporting as follows:

— "More and more economists are forecasting recession."[19]

— "If the dollar continues to plummet, the pressure may prove unstoppable."[20]

— "The mood of the consumer and of business executives indicate a deterioration in expectations about prospective business conditions."[21]

— "The public's...fear of inflation has never been greater than it is today."[22]

Naturally, most investors expected stocks to fall. What would *you* have forecast for the stock market at that time?

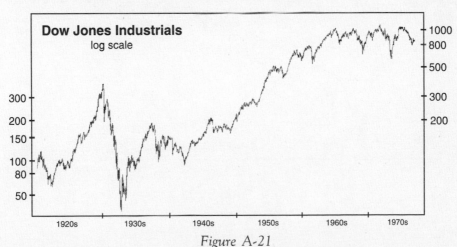

Figure A-21

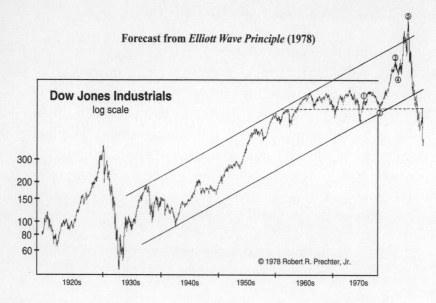

Figure A-22

Figure A-23

Elliott Wave Principle depicted what the authors thought would be a reasonable shape for wave V and its aftermath. This chart is reproduced in Figure A-22. It was derived by inverting the 1929-1937 period and adding it to the low that had just occurred in March of 1978. Our graph called for the DJIA to climb from the 1974 low in "five Primary waves with the fifth extending," carrying beyond the upper trendline of the channel at Supercycle degree, and then to fall below 400. This forecast shows that Elliott wave analysts knew back in those early days the wild upside experience that lay ahead. The first half of that forecast took longer and went higher than anticipated (see Figure A-23), but otherwise, this picture was a darn good guide to the future. The rising portion of the projection ended in 2000. The second half appears to be underway.

THE NEXT STAGE OF THE BEAR MARKET

The underlying trend of human progress us upward. All
bear markets are, at their largest degree, only partial retracements
of previous progress (see Figure 3-1). But those that follow huge
five-wave advances are themselves large enough to be of great
social importance. Once such bear market began in 2000. Figure
A-24 is from Chapter 2 of *Elliott Wave Principle*. It displays a typical
progression of prices and psychology in a bear market. See if the
stock market environment of 2000-2002 fits the classic description
of an A wave:

> During the A wave of a bear market, the investment world
> is generally convinced that this reaction is just a pullback
> pursuant to the next leg of advance. The public surges to
> the buy side despite the first really technically damaging
> cracks in the individual stock patterns.[23]

As demonstrated throughout this Supplement, the psychology of
the old trend always retains its hold on investors through "wave

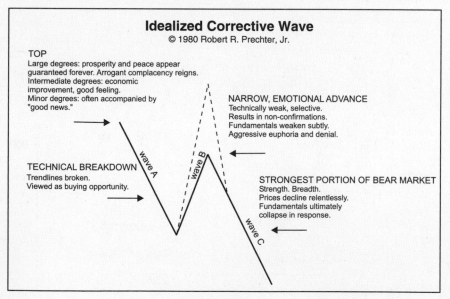

Figure A-24

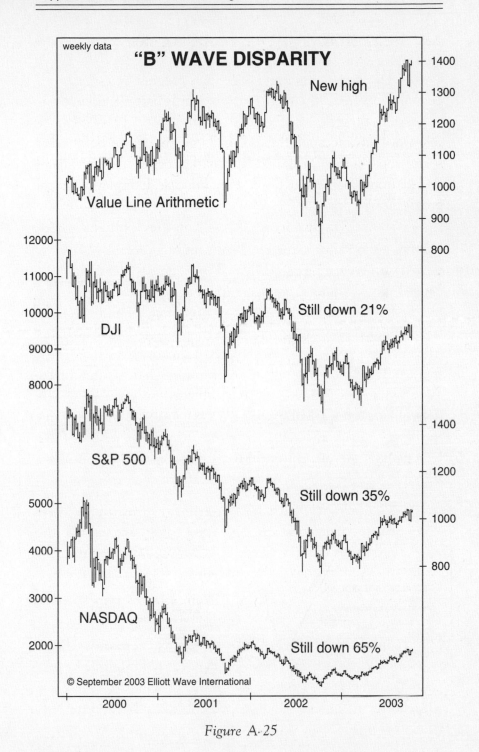

Figure A-25

two" and "wave B" of the new trend. Read what the book says about B waves:

> B waves are phonies. They are sucker plays, bull traps, specu-
> lators' paradise, orgies of odd-lotter mentality or expressions
> of dumb institutional complacency (or both). They often
> involve a focus on a narrow list of stocks, are often "uncon-
> firmed" by other averages, are rarely technically strong, and
> are virtually always doomed to complete retracement by
> wave C.[24]

Does that sound like today, or what? This time, as befits a B wave, there is only one index actually making a new all-time high: the Value Line Arithmetic average, shown in Figure A-25. All other averages are down substantially from their highs. This is the same type of market setup that occurred in the precious metals complex in September 1980. Gold and silver had already begun major bear markets, but the first big rally led gold mining shares to new highs. When that rally ended, the entire complex reversed to the downside and fell relentlessly. That's the juncture we face today in the stock market. To anticipate the ultimate resolution of this bear market, we can again refer to the description in *Elliott Wave Principle* regarding the second major wave of decline:

> Declining C waves are usually devastating in their
> destruction. They are third waves and have most of the
> properties of third waves. It is during these declines that
> there is virtually no place to hide except cash. The illusions
> held throughout waves A and B tend to evaporate, and
> fear takes over. C waves are persistent and broad.[25]

Market analysis is a matter of probabilities, not certainties. But if anything like the pattern shown in Figure A-24 is fulfilled as expected, readers of *Conquer the Crash* will be among the very few who survive and prosper from the experience. Whatever the outcome, I wish you well.

NOTES

[1] Ip, Greg. (2003, May 19). "Having Defeated Inflation, the Fed Girds for War on Falling Prices." *The Wall Street Journal.*

[2] Kirchhoff, Sue. (2003, May 16). "Deflation Fears May Rise as Economy Fights for Traction." *USA Today.*

[3] Hagenbaugh, Barbara, and Barbara Hansen. (2003, June 23). "Economists expect cut; many don't advise it." *USA Today.*

[4] Associated Press. (2003, June 23). "To stop deflation, Federal Reserve may drop interest rate again."

[5] Baum, Caroline. (2003, June 18). "Houston, deflation launch has been scrubbed." Bloomberg News.

[6] Fed Vice Chairman Roger Ferguson, quoted in *The Wall Street Journal*, May 19, 2003 "Having defeated inflation, Fed girds for new for: falling prices," by Greg Ip and Jon Hilsenrath; and by the Associated Press, June 14, 2003, "Price drops could lead to deflation."

[7] Shiller, Robert J. (2003, June 12). "The technology deflator." *The Wall Street Journal.*

[8] Kirchoff, Sue. (2003, June 4). "Greenspan upbeat about economy." *USA Today.*

[9] American Institute for Economic Research. (2003, May 26). "Deflation." *Research Report.*

[10] Lee, Tim. (2003, May 26). "Inflation is a Bigger Danger Than Deflation." *Financial Times* online.

[11] Cosgrove, Michael. (2003, May 21). "The Fed's Complacency." *The Wall Street Journal.*

[12] Headlines in *The Wall Street Journal*, May 16, 2003.

[13] George Von Furstenberg, Indiana University, formerly on the Council of Economic Advisors, quoted in *The Atlanta Journal-Constitution*, May 10, 2003, "Fed deflation warning creates waves," by Michael E. Kanell.

[14] De Rosa, David. (2003, May 7). "Will U.S. Catch Japan's Deflation Bug?" Bloomberg News.

[15] Corrigan, Sean. (2003, May). "Myths of the Crash." *The Free Market.* Ludwig von Mises Institute.

[16] Bugos, Ed. (2003, February 19). "Deflation fears are irrational." *Goldenbar Report,* on the Internet.

[17] Southall, Brooke. (2003, September 1). "Deflation scare is losing air." *Investment News* (excerpt). To be fair, the article quoted one economist who still urges caution about dismissing the possibility of deflation.

[18] Brooks, John. (1999, September). *The Go-Go Years*. New York: John Wiley & Sons.

[19] *Business Week*. (1978, March 8). "The Talk Grows of a Coming Recession."

[20] *Business Week*. (1978, March 20). "The Dollar Fades as a Reserve Currency."

[21] *Business Week*. (1978, May 8). "Business Outlook."

[22] *Business Week*. (1978, May 22.) "How Inflation Threatens the Fabric of U.S. Society."

[23] Frost, A.J., and Robert R. Prechter, Jr. (1978). *Elliott Wave Principle — Key to Market Behavior*. Gainesville, GA: New Classics Library, p. 79.

[24] *Ibid*.

[25] *Ibid*., p. 81.

Media and Misc. References

Chapter 1

Seigler, Mark V. (1998, June). "Real output and business cycle volatility, 1869-1993: U.S. experience in international perspective." *Journal of Economic History*.

Chapter 3

Elliott, Ralph Nelson. (series of books and articles published from 1938-1946). Republished: (1994) *R.N. Elliott's Masterworks – The Definitive Collection*, Prechter, Jr., Robert Rougelot. (Ed.) Gainesville, GA: New Classics Library.

Mandelbrot, Benoit. (1988). *The fractal geometry of nature*. New York: W.H. Freeman.

Frost, Alfred John and Robert Rougelot Prechter. (1978). *Elliott wave principle – key to market behavior*. Gainesville, GA: New Classics Library.

Prechter, Robert Rougelot. (1999). *The wave principle of human social behavior and the new science of socionomics*. Gainesville, GA: New Classics Library.

Prechter, Robert Rougelot. (1982, October 6 and November 8). *The Elliott Wave Theorist*.

Chapter 4

Prechter, Robert Rougelot. (2001, September 11). "Elliott waves and social reality." *The Elliott Wave Theorist*.

Chapter 5

Elliott, Ralph Nelson. (1946). *Nature's law*. Republished: (1994) *R.N. Elliott's Masterworks – The Definitive Collection*, Prechter, Jr., Robert Rougelot. (Ed.) Gainesville, GA: New Classics Library.

Jasen, Georgette. (1994, May 13). "Darts beat pros but losses are the rule." *The Wall Street Journal*.

Jasen, Georgette. (1996, July 10). "Pros lose out to chance, industrials." *The Wall Street Journal*.

Jasen, Georgette. (1997, February 11). "Investment pros defeat darts, but can't top surging market." *The Wall Street Journal*.

Jasen, Georgette. (1997, April 9). "Pros beat darts, but in a losing contest." *The Wall Street Journal*.

Jasen, Georgette. (1998, May 13). "Pros beat darts, but picks trail Dow Jones Industrials." *The Wall Street Journal*.

Jasen, Georgette. (1998, November 5). "Darts draw blood as pro losses far exceed those of Industrials." *The Wall Street Journal*.

Prechter, Robert Rougelot. (1983, August 18). "The superbull market of the '80s – has the last wild ride really begun." *The Elliott Wave Theorist*.

Kendall, Peter Mark. (1998, September 16). "Wave V fundamentals and their implications." *The Elliott Wave Theorist*.

Chapter 6

Prechter, Robert Rougelot, editor. (2002). *Market analysis for the new millennium*. Gainesville, GA: New Classics Library.

Glassman, James K. and Kevin A. Hassett. (1999, March 17). "Stock prices are still far too low." *The Wall Street Journal*.

Birger, Jon. (2002, March). "Faith stocks." *Money*.

Chapter 7

Siegel, Jeremy J. (1999, April 19). "Manager's journal: are internet stocks overvalued? are they ever." *The Wall Street Journal*.

Siegel, Jeremy J. (2000, March 14). "Big-cap tech stocks are a sucker bet." *The Wall Street Journal*.

Glassman, James K. and Kevin A. Hassett. (1998, March 30). "Are stocks overvalued? not a chance." *The Wall Street Journal*.

Dornbusch, Rudi. (1998, July 30). "Growth forever." *The Wall Street Journal*.

Angell, Wayne D. (1999, February 3). "The bubble won't burst." *The Wall Street Journal*.

Glassman, James K. and Kevin A. Hassett. (1999, March 17). "Stock prices are still far too low." *The Wall Street Journal*.

Ip, Greg. (1999, August 30). "Does tech 'explosion' alter market's nature?" *The Wall Street Journal*.

Ip, Greg. (1999, September 13). "New paradigm view for stocks is bolstered." *The Wall Street Journal*.

Gilder, George. (1999, December 31). "The faith of a futurist." *The Wall Street Journal*.

Kadlec, Charles W. (2000, April 18). "Market mayhem. Don't worry, the great prosperity still coming." *The Wall Street Journal*.

Ford, Constance Mitchell. (2000, January 3). "Economists are euphoric about the prospect for 2000 – nearly all surveyed believe expansion will become longest on record." *The Wall Street Journal*.

Ford, Constance Mitchell. (2001, January 2). "Euphoria dominating last year turns to prudence in 2001." *The Wall Street Journal*.

Hilsenrath, Jon E. (2002, January 4). "Economic forecasters expect moderate recovery in 2002." *The Wall Street Journal*.

Hughes, Siobhan. (2002, February 22). "Economists optimistic. Survey says recession likely is already over." *The Atlanta Journal-Constitution*.

Hager, George. (2002, February 28). "'Recessionette' might be at an end." *USA Today*.

Fox, Justin. (2002, March 18). "The profitless recovery." *Fortune*.

Barnes, Angela. (2002, January 10). "Managers bullish on equity markets. Expect double-digit return, survey finds." *The Globe and Mail* (Toronto).

Prechter, Robert Rougelot. (1995). *At the crest of the tidal wave*. Gainesville, GA: New Classics Library.

Leonhardt, David. (2002, March 12). "After Sept. 11, diverging attitudes about the market." *The New York Times*.

Prechter, Robert Rougelot. (2001, September 11). "Elliott waves and social reality." *The Elliott Wave Theorist*.

Altman, Daniel. (2001, December 29). "Positive reports hint at swift recovery." *New York Times*.

Meyers, Mike. (2002, January 6). "Better times coming." *Star* (Minneapolis).

Torres, Carlos. (2001, December 29). "Hope soars in U.S." *Rocky Mountain News*.

Sommar, Jessica (2002, March 1). "Recovery at last." *New York Post*.

Hagenbaugh, Barbara and George Hager (2002, March 8). "Fed chief declares recession at an end." *USA Today*.

Pethokoukis, James. (2002, January 14). "Business bounces back. How to cash in. That old blue-sky feeling." *U.S. News & World Report*.

Curl, Joseph. (2002, January 1). "Bush predicts 2002 will be 'a great year'." *Washington Times*.

Chapter 9
Bolton, A. Hamilton. (1957, February 11). Personal letter to Charles Collins.

Chapter 11

Federal Reserve System. (2001, December 31). "Flow of funds accounts
        of the United States." Washington, D.C: Board of Governors of
        the Federal Reserve System.

The Federal Reserve Bank of St. Louis. "FRED, an economic time series
        database." http://www.stls.frb.org/fred/.

Chapter 12

Prechter, Robert Rougelot. (1979, November 18). "Commodities, inter-
        est rates and inflation: A major top?" *The Elliott Wave Theorist*.

Kondratieff, Nikolai. (1926). "The long waves in economic life." Re-
        published: (1935, November). *Review of Economic Statistics*.

Chapter 13

Norton, Rob. (1997, September 8). "Why not to worry about deflation."
        Fortune.

Wiseman, Paul. (1991, January 17). "Deflation? Not yet. Some prices
        are tumbling but not all." *USA Today*.

Reisman, George and Robert Klein. (1999, November 15). "No infla-
        tion? Look again." *Barron's*.

American Institute for Economic Research. (2002, February 25).
        "Deflation?" *Research Reports*.

Luskin, Donald L. (2001, November 19). "Deflation: The basics." *The
        Luskin Report*.

Quinn, Jane Bryant. (1998, February 16). "In praise of deflation."
        Newsweek.

Shilling, A. Gary. (1998, August 26). "Deflation is nothing to fear." *The
        Wall Street Journal*.

Nevallier, Louis. (1998, August 27). Interview CNBC.

Kanell Michael E. (2001, November 17). "Sliding oil prices a break for
        drivers." *The Atlanta Journal-Constitution*.

Cooper, James C. and Kathleen Madigan. (2001, November 16). "That's
        not deflation ahead, just slower inflation." *BusinessWeek*.

Miller, Karen Lowry. (2001, December 10). "Beware the bugaboo. What's
        worse than inflation? Its opposite." *Newsweek*.

Blackstone, Brian. (2001, April 16). "Fed's Parry: US Economy growing
        at slight positive rate." *Dow Jones Newswires*.

Miller, Rich. (1998, January 7). "Prices under pressure. Deflation could
        slam brakes on economies." *USA Today*.

Birger, Jon. (2002, January). "Can Washington save Wall Street?" *Money*.

Abelson, Alan. (1999, August 30). "Werner visits Wall Street." *Barron's*.

Chapter 16

Birger, Jon (2001, December). "The rock." *Money*.

Chapter 19

Van Dusen, Christine (2001, December 29). "Despite woes, banks well-capitalized." *The Atlanta Journal-Constitution*.

Weiss, Martin. (2002). *Ultimate safe money guide*. New York: John Wiley & Sons.

Chapter 20

The Dick Davis Digest. (2000, January 31 and 2001, January 15). "Top stock pick special." Fort Lauderdale, FL: Dick Davis Publishing.

Chapter 22

Roosevelt, Franklin D. (1933, April 5). "Executive Order 6260." *Federal Register*.

Chapter 26

Prechter, Robert Rougelot. (2001, August). "On the cresting wave – a Q&A with Robert Prechter." *The Elliott Wave Theorist*.

Chapter 27

Lambert, Michael J. and Kristin D. Stanton. (2001, September). "Opportunities and challenges of the U.S. dollar as an increasingly global currency: a Federal Reserve perspective." *Federal Reserve Bulletin*.

New York Times. Article unavailable